POLITICS IN PLURAL SOCIETIES

A Theory of Democratic Instability

ALVIN RABUSHKA

University of Rochester

and

KENNETH A. SHEPSLE

Washington University, St. Louis

Charles E. Merrill Publishing Company
A Bell & Howell Company
Columbus, Ohio

MERRILL POLITICAL SCIENCE SERIES

Under the Editorship of

John C. Wahlke

Department of Political Science

SUNY at Stony Brook

The authors and publisher gratefully acknowledge the following for permission to reprint:

Duke University Press for excerpts from Robert N. Kearney, *Communalism and Language in the Politics of Ceylon* (Durham, N.C.: Duke University Press, 1967).

The Macmillan Company for excerpts from Clifford Geertz, ed., *Old Societies and New States* (New York: Free Press, 1963).

Wesleyan University Press for excerpts from Pierre L. van den Berghe, *South Africa, A Study in Conflict* (Middletown, Conn.: Wesleyan University Press, 1965).

ISBN: 0-675-09114-4 clothbound
      0-675-09113-6 paperbound

Library of Congress Catalog Card Number: 71-187159

1 2 3 4 5 6 7 8 — 78 76 75 74 73 72

Printed in the United States of America

*For Louisa and Risé
who have already spent the royalties*

Acknowledgments

Acknowledgments often sound like post-campaign victory speeches. We do not depart from this practice and accordingly thank our critics, typists, and respective universities. Careful readings of various drafts of the manuscript and helpful comments were given by Eugene R. Alpert, James Bill, Partha Chatterjee, Jane Gilbert, Gerhard Loewenberg, Richard G. Niemi, William H. Riker, Gordon Tullock, Pierre L. van den Berghe, John Wahlke, and a motley crew of graduate students in a seminar on ethnic politics at the University of Rochester. We should especially acknowledge the valuable suggestions of our colleagues, G. Bingham Powell and John D. Sprague. All of these critics made our lives miserable but our book better.

We thank our typists for enduring three drafts of the manuscript: Peg Gross and Janice Brown of the University of Rochester, and Natalie Sekuler, Lillian Ehrlich, and Grace Pickel of Washington University. We also thank Lois Oppenheim who prepared the bibliography.

Financial assistance was provided by our respective universities. A faculty research grant from the University of Rochester permitted trips to several multiethnic societies: Northern Ireland, Belgium, Switzerland, Holland, Trinidad, and Quebec; it permitted two trips to St. Louis during the writing of the manuscript as well. Washington University, in turn, financed a trip to Rochester and supported the writing of the manuscript with a summer faculty fellowship.

We graciously acknowledge the help of all these sources who are not responsible for any errors the book may contain. Any errors of fact or interpretation must, in a co-authored project, be the fault of the other guy.

Contents

PART I

In this part of the book we develop a formal model that provides theoretical expectations about phenomena in one political universe— the plural society. In part two these expectations are subjected to empirical examination in eighteen plural societies.

In chapter 1 a bibliographic and historical review of the plural society concept is traced; here the political universe of concern is mapped. In chapter 2 we present the theoretical tools that are used in chapter 3 to construct a paradigm of politics in the plural society. Here we develop and examine the logical consequences of a model which, in part two, serve as *a priori* expectations to guide empirical analysis.

CHAPTER **1**

The Plural Society

On Tuesday, May 13, 1969, Tengku Abdul Rahman declared a state of emergency in Selangor following clashes between groups of Chinese and Malay youths over a wide area of the Malaysian Federal Capital of Kuala Lumpur.[1] On the next day, the Yang di-Pertuan Agong, the elected monarch of Malaysia, issued a Proclamation of Emergency under Clause 2 of Article 150 of the Constitution. This clause provides the government with wide powers to amend or suspend any written law, suspend Parliament and the electoral process, and even deprive a person of his citizenship.[2]

On October 9, 1969, the National Operations Council, an appointed body that assumed political power in lieu of Parliament, issued its official report on the causes of the May riots. These included:

> 1. a generation gap and differences in interpretation of the con-stitutional structure by the different races in the country, and, con-sequently, the growing political encroachment of the immigrant races against certain important provisions of the Constitution that relate to the Malay language and the position of the Malays, prin-cipally Articles 152 and 153;
>
> 2. the incitement, intemperate statements and provocative be-havior of certain racialist party members and supporters during the recent General Election;
>
> 3. the part played by the Malayan Communist Party and secret societies in inciting racial feelings and suspicions; and

---

1. *Straits Times*, May 14, 1969.
2. *Ibid.*, May 15, 1969.

4. the anxious, and later desperate, mood of the Malays with a background of Sino-Malay distrust, and recently, just after the General Election, as a result of racial insults and threats to their future survival and well-being in their own country.[3]

Race riots are not a new feature of Malaysian political life. Twenty-seven persons were killed and 1,700 were arrested during the November 1967 outbursts on the island of Penang and elsewhere in Northeast Malaya. These riots, presumably sparked by devaluation of the Malaysian dollar, quickly degenerated into racial clashes between Malays and Chinese.[4]

Malaysia is only one of many nations in which ethnic conflict conditions politics. A brief review of ethnic hostilities in plural societies is a very sobering experience. For example, chronic civil strife has plagued Burma ever since Saya San first led a rebellion against British rule in 1930. Since independence in January 1948, Burmans, the dominant ethnic community, have fought against such rebelling minorities as the Karens, a Christian culture, the Shans of northeast Burma, the Kachins of the north, and the Arakanese and Mons of the south. These rebels seek either full independence or increased autonomy.[5]

Intense ethnic conflict also recurs in Ceylon. The major political issues in Ceylonese politics concern protection or advancement of the majority Sinhalese and the minority Tamil communities in either economic, social or political situations. Sinhalese-Tamil tensions materialized into outright violence in 1958, two years after the passage of the Sinhalese Language Act; the death toll mounted into the hundreds. Robert N. Kearney, an informed observer of Ceylon, notes that accommodation of Tamil interests was prevented for nearly a decade by competitive Sinhalese parties, each appearing as the uncompromising champion of Sinhalese aspirations. Kearney concludes that

> the enduring strength of identification with the community and the potential of communal sentiments for mobilizing political support nonetheless remain of manifest and undisputed significance in the contemporary politics of Ceylon.[6]

3. *Ibid.*, October 9, 1969.
4. For an analysis of the Penang incident see Nancy L. Snider, "What Happened in Penang," *Asian Survey* 8, no. 12 (December 1968): 960-75.
5. Charles W. Anderson, Fred R. von der Mehden and Crawford Young, *Issues of Political Development* (Englewood Cliffs, N. J.: Prentice-Hall, Inc., 1967), pp. 98-108.
6. Robert N. Kearney, *Communalism and Language in the Politics of Ceylon* (Durham, N. C.: Duke University Press, 1967), p. 141.

Other ethnic, linguistic, religious, racial or regional disputes in Asia are easy to recognize. Turks and Greeks still maintain a state of armed truce in Cyprus. Christians and Muslims in Lebanon constantly evince mutual distrust and communal self-centeredness. Edward Shils claims that

> even curiosity to know the truth about the confessional composition of the population must be kept in check in order to avoid the provocation of group rivalries and the anxieties which these would stimulate.[7]

As a result, Lebanese authorities have been unable to conduct a census since 1932 out of fear that public knowledge of a shift in the religious composition of the population would provoke militant demands for a change in the allocation of government positions. Parliamentary seats are still allocated on the basis of a Christian/Muslim population ratio that is computed from the 1932 census results.

In still another case, the Kurdish people recently obtained autonomy in the exercise of their national rights from the Iraqi government in March 1970, thus signifying the termination of eight and one-half years of sporadic warfare. Kurds are to receive proportional representation in the Iraqi Parliament and Kurdish is to be an official language in Kurdish areas.[8]

Fijians, receiving independence from Britain in October 1970, had long favored continued colonial rule. Native Fijians were fearful of domination by a larger and more fertile Indian community. Apparently the death of an Indian political leader who advocated the doctrine of "one man, one vote" permitted Indians, Fijians, and resident Europeans to reach a compromise accord; the proposed constitution assures immediate Fijian rule, even though they constitute but a minority of the total population.[9]

Perhaps the most vivid illustration of ethnic conflict in Asia is the Pakistani civil war of April 1971. Bengalis, the residents of the eastern portion of that geographically divided state, had won a clear majority in the nationwide Parliamentary elections held earlier that year. Shortly thereafter the army, commanded and staffed chiefly by the Punjabis of West Pakistan, dissolved the Parliament, declared the Awami League (the Bengali party) treasonous and illegal, and initiated a campaign against dissident Bengali secessionists marked by extensive violence. Thus

---

7. Edward Shils, "The Prospects for Lebanese Civility," in Leonard Binder, ed., *Politics in Lebanon* (New York: John Wiley & Sons, Inc., 1966), p. 4.

8. *The New York Times*, March 12, 1970.

9. *Ibid.*, March 23, 1970, p. 7.

Pakistan's brief experiment with democracy fell victim to intense ethnic passions.

Many countries outside of Asia also display ethnic rivalries. A White minority rules in a now independent Rhodesia, even amidst the fanfare of international disapproval. The Portuguese are continually trying to suppress Black revolutionaries in Portuguese Guinea, Angola and Mozambique, and Indians and Pakistanis are currently victims of social and legal discrimination practiced by Africans in Kenya, Uganda and Tanzania.

Outright killing frequently takes place. Other Nigerian tribesmen killed perhaps a million or more Ibos during the Biafran war. Zanzibar's independence, granted in December 1963, was followed by a Black revolt which seized power from an Arab regime in January 1964, and Blacks have since killed many Arabs and expropriated their property.

In Mauritius, too, communal violence and independence go hand in hand. British troops were called in to quell Muslim-Creole rioting in Port Louis, the capital, in 1968. An uneasy peace has since been maintained, but is continually threatened by intense ethnic animosities. In the Sudan Muslim Arabs oppose a Southern secessionist African movement. Death estimates among Black Sudanese since 1955 range from 500,000 to more than one million out of a total Southern population of three to four million. In the early 1970s a Muslim minority in Chad and an Eritrean minority in Ethiopia are engaging in similar secessionist activities.

Ethnic conflict also appears frequently in the Caribbean and South America. Race riots between East Indians and Creoles in Guyana (formerly British Guiana) disrupted normal constitutional government and on occasion necessitated the use of British troops to maintain order. Guyana, independent since 1966, is now governed by the Peoples National Congress, a Creole Party that won a convincing victory in the 1968 elections. The PNC won with the help of votes cast by an overseas electorate, ninety-three percent of which is Creole.[10] Subsequent attempts to verify the authenticity of these overseas electors cast doubt on the fairness of the 1968 Guyanese elections. Several surveys conducted in America and England have failed to establish the existence of most of these electors. Thus, in Guyana a numerically smaller African community rules a larger population of East Indians.

The same pattern of Creole-East Indian competition characterizes Trinidad electoral politics. Candidates are selected almost exclusively on the basis of their ethnic backgrounds as seen in the 1961 and 1966

---

10. *Ibid.*, December 21, 1968, p. 55.

general elections. As additional evidence, one need only look to the black power riots that shook Trinidad on April 21, 1970, and led Dr. Eric Williams, the Creole Prime Minister of Trinidad, to proclaim a state of emergency. Some attribute these riots to black power extremists who protest white economic rule.

Ethnic conflict illustrates the difficulties that cultural pluralism poses for orderly, democratic government. Ethnic diversity and political instability are not, however, limited to developing countries. If they were, we might expect that economic development and urbanization would eliminate ethnic tensions and facilitate stable government. However, a growing expression of ethnic sentiments in the political processes of several industrialized nations during the 1960s and early 1970s belies this expectation; ethnic politics is indeed not a unique product of the so-called underdeveloped world.

For example, French-Canadians increasingly express their separatist sentiments. Extremist bombings in Montreal have grown in frequency since DeGaulle's momentous visit. In electoral competition the Parti Quebecois, a separatist party, received nearly twenty-three percent of the vote in its very first outing in the April 1970 Quebec Provincial Election. These developments have led some observers to predict more rather than less ethnic conflict during the 1970s. The kidnappings of Pierre LaPorte, who was subsequently murdered, and James Cross in the spring of 1971 by the Front for the Liberation of Quebec, as well as the firm response by Prime Minister Trudeau, support this conjecture.

Ethnic conflict shows signs of intensification in several European societies. For example, British troops since August 1969 have put down religious riots between Catholics and Protestants in Northern Ireland; thousands have actively patrolled the urban areas to contain repeated outbursts of religiously-inspired violence that have plagued the country throughout 1970 and 1971. Northern Ireland is literally an occupied country — the British Army is the police authority. The election of the Reverend Ian Paisley, a Protestant militant, to Northern Ireland's Parliament at Stormont in a by-election in April 1970[11] shows that extremist feelings are running high and that the four-hundred-year history of rivalry, tension and killing remains an important consideration for the Ulster electorate. We should also record that both Paisley and Bernadette Devlin, a Catholic leader, now sit in the British House of Commons; each won, in the 1970 general election, by appealing to extremists in their respective religious communities.

---

11. *Ibid.*, April 17, 1970.

Common adherence to the Catholic faith in Belgium does not prevent Flemings and Walloons from quarreling about language. The language riot at the University of Louvain triggered the downfall of the Belgian government in 1968. The law today separates Belgium into Flemish and French linguistic zones with provision made for the use of either Flemish or French in Brussels. In spite of this legal separation, both Flemish and Walloon nationalist parties now control thirty-two seats in the Belgian House of Representatives following the 1968 election, compared with only one seat in 1961. Their steady growth has contributed to the instability of the unitary Belgian state.

Even little Switzerland has not entirely escaped disputes on the linguistic question. On March 1, 1970, the electorate of the Berne Canton approved a proposal that allowed the predominantly French-speaking districts of the Jura region in northwest Switzerland to decide whether to take steps to split off from the Canton's largely German-speaking majority. The separatist leaders in the Canton accused the German-speaking majority in the Canton of not allowing the French-speaking minority to use French in dealing with local officials. This proposal is the first attempt to redraw Canton boundaries in Switzerland in approximately one-hundred years.[12]

These illustrations of discord in plural societies are not exhaustive. They are, however, typical of their politics — democratic instability, authoritarian government, gerrymandering, and other legal and illegal manipulations. Ethnic conflict is constrained neither by time nor space; the history of plural societies is replete with tragedies of civil strife dating over centuries and located in nearly every region of the globe. Why this is so is the subject of this book.

This chapter contains a review of the scholarly treatment of the plural society concept. It begins with the work of J. S. Furnivall, who developed the concept, and moves quickly through various sociological, anthropological, and political treatments and modifications of it. We conclude the review with our own formulation of the concept that we employ in subsequent chapters.

In chapters 2 and 3 we develop and use an appropriate set of tools to theorize about the distinctive features of politics in plural societies. Evidence for eighteen of these countries constitutes chapters 4, 5, 6, and 7. In

---

12. *Ibid.*, March 2, 1970. See also James A. Dunn Jr., *Social Cleavage, Party Systems and Political Integration: A Comparison of the Belgian and Swiss Experiences* (Ph.D. dissertation, Pennsylvania, 1970) and Kurt B. Mayer, "The Jura Problem: Ethnic Conflict in Switzerland," *Social Research* 35, no. 4 (Winter 1968): 707-41.

the final chapter we extend the treatment to other societies, most notably Switzerland, and discuss the prospects for social engineering.

Bases of Cultural Pluralism

A primary task in plural societies is the subordination of "primordial sentiments" to the requirements of civil politics.[13] Although the nation-state is the legal basis of sovereignty, loyalties to subnational cultural groups often undermine the stability, if not the very existence, of the state. These communal loyalties in themselves contend for ultimate political authority and loyalty; in short, they rival the state for legitimacy.

We identify below the varieties of cultural pluralism that can become salient in the politics of plural societies. Cultural identities — the body of values that constitutes the culture — provide a basis for political cohesion. We intend to show that these primordial sentiments systematically influence cohesion, competition and social interaction in plural societies.[14] Even though each variety of cultural pluralism possesses some unique properties, each displays a similar effect on political behavior.

Race. The concept of race is perhaps the most controversial term in social science. It is often used pejoratively, as the basis for repressive ideologies, or in a scientific sense, in which case it refers to selected phenotypical features: skin color, facial form, stature, hair type, and so forth. Some scholars question whether separate racial groups are indeed identifiable. Malaysia, for example, is viewed as a multiracial society by its inhabitants even though the two major ethnic groups, Chinese and Malays, are each a subcategory of a broader Mongoloid group. Nevertheless, most Malaysians insist that Chinese and Malays belong to different races. Furthermore, most students of Malaysia agree that Chinese and Malays constitute distinct cultural groups and, therefore, they usually classify Malaysia as, at minimum, a multiethnic society.[15]

---

13. Clifford Geertz, "The Integrative Revolution: Primordial Sentiments and Civil Politics in the New States," in Clifford Geertz, ed., *Old Societies and New States: The Quest for Modernity in Asia and Africa* (New York: Free Press of Glencoe, 1963), pp. 105-57.

14. Students of race relations have long observed the effects of one cultural variable — race — on social interaction. See, for example, Brewton Berry, *Race and Ethnic Relations*, 2d ed. (Boston: Houghton Mifflin, 1958), p. 277.

15. We adopt the practice of using local terminology when discussing specific plural societies, e.g., Malaysia is a multiracial society. Very often the inhabitants of plural societies subjectively perceive broad cultural divisions as a surrogate for objective phenotypical characteristics.

The racial configurations of Rhodesia and South Africa pose fewer problems for the construction of classification schemes. Skin color differentiates races and rigorously enforced laws define and accentuate those differences. Whether we use a subjective or objective definition of race, it nonetheless provides a basis for political cohesion that is critical in several plural societies.

Language. Linguistic differences also threaten democratic stability. The breakdown of law and order in Ceylon following passage of the 1956 Sinhalese Language Act, as well as the 1968 Flemish-Walloon riots in Louvain, highlight the potential salience of language as a destabilizing force. In both Ceylon and Belgium, language provides the basis for group cohesion and intergroup conflict as does race in Malaysia and South Africa. Indeed, speakers of different languages often claim that language represents or constitutes the basis of a distinct culture. For example, Flemings and Walloons in Belgium each insist they are the product of a long history of different cultural experiences of which language is only a surface characteristic.[16]

When differences in language become politically salient, stability is often threatened. Adherence to a common language, on the other hand, does not imply or guarantee stable politics. Since they seized power in 1964, Africans have mistreated Arabs in Zanzibar even though both communities speak Swahili; nor has the common use of English prevented civil war in Nigeria or chronic religious discord in Northern Ireland.

Religion. Religion is crucial in the politics of Northern Ireland. Ulster, as the country is commonly called, is a constituent member of the United Kingdom, but possesses a distinct history dating from its conquest and colonization by the English in the seventeenth century. The distinctions between the conquered Irish Catholics and the conquering British Protestants have been scrupulously preserved and often violently expressed in the streets of Belfast and Londonderry. Extensively burned-out sections in West Belfast testify that religious sentiments in Ulster comprise an alternative basis for statehood. As further evidence of this assertion, the results of a survey published in the *Belfast Telegraph* on December 8, 1967, show that a majority of Protestants prefer the existing constitutional links with Britain whereas most Catholics are partial to the idea of an independent united Ireland or a united Ireland linked to Britain.

---

16. For an outstanding treatment of Flemish culture see Patricia Carson, *The Fair Face of Flanders* (Ghent: E. Story-Scientia, 1969).

However, common religious affiliation, like language, need not dampen the destabilizing effects that other salient cleavages create. Nearly all Belgians are Catholics, but Flemings on occasion have attacked French-speaking priests. In still another case, Muslim Africans have not hesitated to mistreat Muslim Arabs in Zanzibar.

Tribe and Custom. Civil wars in the Congo and Nigeria illustrate the difficulties that tribal diversity poses for orderly government. Africans may be racially alike, but are often differentiated on the basis of tribe and custom, a differentiation that has political implications. In the Ivory Coast, for example, tribal categories provide building blocks for party organization, e.g., the Parti Democratique Cote D'Ivoire.[17] Tribal hostilities also provided the justification for South African seizure and rule of South-West Africa; whites claimed their intervention halted a war of genocide waged by Bantu peoples against the Bushmen.[18] Sub-Saharan African history is also replete with examples of tribal conflict.[19] The abrogation of colonial rule in Africa has made tribal divisions especially salient in the political arena.

Different forms of cultural diversity thus display remarkably similar consequences. Ethnic divisions — be they racial, religious, linguistic, or tribal — often coincide with political divisions. This pattern has been observed by several scholars. We turn, in the following sections, to an analysis of their explanations of ethnic politics.

The Theory of Plural Society: J. S. Furnivall

In *Netherlands India* J. S. Furnivall introduced the notion of the "plural society."[20] Furnivall, an economist and colonial administrator, defined a plural society as "comprising two or more elements or social orders which live side by side, yet without mingling, in one political unit."[21] In this study of the tropical dependency of the Netherlands, Furnivall observed that the rulers and ruled were of different races and lived apart from one another in separate communities. He also noted that a similar pattern was

17. Aristide R. Zolberg, "Mass Parties and National Integration: The Case of the Ivory Coast," *Journal of Politics* 25, no. 1 (February 1963): 36-48.

18. Thomas Molnar, *South West Africa: The Last Pioneer Country* (New York: Fleet Publishing Corporation, 1966), p. 13.

19. For an example of the importance of ethnicity in sub-Saharan Africa see Victor T. Le Vine, *The Cameroons: From Mandate to Independence* (Berkeley and Los Angeles: University of California Press, 1964).

20. (Cambridge: The University Press, 1939).

21. *Ibid.*, p. 446.

practiced in Siam (Thailand) and in such nontropical societies as Canada and South Africa.

Because of his training as an economist, Furnivall naturally focused on the economic aspects of the Dutch colony. Observing that each community possessed a distinct set of values incompatible with those of other cultural groups, he characterized the plural society as one lacking consensus or, in his terms, one without "common social demand." To illustrate his point, Furnivall constructed the following example. The buying of cathedrals involves an expenditure of resources much like the purchase of groceries. In a homogeneous society, the purchase of a cathedral provides an indivisible "public good," i.e., every citizen may benefit from its construction. In the plural society, however, the erection of a Chinese temple constitutes a "public bad" for Muslims; in a similar manner, Muslim mosques provide few or no benefits for Chinese. Therefore, in the plural society social demands often result in public expenditures with benefits for one community and opportunity costs for the others. The plural society thus isolates the demands of its separate communities, and fails to aggregate, in Furnivall's terms, common social demand.

Furnivall points to the presence of separate ethnic demands as a basis for differentiating a plural society from its homogeneous counterpart. In the plural society, the only common meeting ground available to the various cultures is the *marketplace*. Although persons differ culturally, Furnivall asserts that they are all similar in their economic wants — each desires profit. In the absence of national consensus (a common social will), economic competition among the separate communities is the only feasible mutual activity. All other activities are determined by the specific cultural values of the separate communities. Since the values of any one specific community cannot be used as a guideline to govern the behavior of the others, their mutual relations must thereby be governed only by a laissez-faire economic process in which the production of material goods is the prime end of social life. The plural state, therefore, cannot be organized for social or normative ends, since these ends vary with the different cultural norms of the respective communities.

Economic activities, Furnivall observed, were congruent with ethnic divisions: Chinese monopolized trade, Indonesians the rural areas, and Europeans the world of business and administration. This congruence reinforced the parochial cultural views that members of the different communities possessed; economic conflict and other social problems (if they erupted) would thus be viewed as exclusively communal.

Since the production of material goods is the prime end of social life, little time remains for leisure and the arts. The native communities are unable to maintain their traditional standards and institutions: native land tenures are distorted, cheap imports disrupt the native economic system, and nationalist leaders very often adopt Western standards in their fight against Western domination. Nationalist movements in colonial plural societies fail to redress native grievances because they often set one community against the other, further aggravating social instability. As a result, the society requires some *external force* to hold it together. Colonial rule is a prime candidate.[22]

Furnivall's major contribution lies in his observation that plural societies are qualitatively distinct from homogeneous ones, and that the different communities of the plural society can meet only in the marketplace. His insistence that outside force is required to maintain order implies that plural societies are inherently prone to violent conflict.

The Theory of Plural Society: Conceptual Development

In the last two decades several scholars have reported results based on research in areas that fit Furnivall's definition of the plural society. Two of Furnivall's implications in particular have frequently been explored: (1) the separate communities incline toward conflictual behavior, and (2) force rather than consensus maintains order. The first three scholars whose works we examine below challenge these implications.

Stephen Morris in 1956 reported on a study of Indians in the East African societies of Kenya, Tanganyika, Uganda and Zanzibar.[23] He records that Africans number approximately 18,000,000, Arabs 79,000, Europeans 50,000, and Indians 198,000 out of a total population of over 18,300,000. Persons in these ethnic groups exhibit distinct cultural habits, speak different languages, and where possible limit social contacts to their own kind. Economic divisions also coincide with ethnicity: Europeans control the political process, Indians form the commercial class, and Africans comprise the bulk of the urban working class and rural peasantry. East African countries seemingly fit the description of a plural society.

Morris reports in his study that Indians are internally organized into various categories and groups. Although Africans, Arabs, and Europeans

22. In a later comparative study of Burma and the Netherlands Indies, Furnivall reached an identical conclusion, namely, that the external pressure of the colonial power was required to hold together an ethnically divided society. See *Colonial Policy and Practice* (London: Cambridge University Press, 1948). See also "Some Problems of Tropical Economy," in Rita Hinden, ed., *Fabian Colonial Essays* (London: George Allen and Unwin, 1945), pp. 161-84.
23. "Indians in East Africa: A Study in a Plural Society," *British Journal of Sociology* 7, no. 3 (October 1956): 194-211. See also "The Plural Society," *Man* 57, no. 8 (August 1957): 124-25.

find it convenient to use the label "Indians," the fact remains that "more important to an Indian in East Africa than being a Hindu or Muslim, or even, on most occasions, than being an Indian is being an Ismaili, a Patidar, a Sikh, a Goan, or a member of a dozen or so other caste or sectarian groups."[24]

Thus Morris insists that divisions within each racial category are more significant in the composition of the total society than the broader racial categories. He observes that factionalism within ethnic groups forestalls perfect ethnic cohesion, leading, on occasion, to alliances of expediency across racial lines.

These broad ethnic categories — "the Indians," "the Africans," "the Arabs," and "the Europeans" — according to Morris, place undue emphasis on differences between ethnic groups and neglect underlying similarities. Morris notes that plural societies begin to resemble nonplural societies when racial or communal categories are divided into subracial units. Conversely, Morris fears that greater emphasis on racial categories institutionalizes relations in plural societies that might reproduce the normatively undesirable condition of apartheid in South Africa.

Morris, in effect, argues that nonethnic cleavages can cut across racial lines and thereby encourage joint pursuit of some common multiethnic objective. In the towns, for instance, significant social and business relationships often occur among African, European and Indian elites. For example, the Ismailis, a subcategory of Muslim Indians, vacillated in allegiance to other racial subgroups as their interests shifted. The failure of all Indians to cohere on every issue vis-à-vis the other communities thus, Morris asserts, disconfirms Furnivall's thesis of ethnic competition.

Before examining the works of other scholars we should mention that Morris drew his conclusions about race relations in East Africa from work he completed before any of those countries became independent. Anthropologists working in other countries, also in the period preceding independence, arrived at conclusions similar to those of Morris. Daniel J. Crowley, as one example, describes Trinidad as a plural society free from ethnic conflict.[25] He identifies thirteen distinct racial and national groups that comprise the social structure: (1) foreign whites, (2) local whites (French Creoles), (3) light coloreds, (4) coloreds of English origin, (5) coloreds from other West Indian islands, (6) Chinese and Chinese-Creoles, (7) Portuguese, (8) Negroes (Creoles), (9) Spanish-speaking Venezuelans, (10) Syrians and Lebanese, (11) Christian East Indians, (12) Muslim Indians, and (13) Hindus. Crowley contends that

24. *Op. cit.* (1956), p. 207.
25. "Plural and Differential Acculturation in Trinidad," *American Anthropologist* 59, no. 5 (October 1957): 817-24.

14   *The Plural Society*

these groups are not exclusive, despite their distinctiveness, and that members of any group are often proficient in or informed about the cultural activities of other groups.

Mutual knowledge in such vital areas as language, folk belief, magic practice, mating and family structure, festivals and music provides the common ground that makes social unity possible in Trinidad. Crowley labels this the condition of "plural acculturation." Persons within each ethnic category retain their own identity yet are familiar with the cultural activities of other groups. Mutual understanding between groups thus prevents the society from fragmenting to the point of dissolution. (How Crowley would use this framework to explain the 1970 black power riots is not clear!)

Burton Benedict's study of ethnic relations in Mauritius based on field work completed during 1955-57 further corroborates the thesis that Morris and Crowley present.[26] Benedict recorded that Mauritius was changing in the 1950s from a society in which the stratification of racial groups is congruent with distinct economic pursuits to one in which each ethnic section pursues a whole range of occupations. This transition, Benedict asserted, encourages a *rapproachment* of communities on class lines, and deemphasizes ethnic distinctions as a basis for political cohesion. Benedict insisted that class rather than ethnic affiliation influenced political alignment in Mauritius in 1962[27] and that Furnivall's model of the plural society was thereby inappropriate since members in each ethnic category are stratified along a whole range of occupational activities. The process of economic modernization, Benedict suggests, creates cross-cutting institutions which, in turn, foster cooperation among different races.

Figure 1.1

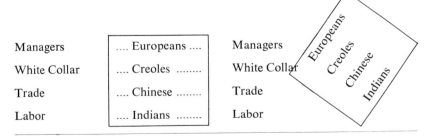

26. *Mauritius: Problems of a Plural Society* (London: Pall Mall Press, 1965), and "Stratification in Plural Societies," *American Anthropologist* 64, no. 6 (December 1962): 1235-46.
27. Mauritius became independent from Britain in 1968.

Figure 1.1 illustrates Benedict's cross-cutting cleavage argument. The congruence of ethnic and occupational categories integral to Furnivall's model appears on the left. In this situation economic competition between ethnic groups creates and intensifies conflict. The cross-cutting cleavage model appears on the right; it shows that each class includes members of several ethnic categories. For example, Europeans, Creoles, Chinese, and Indians all engage in white collar work and trade. Economic modernization thus produces a class-based surrogate for ethnic cohesion.

Benedict admits, however, that ethnic divisions may assume special importance in the political arena. He writes:

> In this paper I have tried to examine social stratification in plural societies. I began by looking at the various statuses of ascription such as ethnic group, religion, and language by which the sections of a plural society are usually differentiated. I found that for Mauritius, and I believe most other societies, corporate groups cannot be differentiated on this basis, *but they sometimes serve as symbols which differentiate blocs in certain political contexts.*[28]

Ethnic conflict in plural societies since 1966 confirms Furnivall's expectations and belies those that his critics have held. Neither intraethnic factionalism, mutual knowledge, cross-cutting cleavages, nor shared values hold together many plural societies today, and normative political consensus does not exist among the respective ethnic strata (even if some *politically irrelevant* shared values do exist).

M. G. Smith, a sociologist with experience in the plural societies of the Caribbean, disagrees with Furnivall's critics.[29] Smith attempts to sharpen the concept of plural society and use it to theorize about ethnic conflict. He defines cultural pluralism as the presence of two or more different cultural traditions in a given population, each possessing a distinct form of the institutions of marriage, the family, religion, property, and the like. Culturally differentiated communities usually vary in their social organization, institutional activities, and their systems of beliefs and values. A plural society is thus a unit only in the political sense: the separate communities are ruled by a single government.

Smith points out that it is erroneous to equate cultural pluralism with "class stratification," since one can vary independently of the other. He uniquely defines a cultural section of a population by its institutional

---

28. "Stratification in Plural Societies," p. 1244 (emphasis added).
29. *The Plural Society in the British West Indies* (Berkeley and Los Angeles: University of California, 1965), pp. xii-xiii.

practices that may or may not be compatible with those of other cultural
sections. Consequently, cross-cutting cleavages of class or ideology need
not mitigate ethnic distinctions—indeed, they may be irrelevant to them.

When the separate communities in a plural society have distinct institutional practices, then the *society relies upon forceful regulation to keep
order*. In Smith's own words

> Given the fundamental differences of belief, value and organiza-
> tion that connote pluralism, the monopoly of power by one cultural
> section is the essential precondition for the maintenance of the total
> society in its current form.[30]

Not all societies composed of diverse cultural groups are plural societies in Smith's view. Plural society is characterized by the coexistence
of incompatible institutional systems and, therefore, force must be used
to maintain order; "pluralistic" societies, on the other hand, contain one
or more relatively distinct subcultures, but their value systems are compatible with the national political consensus. Reliance on force in the
plural society is greatest when the politically dominant communities are
small minorities, e.g., Rhodesia, South Africa.

Smith contributes to our understanding of politics in plural societies
in two ways. First, he demonstrates that cross-cutting cleavages of class
or ideology do not eliminate ethnic distinctions and their political rami-
fications. Second, he draws our attention to the fact that not all societies
containing cultural diversity behave politically as plural societies. Brazil
and the United States, for example, each contain several disparate cultural groups, yet reliance on forceful regulation to compensate for ethnic
conflict is minimal, though perhaps growing since 1960. Furnivall's model
by implication thus applies only where sharp ethnic divisions result in
the political crystallization of communities — the plural society.[31]

Before examining the work of political scientists, we must note that
some sociologists have explored the political implications of a plural social structure. Pierre L. van den Berghe, for example, has tried to specify
the relevant preconditions of democracy in plural societies. He observes:
(1) The prospects for democracy are directly proportional to the degree
of basic value consensus in the society, and inversely proportional to the

30. *Ibid.*, p. 86.
31. For additional contributions to this debate, see J. D. Mitchell, *Tribalism and
the Plural Society* (London: Oxford University Press, 1960); Leo A. Despres,
Cultural Pluralism and Nationalist Politics in British Guiana (Chicago: Rand
McNally and Co., 1967); and Pierre L. van den Berghe, *Race and Racism: A Comparative Perspective* (New York: John Wiley and Sons, Inc., 1967).

degree of cultural pluralism. (2) The prospects for democracy are a direct function of the degree of consensus about the procedural norms of government. (3) The prospects for democracy are a direct function of the norms governing the legitimacy of pluralism and the integrity of each separate community. (4) Stable democracy requires an approximate scientific and technological balance between the constituent groups. (5) Conflict is minimized when cleavages are cross-cutting, rather than coinciding, unless *one type of cleavage assumes overwhelming salience vis-à-vis the others* leading to the disintegration of the polity.[32] Democracy in the plural society is undermined if political parties express purely ethnic sentiments.

Taking stock, we may fairly observe that scholars have thus far been unable to provide a systematic explanation of the conflicts that periodically occur in many plural societies. In part, this inability is due to an intellectual framework that compels the theorist to define society as an integrated set of elements (e.g., "plural acculturation" in Trinidad). This definition leads one to search for common values and practices — the more that are found, the better. By placing an emphasis on the quantity of cross-cutting cleavages and multiple affiliations, social scientists have paid little attention to the *political* salience of these cleavages. They have concluded, then, that the discovery of a core of common values or memberships indicates an integrated society and a low probability of the occurrence of ethnic conflict.

The historical period in which many of these studies were completed reinforced the bias of their analytical frameworks. Social scientists completed most of their field research in Africa, Asia and the Caribbean between 1950 and 1965; during this period ethnic leaders temporarily discarded their differences to join in a multiethnic struggle against the common colonial enemy. *These multiethnic nationalist movements in preindependent plural societies were presumed to foreshadow future patterns of cooperative behavior.* Evidence obtained in the field thus confirmed the consensual character of plural societies that the logic of their analysis implied.

If the proof of the pudding is in the eating, however, then either the recipe or the ingredients are to blame. The scholars whose work we have reviewed are victims of both theoretical omissions (e.g., political salience) and fieldwork restricted to the limited period of postwar, multiethnic nationalist movements. Nationalist politics since the mid-sixties *now*

---

32. "Pluralism and the Polity: A Theoretical Exploration," in Leo Kuper and M. G. Smith, eds., *Pluralism in Africa* (Berkeley and Los Angeles: University of California Press, 1969), pp. 67-81 (emphasis added).

generally entails interethnic political competition, and the cooperative behavior that was predicted to continue is now a virtual memory of the past.

In our review we have thus far neglected the work of political scientists. This does not mean political scientists do not grapple with the problem that cultural diversity poses for sustained democratic stability. On the contrary, the problem occupies the attention of a good many students of ethnic politics, but is couched in different language. Political scientists explore theories of "political integration" rather than theories of plural society. Their overriding concern is to determine whether cultural unity is a necessary and/or sufficient condition for political unity. They have yet to reach full agreement on this point.

Karl Deutsch, for instance, finds a considerable correspondence between general cultural homogeneity, homogeneous political culture, and political integration in his survey of theories of nationalism.[33] In his later study of the North Atlantic area, he and his collaborators find that "mutual compatibility of main values" is an essential condition for certain types of integrated communities.[34] Philip Jacob confirms the findings of Deutsch. He asserts that an integrated community requires compatibility and shared values among its constituent members.[35] Similarly Leonard Binder argues that national integration requires a cultural-ideological consensus,[36] while James S. Coleman and Carl G. Rosberg believe that a homogeneous political community entails a reduction in cultural tensions.[37]

The impression one gleans from a reading of these scholars is that shared values are a necessary prerequisite of political integration. However, not all students of politics view the problem of political integration from this perspective. Lewis Coser and Seymour Martin Lipset, for example, point to the theme of multiple group memberships. Multiple affiliations, they argue, not only prevent a single deep cleavage, and thereby enhance the chances for stable democracy; as well, these associations insulate the individual by binding his fate to that of other kinds

33. *Nationalism and Social Communication* (Cambridge, Massachusetts: Technology Press, 1953), p. 13.

34. Deutsch, et al., *Political Community and the North Atlantic Area: International Organization in the Light of Historical Experience* (Princeton: Princeton University Press, 1957), pp. 58, 66.

35. "The Influence of Values in Political Integration," in Philip E. Jacob and James V. Toscano, eds., *The Integration of Political Communities* (Philadelphia: Lippincott, 1964), pp. 209-10.

36. "National Integration and Political Development," *American Political Science Review* 58, no. 3 (September 1964): 630.

37. *Political Parties and National Integration in Tropical Africa* (Berkeley: University of California Press, 1964), p. 9.

of people.[38] Their point, then, is that the absence of cultural diversity may be positively harmful to the prospects of stable democracy.

For somewhat different reasons Ernst Haas and Amitai Etzioni agree that general cultural homogeneity is not an essential prerequisite of stable democracy and political integration. Haas contends that pragmatic calculations of mutual economic advantage can bring together disparate interest groups and politicians. General cultural homogeneity is not required.[39] Etzioni, on the other hand, argues the point on salience grounds: many cultural characteristics may not be politically relevant — shared culture simply has little effect on political unification, though it may help advance the process to a higher stage.[40] Such differences as religion are amenable to depoliticization and thus become a politically irrelevant cleavage in the general culture.

One other formulation deserves our attention. We refer to the work of Arend Lijphart who offers the concept of the consociational democracy.[41] Consociationalism entails conscious cooperation among elites of different communities to control the destabilizing effects of open, ethnic competition. This is accomplished by elite agreements to restrict the circulation of more extremist junior elites and to resist mass pressures from the electorate for political change. Furthermore consociationalism posits that each community must subscribe to the notion of political autonomy for the other subcultures. As examples of consociational democracies, Lijphart cites Austria, Switzerland, the Netherlands, Belgium, and Lebanon (though events suggest the latter two may no longer fit his model). Thus in the case of the consociational democracy, astute leaders can control the political salience of cultural diversity.

We have learned in this brief review that political scientists, like sociologists and anthropologists, neither have a uniform notion of cultural diversity (e.g., what constitutes a plural society?) nor concur on its political implications. Some of these disagreements, we believe, might be resolved by a fresh focus on the question of salience. Definitional

---

38. Coser, *The Functions of Social Conflict* (Glencoe: Free Press, 1956), pp. 78-79 and Lipset, *Political Man: The Social Bases of Politics* (Garden City: Anchor Books, 1963), p. 77. A similar pluralist argument is posed by William Kornhauser, *The Politics of Mass Society* (New York: The Free Press, 1959).

39. *The Uniting of Europe: Political, Social, and Economic Forces, 1950-57* (Stanford: Stanford University Press, 1958), pp. xv-xvi. In a later paper he changes his mind and suggests that integrative decisions demand either forceful leaders or "a widely shared normative consensus." "*The Uniting of Europe* and the Uniting of Latin America," *Journal of Common Market Studies* 5, no. 4 (June 1967): 327-28.

40. *Political Unification: A Comparative Study of Leaders and Forces* (New York: Holt, Rinehart and Winston, 1965), pp. 35-36.

41. "Consociational Democracy," *World Politics* 21, no. 2 (January 1969): 207-25.

rigor, however, precedes any such resolution. We turn, then, to our own definition of the plural society.

A Definition of Plural Society

This book presents a paradigm of the political process in plural societies. We recall that Furnivall identifies the plural society by the presence of two or more separate communities living side by side, but separately, in the same political unit; economic divisions also coincide with cultural divisions. M. G. Smith sharpens that definition by attributing to the separate communities different institutional structures. Others note that a consensus of social, economic and political values is not present. In short, the existence of separate cultural groups with generally incompatible sets of values constitutes a necessary condition for a plural society.

The presence of cultural diversity constantly strikes scholars as the crucial feature of plural societies. R. S. Milne, a Malaysian specialist, confidently claims:

> More than anything else, the racial composition of Malaysia is the key to understanding the whole picture. It dictates the pattern of the economy, has helped to shape the constitution, and has influenced the democratic process and the party system.[42]

This statement, with appropriate substitutions, applies to many other plural societies.

At the outset, then, we recognize cultural diversity as a necessary condition for a plural society: if a society is plural, then it is culturally diverse. However, nearly every modern society is culturally diverse. Thus, although the existence of well-defined ethnic groups with generally incompatible values constitutes a necessary condition of the plural society, it is not sufficient.

The hallmark of the plural society, and the feature that distinguishes it from its pluralistic counterpart, is the practice of politics almost exclusively along ethnic lines. To put the emphasis differently, in the plural society — but *not* in the pluralistic society — the overwhelming preponderance of political conflicts is perceived in ethnic terms. Permanent ethnic communities acting cohesively on nearly all political issues determine a plural society and distinguish it from a culturally

---

42. *Government and Politics in Malaysia* (Boston: Houghton Mifflin Company, 1967), p. 3.

heterogeneous, nonplural society. In pluralistic countries, where coalitions often vary from issue to issue, the cultural categories tend neither to be carefully demarcated nor always politically salient. Italian-Americans, for example, though they may vote cohesively on some issues, often divide on a great many others. And, in the United States, Italian and Irish highway contractors view themselves as businessmen, not ethnic representatives, in competition.

To summarize, a society is plural if it is culturally diverse *and* if its cultural sections are organized into cohesive political sections. The identification of a plural society, then, becomes a matter of observation. Politically organized cultural sections, communally based political parties, the partitioning of major social groups (e.g., labor unions) into culturally homogeneous subgroups, and political appeals emphasizing primordial sentiments serve as unambiguous indicators of a plural society.[43]

Summary

We began this chapter with a review of recent political disorders in culturally diverse polities. Although the types of cultural pluralism vary widely, we nonetheless observe that most independent plural societies fail to retain, over any sustained period, stable democratic politics.

A recurrent assumption seems to underlie much research on plural societies: *viz.*, mutual interaction and mutual understanding among persons of different communities engenders harmonious relations. Education and other forms of social engineering, e.g., multiracial neighborhoods, are often designed to reduce or eliminate ethnic animosities. The first few pages of this chapter run counter to this belief. Industrialization and education do not eliminate tensions in Belgium or Canada. Even in America, where education is widespread and the color bar considerably reduced, ethnic and racial sentiments are now increasing as any urban resident in northern American cities knows.

Generally speaking, pessimistic conclusions have followed optimistic predictions. The disparity between prophecy and fact demands that we

---

43. Although our definition permits an empirical distinction between plural and pluralistic societies, it does not *account* for the distinction. That is, it does not explain why some culturally diverse societies are plural and others are not. Typically, however, definitions are not called upon to perform such tasks. What is needed is *a theory* — a theory, we argue, of political entrepreneurship. Such a theory would specify the conditions under which political entrepreneurs succeed in converting natural communities into active and antithetical *political* communities. In this book we take the empirical distinction as given. For the present it is beyond our capacity to provide a theoretical explanation for this distinction. It is an interesting and important theoretical question that clearly merits further inquiry.

reexamine the "theory of plural society" and offer explanations that are consistent with more recent developments. The theme of the next seven chapters is that ethnic politics in the plural society is a consequence of logical processes, not fortuitous happenings. To understand and describe that logic requires the development of a theoretical apparatus. Chapter 2 begins on that note.

CHAPTER 2

Theoretical Tools

The Great Depression was a sobering experience for the laissez-faire economist and businessman. Its overwhelming effects cast doubt on his ability to account for and control processes within his area of expertise. Indeed, it undermined confidence in an entire economic Weltanschauung and led some to wonder aloud, "Is the invisible hand losing its grip?"[1]

In more recent years the social scientist's experience with plural societies has been equally sobering, as events reviewed in the previous chapter suggest. Amidst predictions of mutual harmony and progress, multiethnic colonial territories were granted independence during two decades of postwar optimism only to fall victim to internal upheaval, economic stagnation, and communal suspicions. Multiethnic cooperation and compatibility, predictions notwithstanding, dissolved along with the last British, French, Dutch, and Belgian troops. By the same token, more established states have not been spared this fate.

Events in the late 1960s belie the predictions of theorists of the plural society and suggest the necessity of reexamining basic premises. *These premises must be altered to account both for the patterns of conflict, as well as cooperation, which appear at various times in the plural society's experience.* Our task, therefore, is to provide the tools and vocabulary that facilitate such a reexamination. The reexamination employs the language of decision theory. Although the relevance of many of the concepts developed here may not immediately be clear, their complexity suggests that we treat them first in the abstract, unencumbered with substantive interpretations. Chapter 2 is thus a condensation of the appropriate tools of decision

---

1. Herbert Fergus Thompson, Jr., "Is The 'Invisible Hand' Losing Its Grip?" in H. C. Harlan, ed., *Readings in Economics and Politics* (New York: Oxford University Press, 1961), pp. 134-40.

theory. After the logical tools are presented, we turn in chapter 3 to substantive issues; there we develop the theory of politics in the plural society.

Politics and Preference Aggregation

> If the urban areas, constituting more than half the people of Malaya, give their verdict for the winds of change, no leader can afford to ignore it. Parliamentary democracy . . . will work only if people choose rationally from the alternatives they are offered in an election.[2]
>
> —Lee Kuan Yew

During the 1964 election campaign Lee Kuan Yew reminded the citizens of Malaya of an important choice they were to make. He advised them to "choose rationally." Lee's statement is instructive for it focuses on a fundamental component of human behavior in general, and political behavior in particular: choice among alternatives.

Choice is the basic act that transforms essentially private thoughts and values into "public activity," i.e., decisions. While "public activities" are the phenomena with which the behavioral scientist is concerned, the act of choice renders them observable. Since it is incumbent upon the social scientist to explain or rationalize observable behavior, the act of choice, or decision-making, seems a natural focus of analysis.

The Concept of Preference. We begin our theory of the plural society with the individual citizen. He has tastes, values, and preferences concerning a whole range of objects. Most of these tastes are essentially private. They involve private consumption and personal interaction and hence have implications only for their holder and perhaps his close associates: how one dresses, what one eats, who one marries, and so on. Since the consequences of these choices are restricted primarily to the individual chooser, such institutions of aggregation as the marketplace prove quite satisfactory in processing private preference demands. That is, for those "goods and services" with minimal external effects, individual interaction and bargaining, as well as collective devices like the marketplace, satisfactorily aggregate the private tastes, values, and preferences of individuals, constrained only by the law of scarcity.

Other choices, however, may have considerable external effects. One such category involves the private imposition of involuntary costs or benefits on others, as when a manufacturer dumps industrial wastes in a

---

2. Reported in K. J. Ratnam and R. S. Milne, *The Malayan Parliamentary Election of 1964* (Singapore: University of Malaya Press, 1967), pp. 147-48.

public lake or when a philanthropist endows a public museum. Because negative externalities impose involuntary costs on others, and because the marketplace is unable to provide compensation for those who bear these costs, community political institutions are often called upon to resolve the conflicts that are generated. A second category of choices possessing external effects thus results: political choices. This category includes preferences about the public sector, its role in the life of the individual, its scope and authority, and the specific content of its policies — that is, constitutional and substantive choices.

Although the methods of preference aggregation in the marketplace and the political arena differ in notable ways — the most significant being that political decisions are universally binding and hence nonvoluntaristic, whereas markets are characterized by voluntary exchange — the processes involved in each are strikingly similar. Each begins with individual preferences and converts them into aggregate outcomes: market allocations and political decisions, respectively. Preference, then, provides a convenient starting place for theories of social choice — political as well as economic.

For the purposes of analysis we conceive of the individual as a bundle of tastes, values and preferences. We do not engage "in elaborate speculation about the nature of man or the reasons for an individual's desire of some certain thing. We observe that different people want different things, and that the same person will want different things at different times."[3] To proceed we invoke a rather simple assumption, namely that individual preferences are "well-defined" and that individuals act on the basis of their tastes.[4] This assumption has been reasonably well substantiated in the private sector and, indeed, probably conforms rather closely with most personal observations and experiences. People purchase what they desire in the marketplace, constrained only by the scarcity of desirable objects and budget limitations. Political behavior, we suggest, follows this same pattern: people have preferences and seek to satisfy them subject to the political "rules of the game." From the perspective of the individual, the public sector is another source of "goods and services."

---

3. Gordon Tullock, *Toward a Mathematics of Politics* (Ann Arbor: University of Michigan Press, 1967), p. 1.

4. We must be clear about the nature of assumptions. They are analytical devices. Although one may strive to provide intuitive justification, the utility of these assumptions does not depend upon their empirical accuracy. Indeed, at times they seriously distort common sense perceptions. *However, the appropriate criterion by which to evaluate assumptions is the "quality" of the implications which follow from them, not their realism.* For a carefully developed essay explicating this point, see Milton Friedman, *Essays in Positive Economics* (Chicago: University of Chicago Press, 1953), chap. 1.

We do not claim to know why man prefers *what* he does. Nor do we specify what man *should* prefer. We simply observe that individuals have preferences, however arrived at, and that knowledge of these preferences permits us to account for observed behavior.

The major primitive term in our discussion, preference, is characterized by two properties: (1) completeness, and (2) consistency. The former, called *connectivity*, asserts that an individual is capable of expressing preference between the alternatives offered him. That is, for the abstract dyad of alternatives (a, b) the individual either prefers a to b, b to a, or is indifferent between the two.[5] Put another way, we say that preferences are well-defined only for alternatives that possess relevant dimensions of comparison. Thus the preference relation is not well-defined for the dyad (Democratic party, New York Yankees).

The second property characterizing well-defined preferences is *transitivity*. This property stipulates a special form of consistency in expressed preferences. Whereas connectivity is defined on dyads of alternatives, transitivity is a triadic concept. Consider an abstract triad of alternatives (a, b, c). Suppose individual i has connected preferences. Thus, he can express a preference in each of the three dyads (a, b), (b, c), and (a, c). The transitivity condition restricts the form in which preferences on the three dyads may be jointly expressed. In particular, if a is preferred to b and b is preferred to c, it cannot be the case that c is preferred or indifferent to a. If c were preferred (indifferent) to a, then our commonsense notion of consistency would be distorted. Riker expresses this point well:

> Ordinarily we say that a person is quite confused if he says, for example, that he prefers Wallace to Goldwater, Goldwater to Johnson, and Johnson to Wallace. The effect of this axiom [transitivity] is to eliminate this kind of confusion.[6]

Symbolically, then, transitivity is represented by the following logical implication:

$$a \ P \ b \text{ and } b \ P \ c \rightleftharpoons a \ P \ c.$$

The connectivity and transitivity conditions permit us to conceive of individual preferences as *ordered*. Hence, we may speak of *preference*

---

5. Symbolically the connectivity property for the ith individual is written aP_ib or bP_ia or aI_ib, where P_i and I_i are the strict preference and indifference operators for i, respectively. Ordinarily the subscript i is deleted in our discussion unless the context is unclear.

6. William H. Riker, "Arrow's Theorem and Some Examples of the Paradox of Voting," in John M. Claunch, ed., *Mathematical Applications in Political Science* (Dallas: Southern Methodist University Press, 1965), 1: 41-60 (quotation at p. 44).

orderings. Throughout this book the individual is, in effect, represented by his preference ordering. Thus, the fundamental behavioral assumption on which this analysis rests — indeed, upon which all *rational choice models* depend — asserts that individual behavior is motivated by well-defined preferences.

At this point several comments are in order. First, we observe that the preference ordering is a logical construct possessing a logical structure. It does not have anything to do with "truth." An individual may have "wrong" preferences (from the perspective of, say, you, the reader), or may have correct preferences but for the wrong reasons. These considerations are of no account in our analysis, and hence no substantive restrictions are placed on preferences. Second, we note that particular preferences do not imply particular kinds of behavior. The behavior associated with any given preference ordering may vary with the political context. Third, we suppose that preferences are determined *a priori* and are fixed in the short run. Although we do not preclude the possibility of long-term changes in preferences, we do assume that in the short run tastes remain constant.

Collective Choice: The Resolution of Incompatible Preferences. Individuals have preferences; the community does not. Statements alluding to a "general will" or a "community sentiment" are cases of false personification, as is the proverbial invisible hand of the marketplace. Collective choice, as reflected in governmental policies, market allocations, and social traditions, is nothing more than the aggregation, in some fashion, of individual preferences.

The *raison d'etre* of social institutions of aggregation follows from a very simple observation: people are not alike. People have different, often conflicting, ideas about the ways in which the public weal and public authority should be used. In plural societies the conflicts are often so severe that they literally overwhelm the social institutions created to resolve them. However, some collective choice institutions operate rather smoothly. Consider the perfectly competitive market.

People come to the "marketplace" (which may be no farther than the Sears & Roebuck catalogue in the front parlor) with preferences (demands) for various goods and services, and with items of value (which may be a numeraire such as money or simply other goods and services) to exchange. Incompatibilities arise as a result of scarcity. That is, at so-called nonequilibrium exchange rates, the quantity of the commodities demanded by consumers exceeds (is exceeded by) the quantity suppliers are willing to provide.[7] The market mechanism coordinates preferences so

---

7. Learning this lesson is often costly, as the manufacturers of the Edsel automobile well know!

that exchange rates and allocations of productive capacity change in response to demand schedules. In the end "all markets are cleared," as the economist says, and those who desire exchange at the final market exchange rate are satisfied.

Not only is this description of the perfectly competitive market oversimplified, it is "wrong" as well. Nowhere, with the possible exception of bartering for candy on a children's playground, does a market such as the one described above exist. However, this simple model, greatly embellished, has served to generate a number of implications that account for real-world market regularities.

The model of collective choice in plural societies we develop has many parallels to the free market model. However, unlike the free market and its law of scarcity, political choice is governed by the *law of contradiction,* a fundamental axiom of Aristotelian logic. It asserts that the event resulting from the conjunction of two incompatible events is impossible. Consider a two-person polity composed of citizens A and B. Citizen A has preferences about the policies of the collectivity, as does Citizen B. Let us call these preferences a and b, respectively. However, suppose that b implies $\sim a$ (read: not a). The law of contradiction asserts that the preferences of A and B cannot be satisfied simultaneously. There arises, then, the need for a rule, usually embodied in a set of institutions, which transforms individual preferences into a collective choice.

The rule, a *political decision function,* is formulated so as to provide a collective choice for any conceivable combination of individual preferences. Two extreme candidates for "the rule" are dictatorship and unanimity. The former identifies a specific individual (called the dictator, naturally) whose preference is identical to the collective choice regardless of the preferences of other citizens in the polity. The latter rule identifies "the will of all" as the collective choice, if it exists; in the absence of unanimity, the status quo prevails.

The decision function that has most interested scholars, for ideological as well as practical reasons, is majority rule. Methods of majority rule, however, are many and varied. Without getting involved in a host of side issues, we concentrate on certain quantitative characteristics of majority decision rules.

Initially we may distinguish *simple majority rule* from *rule by special majority.* The former specifies the collective choice as that alternative receiving more than fifty percent of the votes cast in pair-wise voting. Thus, if there are N voters (where N is any positive number), the number of votes required for an alternative to be declared the collective choice must be at least as large as d, where

$$d = \begin{cases} \dfrac{N+1}{2} & \text{if } N \text{ odd} \\[2ex] \dfrac{N}{2}+1 & \text{if } N \text{ even} \end{cases}$$

Rule by special majority, in its most general form, subsumes simple majority rule. However, the term "special majority" is typically reserved for schemes other than simple majority rule. A special-majority rule provides a *critical proportion*—the proportion of votes needed for a collective choice. Typically, this proportion exceeds that required in simple majority rule and is often reserved for very important decisions, e.g., constitutional amendments.

Because of egalitarian considerations and certain desirable logical properties,[8] *simple* majority rule is the scheme usually proffered and analyzed by scholars. We, too, restrict our remarks to this rule.

Owing to a number of confusions, it is important to be precise in identifying the properties of simple majority rule. In this light, then, we seek to answer two questions:

1. What constitutes a majority decision? and
2. Does a majority decision necessarily exist?

We define a majority alternative as one that obtains a majority of the votes against any alternative on the agenda. That is, if (and only if) a particular alternative can obtain a majority (*d*-votes as defined earlier) when paired against all other alternatives, each in turn, then (and only then) it is declared the majority alternative. An example illustrates this definition.

Suppose we have an electorate of three voters (I, II, II) that decides upon a collective policy from among three alternatives (*a, b, c*). The voters' preference orderings are:

I	II	III
a	*b*	*c*
b	*a*	*a*
c	*c*	*b*

---

8. Robert A. Dahl, *A Preface to Democratic Theory* (Chicago: University of Chicago Press, 1956); Douglas W. Rae, "Decision–Rules and Individual Values in Constitutional Choice," *American Political Science Review* 63, no. 1 (March 1969): 40-56; and Charles R. Plott, "Individual Choice of a Decision Process," in Richard G. Niemi and Herbert F. Weisberg, eds., *Probability Models of Collective Decision Making* (Columbus: Charles E. Merrill, 1972).

That is, reading down the table, voter I most prefers *a*, prefers *b* next, and *c* last. Similar interpretations hold for II and III. Consider *a*. For the dyad (*a,b*), the preference orderings indicate that voters I and III choose *a*. For the dyad (*a,c*), voters I and II choose *a*. Thus, *a* obtains a majority when paired against each of the remaining alternatives and, according to our definition, is the majority alternative. Note that *a* is not *most-preferred* by a majority of the voters. Only voter I most prefers *a*. Of course, if a majority of voters, like I, ranked *a* highest in their preference orderings, then it would satisfy our definition of majority alternative. We simply observe that this is not necessary, as the example indicates.

The answer to the second question—does a majority decision necessarily exist?—may be somewhat surprising and disconcerting to the reader. It does *not* necessarily follow that the simple majority decision rule provides a majority alternative. To see that some sets of preference orderings, i.e., some electorates, do not possess a majority alternative, consider the following arrangement:

I	II	III
a	*b*	*c*
b	*c*	*a*
c	*a*	*b*

Alternative *a* is preferred by a majority to *b* (I, III), but not to *c*. Voters II and III prefer *c* to *a*. Thus, *a* is not a majority alternative. Neither is *b* since, as we have already seen, *a* is preferred by a majority to it. That leaves *c*: *c* is preferred to *a* (II, III), but voters I and II prefer *b* to *c*. We have, then, an unusual result: *a* is preferred to *b*, but not to *c*; *b* is preferred to *c*, but not to *a*; and *c* is preferred to *a*, but not to *b*. No majority alternative exists.[9]

A majority alternative, if it exists, has the normatively satisfying property of being preferred to *any* alternative by a majority. Furthermore, if it exists, it may be selected even if a pair-wise comparison voting process is not employed.[10] On the other hand, if no majority alternative exists, as

---

9. This occurrence is called the *paradox of voting* or the *cyclical majority problem*. A great deal of attention has been given to it, due in part to its potentially devastating effect on majority rule. For an early consideration of this problem in an explicitly political context, see Duncan Black, *The Theory of Committees and Elections* (Cambridge: The University Press, 1963), pp. 46-51. Also see William H. Riker, "Voting and the Summation of Preferences: An Interpretative Bibliographic Review of Selected Developments During the Last Decade," *American Political Science Review* 55, no. 4 (December 1961): 900-12. For a more recent and more rigorous treatment see Amartya Sen, *Collective Choice and Social Welfare* (San Francisco: Holden-Day, 1970).

10. See Black, *op. cit.*, p. 24. However, some processes, e. g., plurality voting, may eliminate a majority alternative.

in the previous example, and if a collective choice is made nonetheless, then the particular outcome depends upon extraneous criteria like the order of voting or parliamentary skill, and not only upon the preferences of a majority. In fact, the preferences of a majority necessarily will be frustrated: in the previous example, whether *a*, *b*, or *c* is chosen, some majority of voters prefers another alternative.

It is important to emphasize the logic and consequences of this simple argument. Collective choice procedures are instituted to resolve preference conflicts not otherwise resolvable by individualistic mechanisms. With the same certainty as death and taxes, these collective choice procedures always produce outcomes (which includes the possibility of the unaltered status quo). In many instances, under simple majority rule, that outcome is a majority alternative. However, it is entirely possible that the outcome produced does not possess majority-alternative properties. Thus, *a priori*, we observe that majorities may be frustrated in their preferences for collective policies, and that this frustration may have implications for regime legitimacy and stability. *Remember, this is an* a priori *assertion.* Shortly we argue that in certain contexts even majority alternatives are unacceptable.

Outcomes and Expectations. Democratic politics, defined in terms of preference aggregation and collective choice, is clearly outcome-oriented. Political institutions process citizen preferences in order to determine courses of action for the collectivity. Those institutions and their personnel find citizen acceptance, and hence loyalty and allegiance, to the extent that the outcomes their policies produce are compatible with the preferences of citizens.

Is there not, however, another dimension of evaluation separate from, though not independent of, the "effectiveness" of political institutions? Lipset has suggested a second dimension, legitimacy, which "involves the capacity of the system to engender and maintain the belief that the existing political institutions are the most appropriate ones for society."[11] Legitimacy is an affective dimension; effectiveness is instrumental. The former, though related to outcomes, is "procedural," i.e., a judgment of the appropriateness of collective choice procedures. However, by what standards does one judge the appropriateness of collective choice procedures? We do not believe that the abstract concepts of fairness or justice are sufficiently unambiguous to serve as general standards. It is difficult to imagine, for example, a group loyally submitting to a series of "procedurally fair" decisions which, in effect, emasculates its culture. "One man, one vote" in Ceylon is not fair, from the perspective of the Tamil minority, precisely

---

11. Seymour M. Lipset, *Political Man* (Garden City: Anchor Books, 1959), p. 64.

because the Sinhalese majority can legislate restrictions on Tamil culture and language. Fairness, equity, and justice are not universal because they cannot be untangled from preferences and expectations about outcomes. When individuals have incompatible preferences, *and expect these incompatibilities to persist over a number of important issues,* then it is not likely that a consistent "loser" will grant the political institutions legitimacy.

Thus, legitimacy is closely associated with outcomes. Yet, as Lipset has demonstrated, some polities have retained the allegiance of their citizens despite poor performances. That is, citizens have remained loyal to the governing institutions and political leaders even though their preferences have not been well satisfied. We would suggest that the notion of "expectations about outcomes" captures this sufficiently. Individuals remain loyal to a regime so long as they *expect* the regime to implement some of their preferences in the future, despite their unhappiness with current policy outcomes. This is only a necessary condition. Policy satisfaction—effectiveness—must be forthcoming as well. The individual who expects frustration of his goals as a matter of course, who perceives political institutions as biased in favor of goals incompatible with his own, who feels *systematically* discriminated against, is not likely to confer legitimacy on the regime responsible.

Thus, both effectiveness and legitimacy are outcome-oriented. The former is a judgment about current policy; the latter a judgment about future likelihoods and viable alternatives. The *processes* by which outcomes are generated are *not* evaluated in their own right by the actors involved except as those processes relate to outcomes. Although ambiguous political rhetoric and other elite efforts to legitimize process often influence citizen expectations about outcomes, the chronic loser ultimately considers the process itself illegitimate. The mechanisms of collective choice possess significant normative import, but for now it suffices to say that *politics is method*—it is the way in which collective decisions, and hence outcomes, are determined.

In this section we have examined the notion of preference and argued for an outcome-oriented definition of politics. In later chapters we present evidence that suggests this is a useful way to approach political phenomena. First, however, we develop a vocabulary and notation that permits efficient communication and logical deductions. These will serve as the building blocks for our theory of plural society.

Utility and the Risk Environment

In the previous section we assumed that the individual citizen possessed well-defined preferences. In particular, it is assumed that individual preferences satisfy the conditions that define an *ordering,* namely:

1. connectivity, and
2. transitivity.

Second, we posited a behavioral assumption which states that people act on the basis of their preferences, i.e., people reveal their preferences by their political choices (behavior). Provisionally we take this to mean that individuals are maximizers of something—that their behavior is maximizing behavior. This section is devoted to specifying what is maximized.

Utility. We have seen that once our behavioral assumption is accepted, an individual's preference ordering permits us to predict the direction of his behavior. Thus in a voting situation, if a citizen prefers alternative a to b, then we would predict, *ceteris paribus,* that he will vote for a, if he votes at all. Suppose, however, that he prefers a to b and b to c (and by transitivity a to c) but that the alternatives appearing on the agenda (ballot) are:

1. b for certain, and
2. a with some probability p, c with complementary probability $(1-p)$.

The second item on the agenda is a risky alternative. If item (2) is selected by the collectivity then something akin to a lottery is conducted, figuratively speaking: outcome a or c results with probability p and $(1-p)$, respectively.

We believe that choices involving risky alternatives are frequently encountered in the political arena. The political world is an inherently uncertain place. The "random shocks" of external events and the ambiguity generated (at times purposely) by institutions and elites sometimes defy the ordinary citizen to relate the alternatives before him to his underlying values or preferences.

The "ballot box principle" for the selection of officers of democratic collectivities is instructive. Individuals have preferences for certain collective policies or outcomes. In the selection of officers, however, they vote for individuals, not for policies. Furthermore, the relationship between a candidate for office and his actions once in office are but vaguely connected in the mind of the typical citizen. Thus, in effect, in the selection of a candidate, the citizen is choosing among risky alternatives, e.g., if candidate A is elected, then outcome a obtains with probability p and outcome c with complementary probability $(1-p)$.

Given the possibility—indeed, the likelihood—of choice involving risky alternatives, the individual preference ordering in the above situation (a P b, b P c, a P c) is no longer sufficient to predict preference or choice. In order to determine whether the individual prefers b for certain, or the *lottery* $[pa, (1-p)c]$, we need some measure on preferences—a measure of value. This measure is called *utility*.

The history of the theory of utility is a controversial one. Under the label "moral expectation," utility was first treated seriously by such seventeenth- and eighteenth-century philosophers as Pascal, Cramer, and Daniel Bernoulli.[12] It came to full flower in the nineteenth-century utilitarian philosophy of Jeremy Bentham and James and John Stuart Mill. However, during the nineteenth-century development of economic science, and especially after its ordinal revolution, the utility concept lost favor. Its scientific usefulness ended as it became possible to account for economic observations with a much weaker set of assumptions.

The utility renaissance occurred some two decades ago with the publication of von Neumann and Morgenstern's *The Theory of Games and Economic Behavior*.[13] In this volume, the authors make several important contributions to a theory of value.

First, they correct the misunderstanding of the Benthamite utilitarians that utility inheres in objects thus giving them value. Utility, von Neumann and Morgenstern tell us, is a *derivative* concept. It does not inhere in objects; rather, it exists in the mind of an individual, giving the object in question value *for him*. Thus utility is a *subjective* feature of an individual's value system, not an objective property of objects.

Second, they demonstrate that utility is a *relative measure*. The assignment of utility numbers to alternatives is not invariant as the set of alternatives changes. That is, a utility number may be used as a comparative index of value so long as the set of alternatives comprising the basis of comparison remains fixed. This is simply another way of stating that value does not inhere in commodities (or anything else about which individuals express preference) in any absolute sense. The value of an object is relative and thus depends on the nature of alternative objects.

Third, and perhaps most important from a theoretical point of view, von Neumann and Morgenstern produce a set of statements (axioms) that imply the existence of a measure of value.[14] Shortly we illustrate their measure of value and its properties, but for now it is sufficient to say that a measure of value exists, is cardinal (and thus possesses certain desirable quantitative features not present in preference orderings), is unique to positive linear transformations, and is not interpersonally comparable.[15]

---

12. For some historical remarks see George Stigler, "The Development of Utility Theory," *Journal of Political Economy* 58, nos. 4-5 (August-October 1950): 307-27, 373-96; and Jacob Marschak, "Why 'Should' Statisticians and Businessmen Maximize 'Moral Expectation'?" in Jerzy Neyman, ed., *Proceedings of the Second Berkeley Symposium on Mathematical Statistics and Probability* (Berkeley: University of California Press, 1951), pp. 493-506.

13. (Princeton: Princeton University Press, 1947).

14. *Ibid.*, pp. 617-32.

15. These terms may be strange to the reader. Although we explicate them below, the reader may wish to refer to Armen Alchian, "The Meaning of Utility Measurement," *Amercian Economic Review* 43, no. 1 (March 1953): 26-50, for an easily digestible discourse.

After we develop the von Neumann-Morgenstern utility index we shall reexamine the lottery choice posed earlier.

To maintain some degree of generality, suppose a choice must be made from a set of m alternatives $A = \{a_1, a_2, \ldots, a_m\}$. Suppose our chooser Mr. X, ranks them in the order that they appear. That is, his preference ordering is $a_1 P a_2 P a_3 P \ldots P a_{m-1} P a_m$. The set of alternatives, of course, may be composed of practically anything possessing some dimension of comparison.

We quite arbitrarily "anchor" Mr. X's preferences by assigning utility value of unity to his most preferred alternative and a value of zero to his least preferred. Thus $u(a_1) = 1$ and $u(a_m) = 0$, since a_1 and a_m are the most- and least-preferred alternatives, respectively. The function u, a *utility function*, is a mathematical rule that assigns to each of its arguments —in this case the alternatives in the set A—a real number between zero and one inclusive.

Our task now is to assign utility values to the remaining alternatives, viz., $a_2, a_3, \ldots, a_{m-1}$. This assignment should obey several natural conditions:

1. The utility number assigned to a_2 should be less than unity (the value assigned to a_1) since a_2 is less preferred by Mr. X than a_1.

2. The utility value assigned to a_{m-1} should be greater than zero (the value assigned to a_m) since a_{m-1} is more preferred by Mr. X than a_m.

3. The utility values of $a_2, a_3, \ldots, a_{m-1}$ should be in natural order —$u(a_2) > u(a_3) > \ldots > u(a_{m-1})$ — following Mr. X's ordering of those alternatives.

In order to make an assignment consistent with (1) – (3), von Neumann and Morgernstern recommend the following experiment:

Begin with a_2. Present Mr. X with two alternatives from which he is instructed to choose one. The alternatives are

1. a_2 for certain, and
2. $[p\ a_1, (1-p)\ a_m]$.[16]

Now vary the value of p until Mr. X is indifferent between (1) and (2). For example, if $p = 1$ then the choice is effectively between (1) a_2 and (2) a_1. He will obviously choose the latter (a "degenerate lottery") since his preference ordering indicates $a_1 P a_2$. On the other hand, if $p = 0$ then the choice is effectively between (1) a_2 and (2)

---

16. Recall that $[pa_1, (1-p)\ a_m]$ is a lottery which gives Mr. X a_1 with probability p and a_m with complementary probability $(1-p)$.

a_m. Here his choice is the former because his preference ordering indicates $a_2 \ P \ a_m$. What if $p = 0.9$? 0.8? 0.75? Continue to vary p until, for some specific value of p—say, p^*—Mr. X reports he is indifferent between (1) and (2).

Von Neumann and Morgenstern are able to prove that their axiom system implies that $u(a_2) = p^*$. That is, having arbitrarily fixed the utility of a_1 and a_m, the utility of a_2 is found to be the probability number for which Mr. X is indifferent between (1) and (2) above. We may determine the utilities of the remaining alternatives by conducting similar experiments.

Several technical features should be noted, as we promised above. First, the axioms guarantee the existence of a measure of value. Thus, for any set of alternatives and any preference structure satisfying the axioms, utilities may be assigned to individual alternatives in the manner prescribed above. Second, the utility index is an interval-level measure, as compared to the ordinal level of preference orderings. By interval-level we mean that the utility scale is arbitrarily anchored, i.e. arbitrary zero point and unit of measure, and that ratios of utility differences are logically meaningful. Thus we know degree of preference in addition to preference order. That is, if $\dfrac{u(a_i) - u(a_j)}{u(a_k) - u(a_l)} > 1$, we may say that Mr. X prefers a_i to a_j more than he prefers a_k to a_l. This is important when we treat the topic of intensity. A third important feature of the von Neumann-Morgenstern utility index is its uniqueness to a positive linear transformation. In the experiment above we chose the so-called (0,1) normalization, where 0 is assigned to the least-preferred alternative and 1 to the most-preferred. However, we might have chosen 0 and 100 respectively, or –1 and 0, respectively. The very arbitrariness of the two values chosen to anchor the scale permits the following inference:

> If u is a utility function defined on a set of alternatives $A = \{a_1, a_2, \ldots, a_m\}$, then $v = cu + b \ (c > 0)$ is an equivalent utility function.[17]

From this inference it follows that *interpersonal comparisons of utility* are invalid. That is, we cannot meaningfully compare the utility numbers of an alternative for two individuals because those numbers are meaningful only in terms of the anchor values which, in turn, have been arbitrarily assigned by the observer. It is all too easy to treat utility values like any other real numbers—to add them, subtract them, and compare them

---

17. The coefficient c effects a change in the unit of utility measurement, i.e., the difference between the two values which anchor the scale. The intercept term b effects a change in the zero point.

through the use of equalities and inequalities. We must avoid this pitfall. For a particular individual the utility of an alternative is not an objective quantity which is measurable by mere observation of the alternative. Rather it is a *relative* value—it is relative to *his* most- and least-preferred alternatives. Similarly, different individuals have different "zero points" and utility units. Thus, even if we (as analysts) employ (0, 1) normalizations for different individuals, we cannot infer that a utility value of, say, 0.73 means the same thing for different individuals.[18]

Finally, to assuage the skepticism of the more empirically oriented reader, one should not be concerned with the impracticality of the von Neumann-Morgenstern experiment. It was intended only as an abstract intellectual exercise to demonstrate that utility values are, *in principle,* determinable. In any event, it is often the case that theoretical discourse does not rely on particular utility values, but rather on more general characteristics of utility functions.

Nonetheless, the von Neumann-Morgenstern utility index is a powerful theoretical tool, despite the fact that it is only a measure of *relative value.* It permits a number of insights regarding behavior in an uncertain world that are not available if we restrict ourselves to preference orderings. To examine these we return to the problem posed at the beginning of this section.

The Expected Utility Hypothesis. Recall our earlier example in which a citizen, who ordered the alternatives (a, b, c) as aPb, bPc, aPc, was to choose one of the following options:

1. b for certain, or
2. $[pa, (1-p)c]$.

It is clearly impossible to predict his choice on the basis of his preference ordering alone. However, if his utility schedule is known, and if he chooses rationally, then prediction is possible. We use the (0,1) normalization. Thus $u(a) = 1$ and $u(c) = 0$. The utility of the middle-ranked alternative, b, is determined by the von Neumann-Morgenstern experiment. We simply write it as $u(b)$, where it is understood that this value lies in the open unit interval (0,1).

We now have the first piece of required information—the citizen's utility schedule over the alternatives. A description of the meaning of

18. This logically invalid operation — comparing utilities of different individuals — was committed by the Benthamite utilitarians. Indeed, it is symptomatic of a number of scholars interested in social welfare to compute group utility functions (no doubt in order to comply with Bentham's dictum to find the alternative providing "the greatest pleasure for the greatest number of people") composed of summations of individual utilities. This, we have seen, is invalid.

"rational choice" is needed next. That is, we must specify a *decision rule.* For this we turn to the *expected utility hypothesis.* Rational choice implies the criterion of maximizing expected utility, where the latter is a probability-weighted average utility. Thus, the utility of the alternative $[p_1a_1,$ $p_2a_2,\ p_3a_3,\ \ldots,\ p_ma_m]$ is $p_1u(a_1) + p_2u(a_2) + p_3u(a_3) + \ldots + p_mu(a_m)$, where the p_i are probability numbers satisfying the axioms of probability $(0 \le p_i \le 1$ for all i and $\sum_{i=1}^{m} p_i = 1)$. The citizen computes the expected utility of each of the risky alternatives available, the utility of each of the certain alternatives, and chooses the one with the largest (expected) utility, i.e., he is an (expected) utility maximizer.

We may now evaluate the citizen's decision problem:

$$u[\text{option } (1)] = u(b)$$
$$u[\text{option } (2)] = pu(a) + (1\text{-}p)u(c)$$
$$= p(1) + (1\text{-}p)(0) \quad (\text{from the } (0,1) \text{ normalization})$$
$$= p.$$

Our citizen, then, chooses the first option if and only if $u(b) > p$.

To give some substance to this calculation, suppose

$a =$ a European vacation
$b =$ a weekend in New York
$c =$ a weekend grading midterm examinations.

Arbitrarily we let $u(a) = 1$ and $u(c) = 0$. From the von Neumann-Morgenstern experiment, suppose you, the reader, evaluate b as: $u(b) = 0.85$ (which suggests you are quite averse to grading midterm examinations). Clearly, from the expected utility calculation, you would settle for a weekend in New York rather than a fifty-fifty gamble (i.e., $p = 0.5$, $1\text{-}p = 0.5$) on a European trip or a weekend of grading. In fact, unless the probability of the European trip exceeds 0.85, i.e., unless the probability of a weekend of grading is less than 0.15, you will gladly give your regards to Broadway!

When the relationship between the alternatives that confront a citizen and his underlying preferences is ambiguous, he may use the expected-utility rule to determine his choice. Option (2) is of this type. If all the options are like (1) above, then the modifier "expected" is dropped from the decision rule: the citizen is simply a *utility maximizer.* It should be emphasized, however, that if the only options to confront the citizen *qua* decision maker are in the type (1) category, then utility theory is superfluous. Preference orderings suffice in this case. Utility analysis is theoretically valuable because citizens rarely confront decision problems composed of type (1) options exclusively. In the political arena uncertainty is pervasive and affects political institutions in important ways.

Coping with Uncertainty: The Risk Environment. Rational models of political phenomena are sometimes criticized for their overgenerous assumptions about human reasoning ability. Incomplete and imperfect information, not to speak of psychological hindrances, make careful reasoning a difficult task. One of the culprits responsible for this difficulty is uncertainty. Even if we grant the existence of individual goals, i.e., preferences, the task of relating those goals to the ambiguous alternatives from which real-world choices are made is not trivial. The very existence of uncertainty exerts a profound impact on social institutions. As Downs has observed, "Coping with uncertainty is a major function of nearly every significant institution in society; therefore it shapes the nature of each."[19]

Uncertainty plays an important role in our model of politics in plural societies. It is appropriate at this point to trace briefly the "contours" of this concept, leaving more detailed features for later discussion. Uncertainty refers to the fact that knowledge about processes is imperfect and incomplete. In the realm of human behavior, this means that individuals make choices despite their inability to delineate the precise consequences of these choices, i.e., they cannot relate the consequences of their choices (actions) to their underlying preferences (values).

To clarify this point, we follow Luce and Raiffa and partition choice contingencies into three categories:

> [W]e are in the realm of decision making under:
> (a) *Certainty* if each action is known to lead invariably to a specific outcome. . . .
> (b) *Risk* if each action leads to one of a set of possible specific outcomes occurring with a known probability. . . .
> (c) *Uncertainty* if [any of the actions] has as its consequence a set of possible specific outcomes, but where the probabilities of these outcomes are completely unknown or are not even meaningful.[20]

---

19. Anthony Downs, *An Economic Theory of Democracy* (New York: Harper and Row, 1957), p. 13. Other scholars are even bolder in their statements about uncertainty. As Arrow relates, "Risk and human reactions to it have been called upon to explain everything from the purchase of chances in a 'numbers' game to the capitalist structure of our economy; according to Professor Frank Knight, even consciousness itself would disappear in the absence of uncertainty." For a general overview of the subject, see Kenneth J. Arrow, "Alternative Approaches to the Theory of Choice in Risk-Taking Situations," *Econometrica* 19, no. 4 (October 1951): 404-37 (quotation at p. 404).

20. R. Duncan Luce and Howard Raiffa, *Games and Decisions* (New York: John Wiley, 1957), p. 13.

It is important to note that individuals choose *actions* or behaviors. Rational choice implies that actions are chosen with an eye to their consequences (outcomes).

In the certain world there is a one-to-one correspondence between actions and outcomes. The rational chooser's task is quite simple in this contingency. He orders the outcomes from most-preferred to least-preferred, and chooses the action corresponding to the most-preferred outcome. Needless to say this contingency rarely arises in the social realm where outcomes and actions are imperfectly related. For some engineering and natural science situations, certainty (practically speaking, of course) obtains. Technically, however, no human experience falls under the certainty rubric.[21]

In the world of risk (of which certainty is a degenerate case), actions are probabilistically related to outcomes. That is, each action is associated with a *probability distribution* over possible outcomes. The notion of a *lottery ticket* is suggestive. Suppose there are m actions $(a_1, a_2, \ldots, a_m)$ from which to choose, and n "outcome bundles" $(o_1, o_2, \ldots, o_n)$ as possible consequences. A typical action, a_i is represented as a lottery ticket:

$$a_i \equiv [p_1^{(i)} o_1, p_2^{(i)} o_2, \ldots, p_n^{(i)} o_n]^{22}$$

In order to choose an action, the decision maker evaluates each lottery ticket via the expected utility calculus. He chooses that action that provides the largest expected utility.

It is the category of uncertainty that allegedly produces decision-making difficulties, for in this contingency one cannot even specify a probabilistic relationship between actions and outcomes. If we know the probabilistic relationship between actions and outcomes, we can view the decision problem as one of risk (as defined above) and employ the expected utility rule.

One of us has argued elsewhere that the partition of decision contingencies into certainty, risk, and uncertainty is misleading in the sense that it suggests that different decision rules apply in different decision contingencies. The trichotomy, however, may be collapsed for the purpose of selecting and evaluating decision rules. If all decision-making situations are considered under the rubric of *risk,* then the expected utility maximization rule is universally applicable. Since certainty is a degenerate case of risk, it may be subsumed under the rubric of risk. To treat contin-

---

21. This point is nicely made in C. West Churchman, *Prediction and Optimal Decision* (Englewood Cliffs, N.J.: Prentice-Hall, 1961), pp. 174-250.

22. The superscript identifies the action, and the subscript the outcome, with which the probability numbers are associated.

gencies of uncertainty is somewhat more complex. Briefly it may be argued that all proposed rules for making decisions under uncertainty,[23] in effect, remove the uncertainty and substitute subjective judgments. This substitution reduces the problem of uncertainty to one of risky choice. Accordingly, in the remainder of the book we suppose that the decision context is entirely one of risk. We call it the *risk environment*.[24]

Although we promised only to "trace contours" of the uncertainty problem in this section, we deal with one bit of detail before leaving the subject. Behavior under uncertainty[25] is dependent upon two sets of variables. The first describes the nature of the risky alternatives. Some alternatives may be "more" risky than others; some may be degenerate risks (certain alternatives); and so on. That is, decision making (and hence behavior) under uncertainty depends upon the properties of the probability distributions describing alternatives. Probability is one of the necessary components in the expected utility calculation. The second set of variables defines the preference structure of the decision maker. His utility schedule not only orders the alternatives according to preference; it provides an indication of relative valuation as well. The utility schedule is the second component of the expected utility calculation.

The utility schedule enables us to classify individuals according to their reactions to uncertainty. To demonstrate this point, suppose pure alternatives are defined along some underlying continuum. The decision might involve a budgetary matter so that preferences would be defined over possible dollar amounts. Since a continuum represents an infinity of pure alternatives, the decision maker is assumed to possess a continuous utility function instead of a finite utility *schedule*. The *shape* of this utility function, *ceteris paribus,* has important implications for behavior under uncertainty. In fact, individuals who have identical preference orderings often behave differently in contingencies of uncertainty because of differences in the *shape* of their utility functions.

In Figure 2.1 we display the utility functions of three individuals. All three order the alternatives (which, to continue the above example, are

---

23. E.g., minimax, minimax regret, Laplace's law of insufficient reason.

24. This entire argument does not render the above trichotomy a sleight-of-hand. To the contrary, in a number of ways decisions in different "environments" possess qualitative distinctions. For example, decisions under uncertainty undoubtedly are more difficult, more frustrating, and less likely to be "correct" than decisions under certainty. For our purposes, however, these differences are of no concern. See Kenneth A. Shepsle, *Essays on Risky Choice in Electoral Competition* (unpublished Ph. D. dissertation, University of Rochester, 1970), chapter I.

25. Although our position above indicated that we consider all phenomena under the rubric of risk, we nonetheless use the words "risk" and "uncertainty" interchangeably. Unless otherwise specified we always mean risk, technically defined, i.e., a known probabilistic relationship between actions and outcomes.

dollar amounts in a budget for some state activity) in the same fashion—
each prefers smaller budgets to larger budgets. However, the utility functions have different shapes. Suppose that the three individuals must decide
between two alternatives:

1. *B* dollars for certain, and
2. [½ *A*, ½ *C*].[26]

Suppose further that the expected dollar value of option (2) is equal to
option (1):

$$\frac{1}{2} A + \frac{1}{2} C = B$$

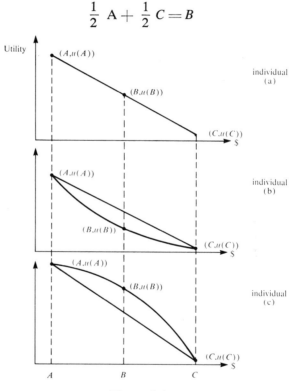

Figure 2.1

That is, given that *B* is available as an alternative, the lottery [½ *A*, ½*C*]
is a "fair gamble."

---

26. For example, the budget amount may be tied to a particular fund-raising
device, e.g., a state betting pool, thus making the amount of money available
uncertain. In this case, to keep things simple, suppose the final budget is either *A* or
C, each equally likely.

It may be shown that each individual reacts differently to the decision problem, despite the fact that each individual has the same preference ordering. The relevant comparison for each individual is the expected utility of the lottery—½ $u(A)$ + ½ $u(C)$, and the utility of the certain option—$u(B)$. For individual (a), ½ $u(A)$ + ½ $u(C)$ = $u(B)$; hence he is indifferent between the two options. Individual (b) prefers the lottery since ½ $u(A)$ + ½ $u(C)$ > $u(B)$, i.e., the midpoint of the line connecting $(A,u(A))$ and $(C,u(C))$ lies above $(B,u(B))$. For individual (c) the inequality is reversed, indicating his preference for the certain option. The different reactions of the three individuals can be traced to differences in the shape of their utility functions. Individual (a), whose utility function is linear, is risk-neutral. Individual (b) is risk-acceptant as a result of a convex utility function.[27] Finally, individual (c), who possesses a concave utility function, is risk-averse.[28] The implication, here, is that the functional form of the utility function reflects reactions to uncertain alternatives. This observation becomes important when we discuss the properties of "ethnic preferences" in the plural society.

In this section a brief survey of the concepts of decision theory has been presented. The important points to digest are:

1. Individuals make choices on the basis of underlying values.
2. These choices are possible even if the relationship between alternatives and underlying values is unclear.
3. Preference orderings, and degree of preference, have implications for behavior, especially behavior under uncertainty.

In the remaining sections of this chapter we embellish the decision model, introducing concepts relevant to an examination of plural societies. The tools presented thus far permit careful specification of these concepts. The first of these is intensity.

Intensity

The intensity problem is the stepchild of democratic theory and welfare economics. Its problematical nature derives from a number of sources, all

---

27. Technically, a utility function is convex if its second derivative is positive. An individual is risk acceptant if the expected utility of the risk exceeds the utility of the expected value of the risk ($\int u(x)\, p(x)dx > u[\int xp(x)dx]$). Convexity implies risk acceptance.

28. A statement analogous to note 27, with all relationships reversed, applies in this case.

closely related to the general task of collective decision making. As Kendall and Carey have noted,

> The problem of intensity as we know it has ... arisen as a special problem in the theory of populistic democracy. It is not, however, peculiar to that theory. Any theoretical answer to the question, "How is the self-governing community to govern itself?" must, soon or late, make a decision as to the extent to which policies are to reflect the individual preferences of members of the community, and as to whether, in order to be reflected accurately, these preferences are ... to be merely counted, or *both* counted and weighed.[29]

The first source of difficulty is normative. In an age in which equalitarianism is the vogue, both in theories of democracy and theories of economic welfare, intensity is confounding. Once popular sovereignty is accepted, the problem of self-governance is reduced to a procedural question: namely, how are individual preferences to be "accurately reflected" in collective choice? The equalitarian response is one of vote *counting*:

> The decision-making group adopts the decision that is "preferred by most members," each member deciding for himself what he prefers, and each expression of preference being counted as of equal "weight" with every other.[30]

However, some of the implications of this procedure are disturbing. The case often cited is the one in which an apathetic majority prevails over an intense minority. "Is it," the student of democratic theory asks, "'fair' to employ the principle of majority rule in this case?" That is, is the RULE (as Dahl calls it) in some way incompatible with other important values, thus implying the use of some nonequalitarian vote-weighting system?

A second source of difficulty arising from a consideration of intensity is definitional. There is confusion over the meaning of preference intensity, the effect of which is an inability to discriminate between it and other important concepts. Eckstein, for example, defines intensity in terms of three criteria:

1. "the amount of 'affect' involved,"
2. the extent of preference incompatibility among individuals, and

---

29. Willmore Kendall and George W. Carey, "The 'Intensity' Problem and Democratic Theory," *American Political Science Review* 62, no. 1 (March 1968): 5-24 (quotation at p. 7).
30. *Ibid.*, p. 6. Also see Dahl, *op. cit.*, pp. 37-38.

3. "the extent to which [preference incompatibilities] have become 'manifest' . . . rather than being merely latent tendencies . . ."[31]

The first criterion identifies the individualistic nature of preference intensity, yet fails to specify the "affect" term or the objects to which it refers. The second criterion confuses intensity of preference and disagreement. Disagreements, i.e., preference incompatibilities, may be "small" but intensely felt by the parties involved, as is often the case in labor-management negotiations. The third criterion defines *saliency*, not intensity, an important distinction we consider at some length below. In sum, intensity is a slippery idea and must be specified more carefully if it is to be of value.

Faulty logic is the cause of yet another source of difficulty. In attempting to build a case for the abandonment of the RULE in favor of some vote-weighting scheme, some scholars rely on interpersonal comparisons of utility in their specification of intensity. As we have observed earlier, individual utility schedules are defined on the basis of an arbitrary zero point and utility unit, and hence are inherently incomparable. A definition of intensity that relies on such comparisons rests on rather shaky logical ground. Any valid treatment of intensity must avoid interpersonal comparisons of utility. Thus we reject those conceptualizations of intensity that employ them.

A fourth difficulty with intensity is empirical. Not only are there the usual measurement problems that plague empirical research, but a more fundamental question arises as well, namely: does it matter? Does a consideration of intensity account for empirical regularities otherwise unaccounted for? Rothenberg puts it thus:

> I think it would be generally agreed, on the testimony of introspection and literature, and, as a matter of fact, on that of our daily behavior toward others, that persons can differentiate preference intensities. Whether this differentiation makes a difference is another question.[32]

We argue shortly that it does make a difference — *even in a political system employing the RULE.* To do this we first examine alternative measures of intensity to identify the difficulties they impose, and then propose our own measure of intensity, tracing its behavioral implications.

---

31. Harry Eckstein, *Division and Cohesion in Democracy* (Princeton: Princeton University Press, 1966), pp. 35-36.

32. Jerome Rothenberg, *The Measurement of Social Welfare* (Englewood Cliffs, N. J.: Prentice-Hall, Inc., 1961), p. 137.

Alternative Measures of Intensity. Intensity, as we mentioned above, is of interest because it has significant behavioral implications. If this were not the case, then a legitimate concern with the intensity problem would follow normative lines exclusively. In fact, most attempts to specify measures of intensity are motivated by normative considerations, and, as a result, are somewhat insensitive to behavioral implications. For this reason alone they are unsuitable for our purposes. However, there are additional difficulties with these measures of intensity. For our purposes three classes of measures are examined and their difficulties exposed. They are:

1.   the "irrelevant alternatives" measure,
2.   the cost-bearing measure, and
3.   the attitude-strength measure.

In each of these cases intensity is taken to be an expression of "degree of preference."

Consider a set of outcomes $O = \{o_1 \; o_2, \; \ldots, \; o_m\}$ and two citizens, Mr. X and Mr. Y. Each rank orders the alternatives as follows:

X	Y
o_1	o_2
o_3	o_1
o_4	o_3
$\vdots$	$\vdots$
o_m	$\vdots$
o_2	o_m

Suppose they are offered a choice between o_1 and o_2. As the preference schedules indicate, for Mr. X $o_1 \, P \, o_2$, while for Mr. Y $o_2 \, Po_1$. The RULE is unable to resolve the choice problem. However, according to the *irrelevant alternatives* measure of intensity, o_1 "should" be the collective choice because Mr. X places more "irrelevant" alternatives between o_1 and o_2 than Mr. Y does between o_2 and o_1. That is, according to this measure, Mr. X is more intense in his preference than Mr. Y.

Quite clearly, this measure of intensity relies on interpersonal comparisons of utility. Specifically, the utility differential between o_1 and o_2 is greater for Mr. X, according to this measure, than for Mr. Y because X includes more irrelevant alternatives between the two outcomes. That is,

$$u_x(o_1) \; - \; u_x(o_2) > u_y(o_2) \; - \; u_y(o_1).$$

This inequality can be rewritten as

$$u_x(o_1) + u_y(o_1) > u_x(o_2) + u_y(o_2).$$

This expression allegedly shows that outcome o_1 provides a larger group utility than o_2. Using the "irrelevant alternatives" measure of intensity, o_1 "should" be chosen. However, as we have made clear several times above, these inequalities are meaningless. Despite the fact that each and every one of us makes interpersonal utility comparisons often,[33] there is no logical basis for such comparisons. To see why this comparison is invalid, recall that a utility index may be multiplied by a positive constant, producing an equivalent utility function. In the case above Mr. Y might remark, "I'll simply multiply my utility function by α (a very large number) so that now $\alpha u_y(o_2) - \alpha u_y(o_1) > u_x(o_1) - u_x(o_2)$." X's response: "I can play that game, too. I'll multiply my utility function by β (an even larger number) so that now $\beta u_x(o_1) - \beta u_x(o_2) > \alpha u_y(o_2) - \alpha u_y(o_1)$" ... *ad infinitum*. The point, of course, is that utility numbers have no comparative meaning among individuals. Thus, however intuitive its appeal may be,[34] an intensity measure based on such a comparison is logically invalid.

Some have argued that *all* collective choices imply interpersonal comparisons of utility. Thus the issue reduces to deciding the kinds of interpersonal comparisons one should make:

> ... as soon as we say that state $[o_1]$ is socially preferred to state $[o_2]$ for two states such that some individuals prefer $[o_1]$ to $[o_2]$ and others prefer $[o_2]$ to $[o_1]$, we are thereby saying that the gains to those who prefer $[o_1]$ are socially more important than the losses to those who prefer $[o_2]$. This implies that we have some basis for comparing the relevant gains and losses. Such a comparison is fundamentally an interpersonal comparison of utilities.[35]

This seems to us to be an end run around the entire issue. A political decision rule, i.e., the RULE, is not a welfare rule. To say that o_1 is the collective choice because it received more votes than o_2 is *not* to say that the utility gains to those preferring o_1 exceed the utility losses to those preferring o_2. Vote counting is legitimate so long as welfare criteria are not employed.

Cost bearing, as a measure of intensity, is subject to the same criticism.

---

33. The parental apology: "This is going to hurt me more than it hurts you," which precedes the spanking of a child, is a case in point.

34. Indeed, originally Mr. Y might have agreed with Mr. X that the latter's utility differential was the larger one and thus that o_1 "should" be the collective choice. Nonetheless the comparison is still invalid, despite the agreement.

35. Clifford Hildreth, "Alternative Conditions for Social Orderings," *Econometrica* 21, no. 1 (January 1953): 81-94 (quotation at p. 90).

The cost-bearing measure of intensity is an index which provides the cost one is willing to bear in order to influence a collective choice. One may bear costs in a variety of ways: time, energy, organizational expertise, psychic costs, etc. Dahl's example from American politics is informative:

> If it is difficult to determine majority preferences on a specific piece of legislation, it is even more difficult to determine whether a hypothetical majority was relatively intense or apathetic. *Perhaps the only available test is the extent to which efforts were made to repass the legislation, to amend the Constitution, to alter the Supreme Court's jurisdiction, to pack the Court, and otherwise to bring about a new outcome.*[36]

Cost bearing is intuitively appealing because it indicates the "value" one is willing to forego (cost) in order to obtain a preferred outcome. However, it should be apparent by now that value is personal. The value of, say, the time invested to form an organization is not comparable among individuals.[37]

We should point out that our statements do not in any way dispute the observation that individuals with intense preferences are likely to have high participation rates. This may very well be true. What we are disputing is the use of participation rates (broadly construed) as an indication of intense preference. The costs of participation are subjective, are measured on individual utility scales which, as we have seen, are arbitrarily anchored, and hence are not interpersonally comparable. Thus participation is an invalid indicator of intensity.

The last measure of intensity we examine is that of *attitude strength*. Popularized by students of public opinion, it is used both as an individual

---

36. Dahl, *op. cit.*, pp. 108-9 (emphasis ours). Dahrendorf uses a similar measure in determining the intensity of a conflict. "A particular conflict may be said to be of high intensity if the cost of victory or defeat is high for the parties concerned."See Ralf Dahrendorf, *Class and Class Conflict in Industrial Society* (Stanford: Stanford University Press, 1959), p. 211.

37. Dahl, it seems, was aware of the difficulties associated with the cost-bearing measure: "It is all too clear, I am afraid, that when we restrict ourselves to *reliable* inferences, we cannot talk with much confidence about our problem." *Ibid.*, p. 109 (emphasis ours). Nonetheless, he never is totally unenamored of the measure, as is indicated by one of his later hypotheses suggesting the close relationship between relative intensity and political activity. See *ibid.*, pp. 134-35. Dahl is not alone on this count. The intuitively pleasing nature of the cost-bearing measure of intensity has found support in other quarters as well. Henry Mayo, to cite another supporter, argues that in the give and take of politics, "those with strong feelings are powerfully motivated to political action in a large variety of ways." See Henry B. Mayo, *An Introduction to Democratic Theory* (New York: Oxford University Press, 1960), pp. 203ff. Also see Eckstein, *op. cit.*, pp. 35ff. for a similar view.

and an aggregate indicator of intensity. At the individual level the measure is derived from responses to statements of the following sort:

"The government should do _____ with respect to _____."

The respondent is asked to express agreement with, disagreement with, or no opinion on this statement. He is queried further as to the strength of his opinion, e.g., strongly agree, weakly agree. An individual is said to possess intense opinions if he holds them strongly. An *aggregate* of individuals is identified by high opinion intensity if at least a minimal proportion of them holds strong opinions.[38] A variant of this measure simply takes the extremeness of the response as a measure of intensity: "The more extreme the stand, the more intensely do people feel about it."[39]

Neither of these measures, in our opinion, has much theoretical consequence. There is an implicit assumption that a natural baseline exists against which "strong" and "weak" agreement (disagreement) are measured. All people who respond in a particular way are lumped into a single category as if to indicate that they hold equally intense opinions. Unfortunately, unlike measures of length or mass, opinions and preferences have no natural baseline. The zero-point is arbitrary. Thus it is not *logically* meaningful to make comparative statements about the strength of individual opinions.

Second, the attitude strength measure is a dyadic concept. Typically there are only two directions of opinion. Thus, in utility terms, there are, in effect, only two points. But we have seen in the previous section that two points are sufficient only to anchor the utility schedule. No inferences about intensity may be drawn in terms of utility differences with only two points because of the arbitrary nature of the "anchor values." Thus, it seems that a minimum of three points is required in order to draw inferences about intensity of preference. This point is taken up shortly when we discuss our intensity measure.

The Lottery Measure of Intensity. Our measure of intensity not only captures the intuitive aspects of the concept without relying on interpersonal utility comparisons, it provides *a priori* behavioral expectations as well that play an integral part in our theory of plural society.

Preference intensity measures degree of preference as a function of utility differences. Yet, as we have seen, utility differences are not inter-

38. See, for example, V. O. Key, Jr., *Public Opinion and American Democracy* (New York: Alfred A. Knopf, 1964), p. 212.

39. Robert E. Lane and David O. Sears, *Public Opinion* (Englewood Cliffs, N. J.: Prentice-Hall, 1964), chapter 9 (quotation at p. 105).

personally comparable. However, *relative* differences are. That is, if we measure utility differences relative to individual utility scales, we may make certain kinds of comparisons. It is for this reason that intensity has no scientific meaning in the absence of less than three points. In fact we specifically define intensity as a triadic concept.

To keep things simple suppose there are three items of preference $\{a, b, c\}$. Mr. X prefers a to b and b to c (and, by transitivity, a to c). To determine his intensity of preference for a *with respect to the set* $\{a, b, c\}$, consider the two alternatives

    1. b for certain
    2. $[pa, (1-p)c]$.

Now we vary the parameter p (recall p is the probability of obtaining a in the lottery) until Mr. X responds that he is indifferent between alternatives (1) and (2). Let that value be p^*.

A large p^*, i.e., a p^* near unity, indicates that item b is sufficiently desirable that it takes a rather high probability of obtaining his most-preferred alternative before Mr. X opts for the lottery. Intuitively this suggests that a is not very intensely preferred vis-à-vis b and c. On the other hand, for very small values of p^*, i.e., a p^* near zero, the implication is the opposite. Item a is so strongly preferred by Mr. X, vis-à-vis b and c, that he is willing to run rather large risks $(1-p^*)$ of obtaining his least-preferred alternative, c, in order to have some likelihood of obtaining a. That is, despite a rather small p^*, Mr. X is not sufficiently enamored of b to opt for alternative (1) above.

Before examining some of the properties of this measure of intensity, we resurrect an earlier example. Suppose Mr. X's decision problem involves the choice set $\{a, b, c\}$, where

    a = a European vacation
    b = a weekend in New York
    c = a weekend grading midterm examinations

and he orders these alternatives $a \, P \, b \, P \, c$. If X is indifferent between b for certain and $(0.9a, 0.1c)$, then our lottery measure of intensity suggests that his preference for a vis-à-vis the set $\{a, b, c\}$ is not very intense. On the other hand, if he were indifferent between b for certain and $(0.1a, 0.9c)$, we would consider him extremely intense in his preference for a.

In the former case $p^* = 0.9$; in the latter $p^* = 0.1$. We take the pa-*rameter* p* *as an inverse measure of intensity. As* p* *increases, preference intensity decreases.*

The first property of our intensity measure to note is its *triadic nature. Intensity is always measured vis-à-vis a set of three alternatives.* We can extend our definition of intensity to larger sets of alternatives in the following sense. An individual is said to hold an intense preference for his first-ranked alternative if for *any* two other alternatives in the available set, the lottery experiment produces a very small value of p^*. For example, suppose the available set of outcomes is

$$0 = \{o_1, o_2, \ldots, o_m\},$$

the elements of which are ranked by Mr. X as $o_1 \ P \ o_2 \ P \ldots P \ o_{m-1} \ P \ o_m$. Mr. X is said to hold an intense preference for o_1 vis-à-vis the set 0 if, for any two outcomes $o_i, o_j \ \varepsilon \ 0 \ (i \neq 1, j \neq 1)$, where (without loss of generality) o_i is preferred to o_j, the indifference relationship between

       1. o_i for certain, and

       2. $[p^*o_1, (1-p^*)o_j]$

holds for a small value of p^*.

From these observations it should be quite clear that, in our view, the statement "o_1 is intensely preferred to o_2" is not meaningful since it relies on dyadic comparison. One who asserts such a statement implicitly assumes that the utility difference, $u(o_1) - u(o_2)$, can be compared to some standard utility metric, which permits the fallacious inference that the difference is "large." However, no such standard metric exists. In addition, the utility difference may be arbitrarily altered.[40] Intensity is an inherently triadic concept and our measure preserves this property.[41]

It is also important to observe that intensity statements depend very much on the particular entities comprising the triad under consideration. In our earlier example, Mr. X might be indifferent between New York (*b*) and the lottery giving a thirty percent chance of a European trip (*a*) and a seventy percent chance of remaining home to grade midterms (*c*), i.e., (0.3*a* 0.7*c*), in which case he is relatively intense (p^*=0.3) about *a*. However, suppose now that for some reason *c* is no longer available, but *d* is, where

    d = death by hanging at dawn.

---

40. Recall that the utility index may be multiplied by a positive constant, yielding an equivalent utility index. But then the utility difference of the transformed utility index is changed. Thus, we cannot draw conclusions from utility differences, per se, because they are not "invariant under positive linear transformations."

41. A thoughtful treatment of the intensity concept is found in the work of Rae and Taylor. Their measure, which is probabilistic in nature, relies on a combination of attitude strength measures and dyadic (interpersonal) comparisons. In light of this and earlier comments we do not find it acceptable. See Douglas W. Rae and Michael Taylor, *The Analysis of Political Cleavages* (New Haven: Yale University Press, 1970). Also see their "Some Ambiguities in the Concept of 'Intensity'," *Polity* 1, no. 3 (Spring 1969): 297-308.

For the triad $\{a, b, d\}$ Mr. X undoubtedly would gladly settle for the week-end in New York (smog and traffic notwithstanding) rather than accept any lottery with more than an infinitesimal chance of obtaining alternative $d!$ The point we emphasize here is that intensity, like utility, is not a property of an alternative. It is subjective, is found (like beauty) in the eye of the beholder, and depends (again like beauty) on the other alternatives available!

One should further note that certain kinds of interpersonal comparisons are valid with this measure. Suppose, for example, that Mr. X and Mr. Y rank the outcomes $0 = \{o_1, o_2, o_3\}$ as follows:

Mr. X	Mr. Y
o_1	o_3
o_2	o_2
o_3	o_1

After conducting the lottery experiment with X and Y, we find, say, that $p^*_x > p^*_y$. We are quite safe in concluding that, *with respect to the set* 0, Y feels more intensely about his first-ranked alternative than X does about his. This conclusion does not follow because Y's utility difference is greater than X's. We have no way of knowing this. *It follows from a behavioral consideration: Y is willing to take greater chances than X to obtain his preferred alternative.*

Needless to say someone might observe that ours is not a "fair" measure of intensity of preference. Mr. Y might be willing to take greater chances in order to obtain o_3 than Mr. X would to obtain o_1 because he (Mr. Y) is wealthier or more secure. That is, our measure does not take account of initial distributions of wealth or other relevant resources. We agree. Initial distributions of wealth and other such considerations are relevant only if one wants to draw welfare recommendations from a measure of intensity. We do not (we almost said "cannot"). Indeed, as we stated at the beginning of this chapter, why men want what they want and why they feel so intensely about their wants are not our concerns. To reiterate, our concern is with the empirical consequences of intensity.[42]

---

42. One final point is worth making: the distinction between utility and intensity. The careful reader may have noticed that our measure of preference intensity vis-à-vis a specific triad of alternatives is identical to the utility of the middle-ranked alternative under the (0, 1) normalization obtained in the von Neumann-Morgenstern experiment. We make intensity comparisons among individuals on the basis of normalized utilities even though we acknowledge the invalidity of interpersonal *welfare* comparisons. This is permissible because the normalization we use, i.e., the (0, 1) normalization, is dictated by the axioms of probability theory (p^*, our inverse measure of intensity, is a *probability number*). The von Neumann-Morgenstern utility measure, on the other hand, has no axiomatic guidelines thus rendering any normalization arbitrary.

Behavioral Manifestations of Intense Preferences. In the next chapter we propose a model of democratic politics in plural societies in terms of the tools developed in the present chapter. At that time we carefully specify the impact of intense preferences on voting behavior and party competition. For now our discussion remains brief and abstract.

A direct consequence of the definition of intensity is the expectation of differences in behavior in contingencies of uncertainty. Consider two individuals with identical preference schedules, but differing preference intensities. Suppose each ranks the set A as: $a\,P\,b,\,b\,P\,c,\,a\,P\,c$, but the first individual has a smaller p^* (is more intense about his most-preferred alternative) than the second individual. Clearly, then, the more intense individual prefers a wider range of lotteries to alternative b than does the second individual. For example, if $p^*_1 = 0.2$ and $p^*_2 = 0.6$, then the first individual prefers all lotteries in the range $[1a, 0c]$ to $[0.2a, 0.8c]$ to the certainty of b, whereas the second individual's range is only $[1a, 0c]$ to $[0.6a, 0.4c]$. In words, the first individual is willing to tolerate considerably more ambiguity in outcomes before opting for the certainty of b than is the second individual.

As we see shortly this fact opens the door to a whole set of strategic possibilities for political parties in their competition for the vote. Once intensity is taken into account, parties may, in a calculated fashion, purposely generate ambiguity in their policy positions in order to take advantage of an opponent whose position has hardened.

A special case of this contingency is displayed in the following example: a hypothetical electorate is composed of twenty-one voters. On the only issue of importance in the upcoming election, the voters partition themselves into three "preference groupings." The issue possesses a continuum of possible positions and is displayed, along with a typical utility function from each preference grouping, in Figure 2.2. Ten voters possess utility functions labelled I; one voter has one labelled II; and ten possess functions labelled III. Suppose one of the political parties advocates position B as its policy stand. This point is the midpoint of the set of most-preferred points $\{A, B, C\}$. It possesses a unique property: B can defeat *any* other point on the continuum in paired comparison by a majority vote. Consider an arbitrary point X to the right of B. The eleven members of groups I and II prefer B to X. Thus B defeats any arbitrary point to its right by at least an 11-10 vote. Similarly, B also defeats any arbitrary point Y to its left by at least 11-10. Therefore, in our earlier terminology, B is the *majority alternative*. Thus, the party which advocates B can be assured of defeating a party taking any other fixed policy position.

Suppose, however, a second political party advocates — though not in so many words — the lottery $(1/2A, 1/2C)$. That is, suppose this second party behaves sufficiently ambiguously so that the twenty-one voters per-

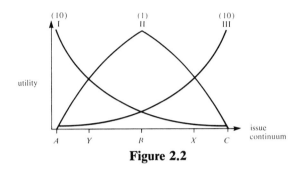

Figure 2.2

ceive it as a "risky alternative." What happens? In Figure 2.3 the calculation for the members of group I is displayed. Via the expected utility hypothesis, the lottery is evaluated. Geometrically, the expected utility of the lottery is the midpoint of the chord connecting the utilities of the components of the lottery. The linear function in Figure 2.3 plots the expected utility of a lottery defined on the outcomes A and C for variable p. The particular point on this function that we identify is the expected utility of the particular lottery on A and C where $p = 1/2$. As is evident the members of group I value the lottery more than the certainty of B.

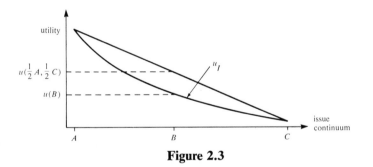

Figure 2.3

Similar calculations for groups II and III show that the former prefers B, the latter $(1/2\ A, 1/2\ C)$. Thus, the risky party defeats the party advocating B by a vote of 20-1. This follows from the fact that voters in I and III *intensely* prefer their most-preferred alternatives (A and C, respectively) — so much so that each is willing to take a 50-50 chance that the final outcome is their least-preferred alternative (C and A, respectively). Together they form a majority capable of defeating the party advocating B. Intensity in this case is a logical consequence of the shape of the utility functions. Voters in groups I and III have *convex* utility functions, *and, with fair lotteries, convexity is a sufficient condition for intense preference.*[43]

In general, the existence of intense preferences in an electorate provides incentives for particular kinds of behavior by competitors for office. In the political world, then, where the premium is placed on winning, we may formulate *a priori* expectations about party competition on the basis of the preference structure of the electorate. Ambiguous campaigning is one of those expectations. This, in turn, has implications for the form of competing political organizations, the absence or presence of logrolling (both in the electorate and in the legislative chamber), the kinds of leaders recruited and their likelihoods of success, and so on.

Once specific assumptions are made, precise statements on these and a host of other topics may be inferred from our theoretical structure. It is this set of consequences that we test against real-world experience in the politics of plural societies. Before beginning this specification, however, we examine one last theoretical element: issue salience.

Salience

Why men prefer the things they do is a question we have purposely avoided. Quite frankly, we do not know the answer. To attribute preferences to socialization is to give what is as yet an incomplete explanation; and until a theory of political socialization is fully articulated we possess but a partial understanding. However, it is evident that great numbers of individuals have preferences on a diverse set of political matters. Moreover, the available evidence further suggests that the sets of issues which interest people, as well as the form of preferences on these issues, vary from person to person. Since it is likely that differences in salience, in addition to incompatabilities in preference, i.e., cleavages, contribute to the political (in)stability of a community, some theoretical attention to the concept of

---

43. For continuous function $u(x)$, convexity is defined by the sign of the second derivative: namely $u''(x) > 0$. A lottery is fair if the expected value of the argument of the utility function, under the probability function of the lottery, is equal to the certain alternative in the case above. (1/2 A, 1/2 C) is fair since $\frac{1}{2}A + \frac{1}{2}C = B$. This example will be pursued in the next chapter. For a more detailed treatment of this and other topics, see Kenneth A. Shepsle, "Parties, Voters, and the Risk Environment: A Mathematical Treatment of Electoral Competition Under Uncertainty," in Richard G. Niemi and Herbert F. Weisberg, eds., *Probability Models of Collective Decision Making* (Columbus: Charles Merrill, 1972); and "The Strategy of Ambiguity: Uncertainty and Electoral Competition, *American Political Science Review* 66, no. 3 (September 1972).

issue "importance" is warranted. We propose to examine the notion of "importance" in this section.

The Public and the Private Sector.   At the outset it is worth noting that behavior aimed at satisfying preferences need not engage the official institutions of the collectivity. This kind of behavior is so obvious and so frequently manifested that it is often overlooked in examinations of the political health of a community. Conflicts in preference may rarely reach the level of public debate. Dimensions of conflict may, for historical or constitutional reasons, be restricted to the private sector for resolution. Certainly, conflicts involving market-like preferences in many societies are manifested and resolved privately. It behooves us, then, to acknowledge that a community's institutional stability may, in very profound ways, depend upon the community's ability to restrict the kinds of issues eligible for public resolution. As Mayo has observed, " 'Government by discussion and majority vote works best when there is nothing of profound interest to discuss' and when there is plenty of time to discuss it."[44]

From these brief remarks, and our remarks on outcomes earlier in this chapter, an important, though perhaps obvious, implication follows: political equanimity obtains in the absence of *salient* issues in the public sphere. This is but a variant on the theme (with normative implications removed): "that government is best which governs least." If a polity finds itself in the fortunate position of possessing few value conflicts scheduled for *collective* (public) resolution, then it can expect to experience few destabilizing events. This, of course, does not mean that the polity is, in some sense, good. Nor does it mean that the citizens of the polity have compatible preferences. It simply means that for historical or accidental reasons the weight of conflict does not fall on the community's official institutions.

The distinction between the private sector and the public sector as alternative arenas for conflict resolution is important (though we should acknowledge the role of government in the private sector, e.g., the enforcement of contract). If the private sector is relatively unconstraining, and if individual expectations of success through private channels are high, then it may well be that "there is nothing of profound interest to discuss" publicly. The plight of blacks in the United States, French-Canadians in Canada, and Catholics in Ulster is disturbing precisely because of the inability of these groups to succeed within the private sectors of these democracies (perhaps because the dominant communities use the instruments of government to influence private opportunities). The absence of success and of expectations of private redress not only provides incentives

---

44. Mayo, *op. cit.*, p. 298.

for "political entrepreneurs" to take their cases to public arenas; it alters expectations and political activities of others as well — what Schattsschneider calls "the contagiousness of conflict."[45] It is important to note, then, that an open, unfettered private sector serves as a cushion for political institutions.

Salience and the Cross-Cutting Cleavages Hypothesis. The last section serves as an introduction to the notion of political salience by suggesting a rather broad distinction between collective and private conflict resolution. Some issues, though subject to conflicts and disagreements, are simply not political. We now turn to somewhat finer distinctions. The vehicle for this discussion is the cross-cutting cleavages hypothesis.

A principle tenet of pluralist theories of democracy suggests that the stability of a regime is "enhanced to the extent that groups and individuals have a number of cross-cutting, politically relevant affiliations."[46] Dahl puts it as follows:

> . . . the severity of a conflict depends on the way in which one conflict is related to another. A society offers a number of different lines along which cleavages in a conflict can take place; differences in geography, ethnic identification, religion, and economic position, for example, all present potential lines of cleavages in conflicts. If all the cleavages occur along the same lines, if the same people hold opposing positions in one dispute after another, then the severity of conflicts is likely to increase. The man on the other side is not just an opponent; he soon becomes an enemy. But if . . . the cleavages occur along different lines, if the same persons are sometimes opponents and sometimes allies, then conflicts are likely to be less severe. If you know that some of your present opponents were allies in the past and may be needed as allies again in the future, you have some reason to search for a solution to the dispute at hand that will satisfy both sides.[47]

Mutually reinforcing cleavages are, according to this theory, the *bete noire* of stable democracy. Eckstein calls these *segmental cleavages* of which he reports:

> . . . one often gets the impression that politics is struggle between distinct, only nominally unified subsocieties, each pursuing not only

---

45. E. E. Schattschneider, *The Semi-Sovereign People* (New York: Holt, Rinehart and Winston, 1960), pp. 1-20.
46. Lipset, *op. cit*, p. 77.
47. Robert A. Dahl, *Pluralist Democracy in the United States* (Chicago: Rand McNally, 1967), p. 277.

policy and procedural preferences, but above all autonomy from, or domination over, others, and sometimes these ends alone. The present world of emerging nations teems with examples not only of tribal cleavages, but of territorial, generational, religious, linguistic, racial, and sexual ones as well.[48]

Despite the emphasis on "cross-cutting, politically *relevant* cleavages" in each of these definitions, pluralist scholars have been unable to establish criteria of political relevance. Yet it is obviously the case that some cleavages (preference incompatabilities) are more significant than others, both for individual preferences and political stability. In the absence of explicit criteria, i.e., measures of *salience,* several embarrassing contradictions come to light. Eckstein's own case of Norway, as well as Lijphart's case of the Netherlands, are *"prima facie* contrary to the cross-cutting cleavages propositions."[49] In the case of Norway, Eckstein argues that the "theory" of cross-cutting cleavages provides us with no *a priori* expectations about the consequences of cleavage patterns for political integration and stability. In fact, "the possibility that cross-cutting divisions might actually *intensify disintegration* is certainly borne out by the Norwegian party system. . . . This suggests that empirically as well as logically, overlaps, aggregation, and cooperativeness are only weakly related, if at all."[50] That is, in the absence of some manner of *weighing the significance of cleavages,* no *a priori* relationship between the existence of cross-cutting cleavages and stability follows.

Lijphart arrives at the same uncomfortable conclusion in his excellent study of Dutch politics. As he reports, "It is the combination of deep social cleavages [primarily religious] and clearly viable democracy which makes Holland an eminently significant case for pluralist theory. It is a nation divided, but not one divided against itself."[51]

How are these contrary cases rationalized? In our view the proposed solutions are *ad hoc.* In Norway, Eckstein argues that a "sense of community," encouraged by the congruence of governmental and social authority patterns as well as by characteristics of Norwegian interpersonal relations which emphasize noninstrumental rather than calculating Gesellschaft values, accounts for stable political arrangements.[52] In the case of Holland, Lijphart argues that "mass deference," "elite accom-

---

48. Eckstein, *op. cit.,* p. 34.
49. Arend Lijphart, *The Politics of Accommodation: Pluralism and Democracy in the Netherlands* (Berkeley: University of California Press, 1968), pp. 14-15.
50. Eckstein, *op. cit.,* p. 75 (emphasis added).
51. Lijphart, *op. cit.,* p. 70. Lijphart goes on to state that "democratic government has proved both legitimate and effective. In fact, Dutch politics appears to be not just healthy and stable, but decidedly dull and unexciting" (p. 77).
52. Eckstein, *op. cit.,* chapter 5.

modation," and competition "within the confines of the total system" auger well for political stability.[53]

It appears that the inability to distinguish salient political divisions from nonsalient ones has forced *ad hoc* "explanations." To account for two alleged contradictory cases of the cross-cutting cleavages hypothesis, Eckstein and Lijphart must invent explanations that are little more than restatements of the event requiring account.

To disentangle the confusion surrounding the cross-cutting cleavages hypothesis, and to avoid begging the question, a careful specification of the concept of political salience is a first-order priority. The existing confusion is quite real, we have discovered, because of the difficulty of this task. However, once it is realized that politicians, desirous of political office and its concomitant perquisites, are in a position to organize political debate, some light is shed on salience.

Political Entrepreneurs, Demand Generation, and Salience. In Holland the political parties, reflecting a deep-seated, long enduring cleavage, are divided along religious lines primarily. Of religious issues Lijphart asserts that "although these are sensitive questions *they are not issues of major importance*. It is important to realize that in almost all countries where religion is a divisive factor, the crucial issue concerns the relationship between the state and private denominational schools. Once this question is resolved, religious issues lose much of their *political salience.*"[54] What we seek is an explanation, not only for the specific case that Lijphart provides, but for the general *post hoc* observation of differential issue importance. Why are some cleavages salient in the political life of the community while others, though perhaps equally invidious, lie dormant? Politicians, their motives, and hence their behavior provide the missing links.

Politicians are office-seekers. For whatever reasons—prestige, power, material perquisites—they are in the business of winning elections. And in order to win elections, they must assemble electoral organizations (coalitions).[55] The natural cleavages that divide men in the community provide the obvious and perhaps strongest nuclei around which coalitions are built. The astute politician latches on to an issue precisely because of the groups he believes it will *activate*. This "political entrepreneur" seeks political profit—electoral victory. Profit accrues to those who choose the issues—

53. Lijphart, *op. cit.*, pp. 78, 102-4, 200.
54. *Ibid.*, p. 118 (our emphasis).
55. See William H. Riker, *The Theory of Political Coalitions* (New Haven: Yale University Press, 1962). Additionally the reader is directed to Sven Groennings, E. W. Kelley, and Michael Leiserson, eds., *The Study of Coalition Behavior* (New York: Holt, Rinehart and Winston, 1970).

define the situation—in ways that activate winning electoral coalitions. The successful political entrepreneur, then, is the person who manipulates natural social cleavages, who makes certain of those cleavages *politically salient,* who exploits, uses, and suppresses conflict.[56]

Politicians, however, do not have a free hand in the activation of social cleavages. In addition to particularistic constraints on individual politicians, there is a more general constraint: community institutions. Social arrangements, citizen preferences, and official political institutions dictate, in important ways, the kinds of political appeals that can be made and that are likely to be successful. Once these "givens" are established, the politician is in a position to sensitize the electorate to the issues at stake in an election. The dynamic interaction between political appeals on the one hand, and mass perceptions and interpretations of those appeals on the other, is the primary determinant of issue salience.

The question may now be put: Why are some social cleavages more salient than others? Or to put it another way, admitting that "the essence of all competitive politics is the bribery of the electorate by politicians,"[57] why does the "bribe" take one particular form rather than another? Any answer to this question is speculative. Though our treatment of salience is not formal, we believe an understanding of it lies in an examination of the motives of political entrepreneurs. Politicians want to win, and they choose their mass appeals with this in mind. In particular, their appeals are aimed at "defining" the election in terms of the issues on which they feel advantaged. Like the automobile manufacturer who profits from the sale of his product (which may emphasize, say, large tail fins), and who accordingly chooses the advertising campaign that best *generates demand* for it, the politician seeks out issues which advantage him and gauges his appeals accordingly. The quest for electoral dominance, then, is not only a search for optimal positions on *fixed* issue dimensions; it is a search for advantageous dimensions as well. Schattschneider's perceptive observation deserves citing:

> The definition of alternatives is the supreme instrument of power . . . .
> He who determines what politics is about runs the country because

56. The notion of "political entrepreneur" was first formulated by Richard E. Wagner. See his "Pressure Groups and Political Entrepreneurs: A Review Article," in Gordon Tullock, ed., *Papers on Non-Market Decision-Making* (Charlottesville: Thomas Jefferson Center for Political Economy, 1966), pp. 161-70. Also see Alvin Rabushka and Kenneth A. Shepsle, "Political Entrepreneurship and Patterns of Democratic Instability in Plural Societies," *Race* 12, no. 4 (April 1971): 461-76, and Norman Frohlich, Joe A. Oppenheimer, and Oran R. Young, *Political Leadership and Collective Goods* (Princeton, N.J.: Princeton University Press, 1971).
57. Dahl (1956), *op. cit.*, p. 68.

the definition of alternatives is the choice of conflicts, and the choice of conflicts allocates power.[58]

Our final question: How do politicians know on which issues to generate demand? An answer to this question requires a careful definition of political astuteness, a topic we dare not entertain! At this point politics becomes art, not science. Or at any rate it becomes psychology, not political science. To say that astute politicians are "good observers of human nature" is to beg the question. To account for political astuteness with observations of political success is circular. Yet we are not prepared to be more specific. What is clearly needed is a *theory of political entrepreneurship*. Although we pursue this matter briefly in chapter 3, we do not claim to have filled this important theoretical void. It still remains an open question. However, for our purposes it is sufficient to assert that the law of survival in free competition implies that the more valuable prizes will be contested by relatively sophisticated, astute candidates. Our assumptions of political calculation and machination, e.g., demand generation, are probably descriptively accurate for this group of politicians.

Summary

The reader, no doubt, is rather winded from the sprint through the material in this chapter. He may also be puzzled about the relationship between the abstract concepts developed and the politics of plural societies. We have no intention of resolving this problem in summary fashion. As a result, the next chapter is devoted in its entirety to an analysis of politics in the plural society using the tools and language of this chapter.

---

58. E. E. Schattschneider, "Intensity, Visability, Direction and Scope," *American Political Science Review* 51, no. 3 (September 1957): 933-42 (quotation at p. 937).

CHAPTER 3

Distinctive Features of Politics in the
Plural Society: A Paradigm

In chapter 1 we began with Furnivall's definition of the plural society. A plural society, according to Furnivall, is one comprised of "two or more elements or social orders which live side by side, yet without mingling, in one political unit."[1] We then traced the intellectual development of the plural society concept, at last arriving at our own meaning. For our purposes a plural society is identified by

1. cultural diversity,
2. politically organized cultural communities, and
3. the salience of ethnicity.

A cursory glance at the social composition and organization of nearly all extant nation-states suggests that the first feature is simply the reflection of a social truism: rarely are modern societies culturally homogeneous. It is the latter two features (ethnic politics), however, that distinguish the *plural* society from its *pluralistic* counterpart.

In the following pages we present a paradigm of politics in the plural society. We begin with a verbal description of individual preferences and then provide a formal representation, relying on the materials developed in the preceding chapter. It is important to observe throughout that ours is essentially a *political,* not a sociological, theory. Quite obviously this is a matter of emphasis since the distinction between the political and the sociological is fuzzy at best (except in the corridors of university social science buildings). However, this distinction does provide some manageable limits to our inquiry. We focus, as a result, on the *political consequences* of cultural pluralism, rather than on dynamic changes in the social structure itself. For example, we do not investigate changes in practices of

---

1. *Netherlands India* (Cambridge: The University Press, 1939), p. 446.

kinship, marriage, religion, etc., though they may be important to sociologists and anthropologists.

A second point is also germane: our concern is with the consequences of ethnicity for the practice of democratic politics in the plural society, not with "politics in general." More specifically, we examine the juxtaposition of ethnically organized politics and democracy, "that institutional arrangement for arriving at political decisions in which individuals acquire the power to decide by means of a competitive struggle for the people's vote."[2] With these points in mind, let us turn our attention to an examination of ethnic preferences.

Ethnic Preferences

In the plural society competitive politics is characterized by ethnic politics. That is to say, ethnicity is the (only) major basis for the "authoritative allocation of value." The salience of "primordial sentiments" has been accurately observed by Geertz:

> The network of primordial alliance and opposition is a dense, intricate, but yet precisely articulated one, the product, in most cases, of centuries of gradual crystallization. The unfamiliar civil state, born yesterday from the meager remains of an exhausted colonial regime, is superimposed upon this fine-spun and lovingly conserved texture of pride and suspicion and must somehow contrive to weave it into the fabric of modern politics.[3]

The primordial communities that partition the plural society are what Emerson calls *terminal communities*: "the largest community that, when the chips are down, effectively commands men's loyalty."[4] They provide a natural base for political organization and a source of divisiveness as well. And in the plural society primordial sentiments are (by definition as well as by observation) manifest and politically salient.

The Salience of Primordial Sentiments in the Plural Society. We have argued in chapter 2 that issues are politically salient partly because poli-

---

2. Joseph A. Schumpeter, *Capitalism, Socialism and Democracy,* 3d ed. (New York: Harper and Row, 1950), p. 269.

3. Clifford Geertz, "The Integrative Revolution: Primordial Sentiments and Civil Politics in the New States," in Clifford Geertz, ed., *Old Societies and New States* (New York: Free Press, 1963), pp. 104-57 (quotation at p. 119).

4. Rupert Emerson, *From Empire to Nation* (Cambridge, Mass.: Harvard University Press, 1960), pp. 95-96. Cited in Geertz, *op. cit.,* p. 107.

ticians and community leaders view them as such. We endeavor to show here that it is reasonable for ethnicity to dominate political conflict in those societies in which ethnic communities are politically organized. The subcommunities of the plural society have permanent and separate histories, separate social institutions, customs and practices, and separate leaders. When several of those communities are agglomerated into a single political entity, it is only natural that the local politician uses his community as a base of operations. This calls for appeals aimed at the dominant community sentiments that distinguish it from competing, sometimes alien, communities. As Melson and Wolpe suggest, "In a competitive political system, the social . . . separation of communal groups encourages the development of communally-based political institutions and strategies."[5]

If historical-sociological processes influence the perceptions, and hence strategies, of community leaders, then purely political rules tend to reinforce this view. The territorial basis of representation that characterizes most democratic arrangements, and the resulting cultural homogeneity (or nearly so) of most constituencies, generally dictates the necessity of communal strategies for elite survival. Thus segregation reinforces the political salience of communalism.

Further support for the salience of primordial sentiments is found in the political, social and psychological discontinuities that result in the creation of a modern state. As Kearney observes, "creation of a modern state seems to [stimulate] communal and other particularistic sentiments by providing a new arena for competition and a more valuable prize for which to compete."[6]

To this point, as in the last chapter, a bothersome question remains. We have not precluded other issues from stimulating political conflict in the plural society. Why, for example, are conflicts in such societies not organized along economic lines? Our answer is that politicians exert control over the definition of political alternatives, often relying on ethnic appeals. But why this *particular* choice?

Part of the explanation for the choice of "ethnicity" lies in the existence of mobilized resources and organizations, well-suited for political deployment on ethnic issues. Politics becomes a rather serious matter "in view of the fact that communal groups are usually more readily organized for political action and are capable of more sustained effort than other forms of pressure groups."[7] Politics, according to this explanation, "naturally"

---

5. Robert Melson and Howard Wolpe, "Modernization and the Politics of Communalism: A Theoretical Perspective," *American Political Science Review* 64, no. 4 (December 1970): 1112-30 (quotation at p. 1119).

6. Robert N. Kearney, *Communalism and Language in the Politics of Ceylon* (Durham, North Carolina: Duke University Press, 1967), p. 15.

7. K. J. Ratnam, "Constitutional Government and the 'Plural Society,'" *Journal of Southeast Asian History* 2, no. 3 (October 1961): 1-10 (quotation at p. 1).

follows ethnic lines. However, there is good reason to believe that the hardening of politics along the ethnic dimension additionally requires that the organizational and institutional "naturalness" dovetails with individual perceptions and preferences. If, for example, the ethnic issue were a facade foisted upon an electorate not receptive to those issues simply to suit the motives of strategically advantaged politicians, then one might expect successful political recourse to be taken by the "losers."

Although other issues may affect politics in plural societies, we here assert the preeminence of ethnicity. We are not able to explain its genesis. A satisfactory resolution of this problem awaits two developments:

1. a formal explanation of the formation, development and endurance of values and preferences, and
2. a positive theory of political entrepreneurship.

The first is self-explanatory: until we better understand how individual values and preferences develop, decision-theoretic methods require *assumptions* about them. They are, in effect, primitive terms.

The second proposed development, a positive theory of political entrepreneurship, would, in our view, provide an explanation for the ways in which political entrepreneurs structure partisan debate and competition in order to achieve their goals. More specifically this theory would explain (1) how political elites behave when the issues of a given contest are well-defined, and (2) how these elites shift the issues of politics for partisan gain, i.e., redefine the focus of political conflict.

With these two developments, then, we could more persuasively account for the preeminence of ethnicity in the plural society. *However, we do not need this account in order to trace the course of democratic politics once ethnicity becomes salient.*

In conclusion, we recognize, with Kearney, the primacy of ethnicity in plural societies:

> The community frequently is the most inclusive group possessing a claim on the loyalty of the individual and with which he can readily identify. An individual is born into a community, and membership in that community and exclusion from all others remains with him throughout his life. . . . Virtually every permanent inhabitant of [a plural society] identifies himself and is identified by others as belonging to one and only one community.[8]

Value conflicts between these communities complicate political processes. As Geertz indicates, individuals in the plural society

---

8. *Op. cit.*, p. 6.

tend to regard the immediate, concrete, and to them inherently meaningful sorting implicit in such "natural" diversity as the *substantial content of their individuality.* [To] subordinate these specific and familiar identifications in favor of a generalized commitment to an overarching and somewhat alien civil order is *to risk a loss of definition as an autonomous person,* either through absorption into a culturally undifferentiated mass or, what is even worse, through domination by some other rival ethnic, racial, or linguistic community that is able to imbue that order with the temper of its own personality.[9]

Not only do communal values in conflict inhibit a strategy of ethnic de-emphasis; they prevent compromise solutions as well. *Ethnic preferences are intense and are not negotiable.* To promise less for one's group in the name of harmony and accommodation is to betray that group's interest.

The shadows of the logic of politics in plural societies are slowly coming into focus. Separate communities with separate institutions and patterns of socialization—indeed, separate and incompatible values—are agglomerated into an artificial political entity as a result of historical forces and random events. The members of these separate communities, now co-nationals, have internalized a history of intergroup conflict that has a new institutional framework in which to be manifested: the nation-state. We demonstrate and document in the remainder of this book that politicians reinforce perceptions of incompatible communal values, sooner or later, through the widespread use of ethnic appeals; that *intragroup* politics soon becomes the *politics of outbidding;* that brokerage institutions, e.g., the political parties of pluralistic democracies, become inefficacious; that communal institutions of aggregation are rapidly converted into corporate representatives of communal values; and that competitive politics ultimately leads to winners and losers whose temporary status is made permanent through the *manipulation of the electoral machinery.*

Ethnic Preferences: A Theoretical Description.   Politics in the plural society, by assumption, is restricted to the single dimension of ethnicity. To this point our treatment has been intuitive. We have shown that primordial sentiments provide a gestalt that defines the available political alternatives. Unlike politics in pluralistic societies, where fluid coalitions, shifting alliances, and changing world views are preeminent, "the patterns of primordial identification and cleavage within [plural societies] . . . are definitely demarcated."[10]

Here we begin a formal treatment of ethnic preferences in terms of individual values. This requires the specification of several assumptions.

---

9. Geertz, *op. cit.,* pp. 108-9 (emphasis added).
10. *Ibid.,* p. 118.

The first assumption follows from a presumed uniformity of preference within communities.[11]

> **A.1 intracommunal consensus:** the members of an ethnic community perceive and express preferences about political alternatives identically. Thus all members may be represented by identical "ethnic preference functions."

On the basis of those cultural tastes and values that define his community, this assumption asserts that each member of any given community ranks the alternatives available, say $\{a, b, c\}$, in a manner identical to those of his communal compatriots. That is, of the six logically distinct preference orderings, *viz.*

(1)	(2)	(3)	(4)	(5)	(6)
a	a	b	b	c	c
b	c	a	c	a	b
c	b	c	a	b	a

the same one is selected by each member of a given community.[12]

The second assumption relates the consensually held preferences of one community to those of others:

> **A.2 intercommunal conflict:** communities are in disagreement on all issues that face the collectivity.

By this we mean that among communities, preferences on collective decisions, and hence underlying cultural values, are in conflict — that if community A prefers alternative a, then community B not only prefers alternative b, but believes that b implies $\sim a$ (read: not a) as well. In short, the political world of the plural society is, to a greater or lesser extent, Hobbesian.[13]

Numerous empirical cases suggest that these two assumptions capture the nature of politics in plural societies. Although part two of this study

---

11. Recalling the relevant discussion in chapter 2, the reader should note that whenever reference is made to individual preferences, we mean connected, transitive, preference orderings.

12. Assumption A.1 is consistent with the frequent observation that the plural society is a collection of highly cohesive communities. In a manner of speaking, preferences are narrowly distributed about the modal preference ordering of the community.

13. On the topic of preference conflict in terms of utility theory, see Robert Axelrod, *Conflict of Interest* (Chicago: Markham Publishing Company, 1970).

examines these assumptions and their consequences in a broad variety of empirical settings, for now two examples suffice:

> 1. In Northern Ireland "there are three tiers of constitutional elections. . . . With few exceptions in the fifty years of Northern Ireland's existence, all these elections have been fought on the issue of 'for or against' the continuance of Northern Ireland as a separate political entity linked with Great Britain, *and virtually all votes have been cast on strictly sectarian lines.* . . . In many constituencies the results have been so predictable—*with voting strictly reflecting the main religious division*—that no elections have taken place in a great many years, candidates (mostly Unionist) being returned unopposed."[14]

> 2. Ceylon is partitioned into two primary communities, Sinhalese and Tamil, the former comprising an overwhelming majority. During the period shortly before independence, the dominant political question was of a constitutional nature: how should the newly independent country govern itself? "If the belief had been prevalent that ethnic and linguistic differences were irrelevant to the issues confronting a modern state, no reason would have existed for disputing the claims of majority rule. However, *the expectation of solidarity within and competition between communities on political questions was clearly evident,* particularly among those who spoke for the Tamil community . . . [A]s their concern over the enhanced political strength of the Sinhalese mounted, Tamil leaders supported selective use of *communal* representation and sought other devices to curtail the political power of the Sinhalese."[15]

In each of these examples the ethnic community is perceived, by actors and observers alike, as a consensual corporate group (A.1) in conflict with similar corporate entities (A.2). These expectations become self-fulfilling prophecies in the sense that the disagreement *within* communities and the cooperative tendencies *between* communities that may have existed become less salient.

The third assumption is that of a common perceptual frame:

---

14. *Orange and Green: A Quaker Study of Community Relations in Northern Ireland* (Northern Friends Peace Board, 1969), pp. 13, 16 (emphasis added).

15. Kearney, *op. cit.*, pp. 32-33 (emphasis added). It is interesting to note that after reviewing the dimensions of political conflict in pre- and post-independence Ceylon, Kearney arrives at a position quite compatible with our own, namely the pervasiveness of communalism: "The existing sense of communal identification and loyalty dictated that communal interests and aspirations be protected and promoted in the political sphere. . . . The benefits and deprivations dependent on political action had multiplied with the rapid expansion of the functions of the modern state. It was, therefore, *almost inevitable* that growing communal rivalry should accompany the emergence of a modern participant political process. . . ." *Ibid.*, p. 40 (emphasis added).

A.3 perceptual consensus: alternatives are viewed according to a perceptual frame common to all actors.

Although undoubtedly restrictive,[16] we suppose that among the various communities, and especially among the elites, there is agreement as to what constitutes the set of available alternatives. Moreover, how these alternatives benefit or harm each community is readily apparent.

That perceptual consensus on the set of political options (A.3) can exist in the midst of preference conflict between communities (A.2) is illustrated by Greek and Turkish views of the 1960 Cypriot Constitution:

> The persistent bi-communal groupings reflected the attitude of the two communities toward the 1960 Constitution. On the one hand, the Greek Cypriots felt that the Constitution established a "privileged position" for the Turkish Cypriot community and from the start challenged the Constitution's basic provisions. On the other hand, the Turkish Cypriots viewed the Constitution as securing absolutely minimum guarantees for their effective participation in Government.[17]

Oddly enough, then, there is a "definitional consensus" among all the communities of the plural society, namely, that politics is ethnic in character and that communal values are in conflict. *In the plural society the lines of conflict are drawn, hardened, and in full view of everyone.*

We are now prepared to describe the technical characteristics of preferences in plural societies. Technical accuracy requires distinctions in *dimensionality*. That is, *a priori* it is important to distinguish between plural polities with two, three, . . . , and *n* ethnic communities. For a great many situations, however, the case of two communities suffices for our analysis.

In the case of two ethnic communities, call them A and B, we suppose that the available alternatives can be arrayed along a single bounded dimension, where the preferred position of each community is an endpoint (figure 3.1). Several features of this particular representation of the alter-

A   B

Figure 3.1

16. See Donald E. Stokes, "Spatial Models of Party Competition," *American Political Science Review* 57, no. 2 (June 1963): 368-77, esp. p. 374.

17. Stanley Kyriakides, *Cyprus: Constitutionalism and Crisis Government* (Philadelphia: University of Pennsylvania Press, 1968), p. 75. Here Kyriakides notes that the common perception of the special status of the Turks in this constitution did not preclude differential evaluation of it by the respective communities.

natives need to be noted. First, from A.1 it is appropriate to represent a community's most-preferred alternative by a single point—hence, the points A and B in figure 3.1. From A.2 it follows that these points are distinct from one another, although the extent of the distinction, i.e., the "amount" of preference conflict, remains unspecified. Finally, assumption A.3—perceptual consensus—permits the use of a dimension common to all actors to depict the set of alternatives. Although we argue that perceptual consensus is a manifestation of an ethnic definition of politics, this does not preclude a multidimensional representation of the alternatives if (or when) ethnicity is not salient; the single dimension simply reflects the (inverse) relationship between the ethnic preferences of the two communities.[18]

Individual preferences are characterized by von Neumann-Morgenstern utility functions (see chapter 2) defined on the continuum of alternatives. In figure 3.2 preference functions for the two-community case are pre-

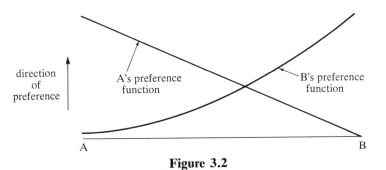

Figure 3.2

sented. As A.1 and A.2 suggest, each community prefers the point that reflects its own communal values most, with preference decreasing as alternatives more and more "distant" from that point are considered. In fact, for the two-community case, A.2 means that slopes of the respective

18. Our use of a *continuum* to specify the set of alternatives is incomplete since a metric has not been provided. It must remain so since political scientists, unlike economists and natural scientists, do not yet possess well-defined "units" with which to measure phenomena. Thus, any of our results that ultimately depend on particular units are, for the time being, suspect. However, as is seen below, most of our results depend only in a limited way upon the metric properties of the continuum. In particular, if the units of the continuum in figure 3-1 are altered by (positive or negative) linear transformations, our results are unaffected. In fact, for some kinds of nonlinear transformations our results remain invariant. Although political research would undoubtedly benefit from the discovery of a metric like dollars or Euclidean distance, until that time it makes good sense to formulate problems in a manner which makes only "limited use" of metric properties.

community preference functions are of opposite sign at every point in the interval [A, B].

Notice that the preference curves may take on a variety of shapes, so long as they continually slope downward as the argument of the function is more and more distant from the community preferred point. Shortly, we restrict this variety somewhat when we take intensity into account.

Second, one should observe that, despite our labelling which identifies preference functions as "community preferences," the functions are, in fact, those of individuals. *However, from the assumption of identical preferences within communities (A.1) we may take any individual preference as representative of community sentiment without running the risk of false personification.*

Although we have argued that it is reasonable to deal with a continuum of alternatives bounded by communal preferred points, the possibility of an unbounded continuum, as in figure 3.3, is not precluded. However,

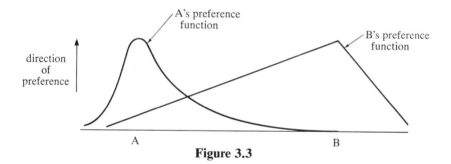

Figure 3.3

throughout this analysis we employ the interpretation displayed in figure 3.2 (polar extremes case), rather than the one in figure 3.3, because in the latter it may be seen that the only "relevant" alternatives fall in the interval [A, B]. Compared to points to the left of A, *both* communities prefer A. Similarly, both communities prefer B to any point to its right.

The case of three (or more) ethnic communities is geometrically more complex, but poses no major analytical difficulties. The preference "space," the analogue of the preference continuum of figure 3.2, is depicted in figure 3.4, where (A, O, O), (O, B, O), and (O, O, C) represent the preferred points of three ethnic communities. Notice, however, that under this geometric interpretation the point with coordinate (A, B, C) is admissible. This violates A.2 — the assumption of interethnic conflict — for it allows the preferred points of all three communities to be realized simul-

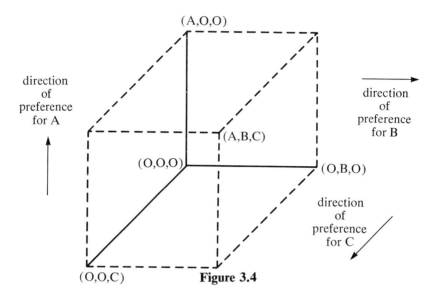

Figure 3.4

taneously. Thus, we must modify our geometric representation accordingly. To do this we pass a plane through the rectangular solid in figure 3.4 that intersects the extreme points (A, O, O), (O, B, O), and (O, O, C). The intersection of the plane and the "unmodified" preference space produces a triangle, as shown in figure 3.5. We define the triangle T as the preference space. Each community's preferred point is possible, but no two (or

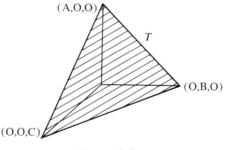

Figure 3.5

more) communities simultaneously obtain their preferred alternatives — an indication of preference conflict.

Preference functions are defined on the triangle T in a manner that parallels our treatment in the two community case. The extreme points of T represent communal most-preferred alternatives, with communal preference decreasing for points increasingly removed.

One new factor appears in the three- (and higher-) dimensional cases —
the possibility of coalition formation among communities. Although communities prefer their respective extreme points in T, their utility functions
need not be symmetric with respect to the other communities. Thus, members of community C (see figure 3.5) naturally prefer (O, O, C) most, but
they may distinctly prefer movement along the axis between (O, O, C)
and (O, B, O) to analogous movement on the axis between (O, O, C) and
(A, O, O). In this tricommunal instance C's preference function is said
to be *skewed* toward (O, B, O). If B's preference function happens to be
skewed toward (O, O, C), then, despite each community's preference for
its respective extreme point, they may be willing to cooperate (implicitly
at least) in order to prevent an outcome near the point (A, O, O). If B
and C are minority communities, for example, then they may coalesce
against the dominant community. The case of Malaya is instructive. There
the Chinese and Indian communities, acting in concert, advocate multi-
lingualism (though each undoubtedly would prefer their own as the sole
official language) to inhibit the implementation of Malay as the official
language (see chapter 4 for additional details).[19]

In much of our analysis ("fragmented" societies excepted) we reduce
the dimensionality to the two-dimensional case, as it is often evident that
many of the disadvantaged communities (implicitly) coalesce against the
dominant group. Thus, in many multicommunal instances, politics takes
on a "dominant community vs. coalition" quality.[20]

We make one final comment about ethnic preferences before examining
their implications: they are *intensely* held. As a result, preferences cannot
stand even the tiny chips of moderate frustration. When ethnicity is involved, many are willing to "go for broke." Technically, intensity is
characterized by the propensity to accept fair lotteries — recall our definition of *risk acceptance* in chapter 2. In mathematical terms, this means
that preference functions are convex, rather than linear or concave, in the
relevant range of alternatives. Thus preferences in the plural society are
of the same functional form as those in figure 3.6(a), whereas in *pluralistic* societies, preferences along the cultural dimension are more like those
in figure 3.6(b). The important feature in this comparison is the shape of
the respective utility functions. Convexity provides a mathematical char-

19. The mechanics of coalition formation are not formally treated in our analysis.
On occasion, we make reference to coalitional possibilities.

20. It should be noted, parenthetically, that figures 3.4 and 3.5 can be generalized
to any number of dimensions, although higher dimensions escape geometric representation. One would begin with an n-dimensional hypercube, analogous to figure
3.4, pass an $(n\text{-}1)$-dimensional hyperplane through the extreme points, which would
produce an $(n\text{-}1)$-dimensional hypersurface or generalized triangle analogous to T
in figure 3.5. The analysis could then proceed in a similar fashion.

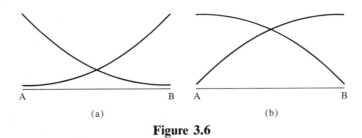

(a)   (b)

Figure 3.6

acterization of the "go for broke" attitude prevalent when enthnicity is salient. In the section that follows, we show that intensity, as represented by convexity, profoundly shapes and ultimately undermines democratic politics in the plural society.

A Paradigm of Politics in the Plural Society

In the last section we focused on the features of individual preferences in the plural society. Using those features we examine, in this section, the dynamics of ethnic competition and derive some theoretical results. An overview of those dynamics reveals five distinct features. They are:

1. preindependence ethnic cooperation;
2. postindependence ethnic cooperation: ambiguity;
3. demand generation and the increased salience of ethnicity;
4. outbidding and the decline of the multiethnic coalition; and
5. electoral machinations and mistrust.[21]

Preindependence Ethnic Cooperation. An examination of the historical experiences of most plural societies reveals the first significant regularity: the existence of elite-level ethnic cooperation in the preindependence period. During this period, ethnic communities were not so much competitors with one another as they were in competition with a common opponent. The existence of alien rule provided the impetus for interethnic cooperation

---

21. Two caveats are in order. First, by "independence" we do not intend the literal, legal meaning of the word. Rather, we have a more psychological definition in mind, captured in part by the expression: "when de facto independence appears imminent." Second, although many of today's plural societies are the so-called developing or modernizing nations, our comments and observations are not restricted to them. Thus, on some occasions we speak of the "colonial experience," e.g., Guyana, while on others we refer to the "prenational period," e.g., Yugoslavia.

and the submergence of ethnic differences. Indigenous middle classes, who bore the brunt of alien rule, were painfully aware of the opportunities foreclosed to native populations.[22] While the indigenous masses were able to rationalize whatever indignities they suffered (and it is doubtful that the indignities lessened much after independence), the middle class could not. Thus, Sir Kamisese Kapaiwai Tuimacilai Mara, Fiji's new political leader, is described by the *New York Times* as a middle-class Fijian who felt resentment towards the ruling British colonial authorities. "It is said that his resentment at receiving a lower salary than that of Britons doing the same job intensified the highly educated young chief's nationalist tendencies."[23] Perceptions of inequities, indignities, and the general foreclosure of opportunities for self-gain and self-aggrandizement were reinforced by frequent dealings with alien administrators (e.g., professional licensing, business negotiations, etc.). Members of the middle class had, as a result, incentives to cooperate with one another in order to render outside exploitation as costly and as unsuccessful as possible.

There were other incentives as well. Broad-gauged resistance and demands for increased opportunities had the effect of supplying the mother country with a convenient rationale for disengagement. In addition, the fact that the colonialists held the larger piece of the economic pie and the authority to allocate it, and that coordinated efforts were required to wrest it from them, augered well for mutual cooperation. The net result of these factors is, as Shils informs us, an intensely nationalistic elite little bothered by communal divisions in their ranks.[24] The case of Ceylon is representative:

> Early in the life of the movement for political autonomy, some hope and expectation existed that the struggle for Ceylonese self-government would unify the Sinhalese and Tamils in common cause. The politically active middle class was multicommunal in composition and relatively cosmopolitan in outlook. . . . While even within this class, communal identity was not obliterated and marriage seldom leaped communal barriers, relations between Sinhalese and Tamils were not only free of tension but were often cordial and warm. It was a sign of "modernity" to reject communal sentiments as barbarous and atavistic.[25]

---

22. For supporting arguments, see, for example, T. B. Bottomore, *Elites and Society* (Harmondsworth, England: Pelican Books, 1966), pp. 99-100.

23. *New York Times,* October 10, 1970, p. 2.

24. Edward Shils, "On the Comparative Study of New States," in Geertz, *op. cit.,* pp. 1-27 (citation at p. 2).

25. Kearney, *op. cit.,* p. 27.

As independence was granted or became imminent, the multiethnic coalition that dominated the struggle for independence became strained. However, to a certain extent, the cooperative behavior among ethnic elites had become institutionalized in the form of economic and especially political associations. The postindependence period, then, witnessed attempts to hold an oversized multiethnic coalition together.

Postindependence Ethnic Cooperation: Ambiguity. Geertz aptly describes the problem facing the multiethnic coalition or political association:

> The pattern that seems to be developing, and perhaps crystallizing, is one in which a comprehensive national party . . . comes almost to comprise the state and is multiply assailed by a field of small parties . . . each of which is trying to knock chips off one or another part of it by attacking the points of strain that develop within it as it functions and by appealing more openly to primordial sentiments.[26]

The strains that develop in the ranks of the multiethnic coalition are traceable directly to the changes in the "rules of the game." After independence, the content of politics is distribution. The colonial power (or its equivalent) is no longer a contender, leaving only fellow nationals to dispute "who gets what, when, and how." That is, from the point of view of the multiethnic coalition, the game has been reduced from one against the colonialist to one turned against itself. The political situation, formerly a *game of extraction*, i.e., extraction of gains from a dominant group, has been converted into a *game of division* among the members of the victorious coalition. Gain *at the expense of coalition partners* now becomes a distinct possibility.

Despite the invidiousness of the new context, political activists who participated in the drive for independence have an immediate interest in preserving the multiethnic political organization. It is psychologically difficult and politically dangerous for these intense nationalists to desert the cause (and its institutional manifestation — the multiethnic coalition) for which they fought so long.

How, then, does the oversized multiethnic coalition resolve the strains it encounters and, more specifically, how does it deal with the more open appeals to primordial sentiments that opposition leaders voice? The technique it employs is essentially two-fold. On the one hand, leaders *generate demand* for national (as opposed to communal) issues, e.g., economic development, territorial integrity. On the other hand, they treat divisive communal issues *ambiguously*.

---

26. Geertz, *op. cit.,* pp. 135-36.

The first technique — demand generation for national issues — allows the multiethnic coalition to avoid the divisiveness of a politics of distribution. Those small parties that seek communal distributive advantage are easily accused of undercutting attempts at nation building, both by inhibiting economic growth and by endangering the political viability of the new regime. External enemies are conveniently "found" or exaggerated by the coalition to justify their claims of treasonable behavior on the part of communal interests. Indeed, in some instances democratic prerogatives are suspended in the interest of preserving the integrity of the new state.

The generation of demand for issues of national importance is an eminently sensible strategy for the multiethnic coalition, primarily because it is ordinarily the only national political organization. The *raison d'etre* of its smaller competitors is *communal* interest. The coalition is the only party, then, that has a legitimate claim to a national constituency. Its dominant position on broadly defined national issues that it keeps salient allows it to retain leadership.[27]

To deal with the potentially divisive set of communal issues, the multiethnic coalition *purposely generates ambiguity.* Individuals in the plural society have, as we argued earlier, intense preferences along this dimension. Given this condition it may be demonstrated mathematically that ambiguous policy stands bear electoral fruit.

In figure 3.7, for example, we display the bicommunal case. Each community intensely prefers its own set of values, as is suggested by the convexity of the preference functions. How would each community react to ambiguous statements on this dimension? In particular, suppose the multiethnic coalition, through appropriate behaviors and expressions, is perceived by all citizens as a *lottery*, e.g., ½A, ½B). Employing the expected-utility decision rule,[28] one may determine the "value" each com-

---

27. Our theoretical point here is that demand generation—the determination of issue definition and salience—is an important strategic device that leaders may use. Unlike some recent models of political competition which follow in the tradition of Anthony Downs (*An Economic Theory of Democracy* [New York: Harper and Row, 1957], esp. chap. 8), we do not presume a *fixed political structure* within which political activists compete. To the contrary, we suppose that the structure, itself, is a critical variable which may be altered by the behavior of "political entrepreneurs." The interactions of political entrepreneurs define issues and determine salience. Demand generation, in our view, is to political competition what advertising is to economic exchange; and political entrepreneurs, like advertisers, sensitize the electorate to the dimensions and importance (read: salience) of choice. It should be pointed out, however, that entrepreneurs in neither field are completely unconstrained in their behavior nor invariably successful. Like the effectiveness of a lighthouse which depends not only on which direction it is pointed, but on what is actually "out there," the success of demand generation depends both on the choice of issues and the degree to which this choice dovetails with individual preferences.

28. See chapter 2.

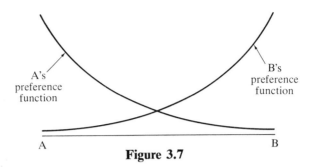

Figure 3.7

munity places on the multiethnic coalition. A geometric representation of this calculation for a citizen in community A is presented in figure 3.8. The utility of the lottery $L = (\frac{1}{2}A, \frac{1}{2}B)$, i.e., A and B each with a probability of 0.5, is represented by the midpoint of the chord connecting the points $(A, u(A))$ and $(B, u(B))$. Note that the expected utility of this lottery, $u_A(L)$, is equal to the utility of the certain alternative x^*, and that x^* is a position relatively close to community A's preferred point.[29]

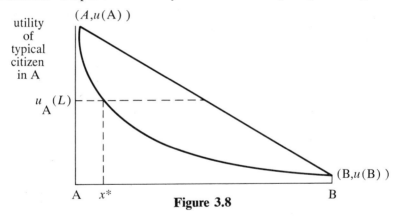

Figure 3.8

In figure 3.9 the analogous calculation for a citizen in community B is displayed. The expected utility of the lottery L is equal to the utility of the point y^*. That is, y^* is B's certainty equivalent of L. Again, note that y^* is relatively close to community B's preferred point.

---

29. The point x^* is usually called the *certainty equivalent* of the lottery L. See John W. Pratt, Howard Raiffa, and Robert Schlaifer, "The Foundations of Decision Under Uncertainty: An Elementary Exposition," *Journal of the American Statistics Association* 59, no. 36 (June 1964): 353-75.

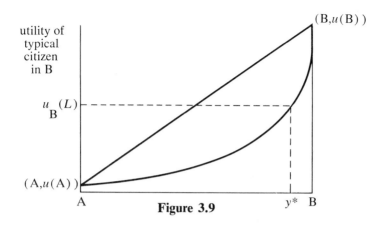

Figure 3.9

Figures 3.8 and 3.9 dramatically illustrate that *despite conflicting preferences — indeed, because of conflicting preferences — each community places high value on the lottery* L = (½A ½B). For A, the lottery is as preferred as x^*; for B, it is as preferred as y^*. *And each community is relatively well-satisfied with its respective certainty equivalent.*[30]

Though this result is not obvious, our logical account persuades us that purposeful ambiguity, by permitting appeals to groups with conflicting preferences, is an efficacious and hence rational strategy. If the multiethnic coalition succeeds in focusing attention on national (nonethnic) issues, and if it neutralizes divisive ethnic issues via ambiguity, then it should retain its leadership role. Though it can be marginally outbid on ethnic issues,[31] the coalition is successful because those ethnic issues are simply not salient.

An example of the use of ambiguity as a political strategy that keeps communalism temporarily at bay is found in Malaya's Alliance Party, a coalition of three explicitly ethnic parties. In the 1959 election the Alliance behaved ambiguously on communally based issues that might have split the Malay, Chinese and Indian constituents of the coalition. With the society racially divided, the coalition developed an approach to racial issues that did not require irrevocable commitment to one side or the other.

---

30. Moreover, each community prefers the lottery, and hence its certainty equivalent, to some compromise position—say, a point z midway between A and B; i.e., x^* is preferred to $z = \dfrac{A+B}{2}$ by community A and y^* is preferred to $z = \dfrac{A+B}{2}$ by community B.

31. Members of community A prefer points in the interval [A, x^*] at least as much as L, while members of community B prefer points in [y^*, B].

During the campaign the Alliance leadership exhibited some ambivalence toward communal issues. On the one hand Tunku Abdul
Rahman made a communal appeal for the support of the Malays,
stressing such issues as "the alien danger" and the threat to the Malays posed by the immigration of "foreigners." On the other hand, he
defended the Alliance manifesto which attributed the "alien danger"
to the restrictive citizenship requirements which made it difficult for
non-Malays to acquire full status as Malayan citizens. Thus, the
Alliance tended to utilize the "foreign threat" issue in appealing to
the Malays, but hastened to explain to its [Malayan Chinese Associa-
tion] and [Malayan Indian Congress] members that the loyal Chinese
and Indians in these two organizations were not a part of that "foreign threat." *This is just one of the many examples of ambiguous
terms being employed successfully to keep incongruous elements
united for common political action.*[32]

That the strategy of demand generation for national issues and purposeful ambiguity for ethnic issues is appropriate has been demonstrated formally. That it was employed in a number of plural societies is verified in
part two. However, as the examination in the next section indicates, the net
result of this strategy, in case after case, is the emergence of ethnicity as
the dominant political consideration. Demand-generating activity on the
part of the multiethnic coalition may suppress temporarily an ethnic
definition of politics, but it neither alters preferences nor entirely removes
ethnic considerations.

Demand Generation and the Increased Salience of Ethnicity. Loyalty in the
plural society is *communal*, not *national*. And communal preferences are
intense. National issues, though salient for a time, do not have staying
power.[33] The multiethnic coalition is short-lived as a result.

What sparks the manifestation of communalism? The answer is obviously complex, and ultimately depends on historical happenstance. Yet
from our emphasis on (and assumptions about) individual preferences
and political motives, several explanations are indicated and, as a consequence, a number of empirical regularities are uncovered.

A first source of increased communalism is the distributive character
of the postindependence period. As government becomes more responsive
to indigenous interests, internal rules of distribution become especially
salient. Citizens of different communities, as a result, are turned against

---

32. Gordon P. Means, *Malaysian Politics* (New York: New York University
Press, 1970), p. 165 (emphasis added).
33. As Geertz notes, communal preferences are intense, though sometimes latent.
Given appropriate circumstances, however, they become manifest. "Primordially
based political solidarities have a deeply abiding strength in most of the new states,
but it is not always an active and immediately apparent one." Geertz, *op. cit.,* p. 114.

one another. Scarcity of resources, as well as more serious incompatibilities, implies that some people's preferences are satisfied at the expense of others'. The fact that government becomes an increasingly important indigenous force in the allocation of these resources merely exacerbates matters.

A second source of increased conflict, which eventually takes a communal turn, is the *oversized* condition of the multiethnic coalition. With the creation of the new state, and the departure of the colonial power (if it existed), the multiethnic coalition becomes, in effect, the coalition-of-the-whole. And, for the most structural arrangements, the coalition-of-the-whole is larger than necessary for making collective decisions. There are often positive incentives for some subcoalition to expel the remaining members.[34] Communal criteria often determine who is expelled and who remains.

These factors — the distributive character of politics and the existence of an oversized coalition — when combined with independent decision-making authority, incite communal sentiments. Given the institutionalization of primordial sentiments, and the existence of communal fears and insecurities, the new rules of distribution invariably follow communal lines.

Something, however, must set this whole process in motion. Historical events provide the catalyst in some instances, e.g., external events, deaths of political leaders, exogenous changes in the economy, etc. Of more interest is the behavior of communal politicians. The ethnic leader, who is either expelled from the multiethnic coalition or whose community is systematically ignored, perceives incentives to "ethnicize" politics. That is, as a response to the deemphasis of communalism by the ruling coalition, excluded politicians have incentives to "fan the flames" of ethnic chauvinism. Geertz, as usual, says it well:

> . . . there swirls around the emerging governmental institutions of the new states, and the specialized politics they tend to support, a whole host of self-reinforcing whirlpools of primordial discontent, and this parapolitical maelstrom is in great part an outcome—to continue the metaphor, a backwash—of that process of political development itself.[35]

---

34. That there is an inherent tendency for coalitions to reduce their size, as much as situational constraints permit, to the minimum proportion consistent with winning is a well-known result of game theory. It has been given a political significance by William H. Riker, *The Theory of Political Coalitions* (New Haven: Yale University Press, 1962), pp. 32-101 and has been tested with varying success in a variety of empirical political contexts in Sven Groennings, E. W. Kelly, and Michael Leiserson, eds., *The Study of Coalition Behavior* (New York: Holt, Rinehart and Winston, 1970), part I.
35. Geertz, *op. cit.,* p. 127.

There are, then, two important conclusions to draw. First, the multi-ethnic coalition is inherently unstable, being vulnerable to a sort of reverse demand generation focusing on ethnic chauvinism. Second, there are politicians whose interest demands the encouragement of ethnic chauvinism. The likely consequence: an increasing frequency of ethnic appeals that strains the unity of the governing coalition. Vivid examples include: "apanjaht"[36] politics in British Guiana, "Sinhalese only" in Ceylon; apartheid in South Africa and Rhodesia; the "Enosis"[37] movement in Cyprus; anti-Catholicism in Ulster; "black power" in Trinidad; separatist sentiments in Belgium; secessionism in Nigeria, Chad, and Ethopia; pan-Indonesian sentiments in Malaya; and hostility toward Indians and Arabs in former British East Africa.

Outbidding and the Decline of the Multiethnic Coalition. Our argument to this point is that politics in the postindependence period takes on a distributive quality, that the criterion of distribution racks the multiethnic coalition producing strains, and that its eventual split accompanies an increased salience of the ethnic dimension. "In this struggle ethnic . . . affiliations . . . become important symbols of political alignment, *symbols which ambitious politicians attempt to manipulate.*"[38]

The consequences of the increased salience of ethnicity are deleterious for the multiethnic coalition and other representatives of political moderation. As Sartori observes, "Unlike the market place, in politics there is no way to protect against 'unfair competition' — demagogy, outbidding, promises without substance."[39] Yet in the plural society, sooner or later, "outbidding becomes the rule of the game. Somebody is always prepared to offer more for less, and the bluff cannot be seen . . . . [T]his is no longer a situation which allows the survival of a political system based on competitive principles. Beyond certain limits, the politics of over-promising and outbidding is the very negation of competitive politics."[40]

---

36. "Apanjaht" is a Hindi word that means "vote for your own kind." See Leo A. Despres, *Culture Pluralism and Nationalist Politics in British Guiana* (Chicago: Rand McNally, 1967), pp. 228-29.

37. The "Enosis" movement was a Greek Cypriot movement to unite Cyprus with the rest of the Greek world. See Kyriakides, *op. cit.*, p. 7.

38. Burton Benedict, *Mauritius: Problems of a Plural Society* (London: Pall Mall Press, 1965), pp. 65-66 (emphasis added).

39. Giovanni Sartori, *Democratic Theory* (Detroit: Wayne State University Press, 1962), pp. 67-68.

40. Giovanni Sartori, "European Political Parties: The Case of Polarized Pluralism," in Joseph LaPalombara and Myron Weiner, eds., *Political Parties and Political Development* (Princeton: Princeton University Press, 1966), pp. 137-76 (quotation at p. 158).

The theoretical features of these observations bear repeating. First, ambitious politicians not included in the multiethnic coalition have incentives to generate demand for communal rather than national issues. As the only national party, the multiethnic coalition is not likely to lose when national issues are salient. Its position becomes more tenuous as the salience of communal issues increases. Second, as figures 3.8 and 3.9 reveal, communal politicians can defeat candidates of the multiethnic coalition, whose position on the ethnic issue is ambiguous, only by taking extreme positions. That is, only points in the intervals [A,x^*] and [y^*,B] are preferred to the lottery of the multiethnic coalition by the respective ethnic communities. In short, communally based political entrepreneurs seek to increase the salience of communal issues and then to outbid the ambiguous multiethnic coalition.[41]

The consequences of the increased salience of ethnicity are manifold. The first notable consequence is the *disappearance of brokerage institutions*, the prime example of which is the multiethnic coalition. Bargains are struck, and cooperative behavior is manifested, only when mutual gain is possible. It is difficult, however, for members of so-called brokerage institutions to cooperate with one another while simultaneously "mending fences" in their own ethnic communities, an activity necessitated by the "flame-fanning" behavior of ambitious ethnic politicians.

The case of Ulster is instructive. Even before the Reverend Ian Paisley arrived on the scene, cooperation between Catholics and Protestants was difficult. In the mid-sixties Captain O'Neill (Unionist premier of Northern Ireland) made attempts at bridge building, symbolically represented by his invitation of the prime minister of the Irish Republic to Belfast. Catholic partisans "saw it as an honest attempt at reconciliation, and it encouraged them, under the restrained leadership of Mr. Eddie McAteer, to become for the first time the Official Opposition in Stormont."[42] However, the premier's position was untenable, as was indicated by the unpopularity of the visit in Unionist circles. It "caused alarm among the hard-liners, and in the following year a back-bench group was formed to keep a watch on Captain O'Neill's future actions . . . ."[43] Shortly thereafter Reverend Paisley began his campaign of public protest and was arrested and imprisoned for the first time.

---

41. The above theoretical account provides, as well, a dynamic account of political change in the plural society. Specifically, this dynamic portrays the steady growth of ethnicity and extremism, ultimately culminating in the collapse of the multiethnic coalition. These observations should disabuse the reader of the notion that rational-choice models of political behavior are inherently static.

42. *Orange and Green, op. cit.*, p. 45. Stormont is the Ulster parliament.

43. *Ibid.*

Not only do parties fail to remain broad-based brokerage institutions, becoming instead communally oriented; interparty communication and cooperation resist nurturing as well. One manifestation of this is suggested by a theoretical proposition of Haefele's. He shows that "if the scope of [a] decision body is restricted to one issue, so that all issues that come before it are likely to be strongly interdependent, then vote-trading can play only a small role in decision-making."[44] That is, if a single substantive criterion defines the value of all issues for all actors, then bargaining, logrolling, and other *quid pro quo* activities are precluded. Such activities are possible only when several important kinds of issues arise — those are amenable to bargaining solutions. However, in the plural society all issues are viewed in terms of their ethnic implications. And, from A.2, values are incompatible on all issues that arise. The premise, then, of Haefele's proposition is met; the conclusion follows: there are no logs for rolling!

A third consequence stemming from the increased salience of ethnicity is the *ethnicization of collectively provided goods*. In pluralistic societies, a number of goods produced by political decisions are jointly consumed, e.g., education, defense, police protection. Consumption of these goods, in many cases, is independent of cost-bearing ability or purchasing power, distinguishing them from the private goods that are supplied in the marketplace. That is, to take the case of defense as an example, all U. S. citizens "benefit" from the United States Government's nuclear arsenal whether they pay for it or not. Indeed, the ability of a tax-evader to "consume" this good suggests the two distinguishing characteristics of collective goods:

1. jointness of supply — consumption by some individuals does not preclude consumption by others, and
2. nonexcludability — criteria distinguishing those permitted to consume the good from those prohibited do not exist.[45]

This, of course, should not be taken to mean that there is no conflict in the allocation of public-sector goods in the pluralistic society. To the contrary, there are at least two kinds of conflict. First, opportunity costs

---

44. Edwin T. Haefele, "Coalitions, Minority Representation, and Vote-Trading Probabilities," *Public Choice* 8 (Spring 1970): 74-90 (quotation at p. 85).

45. Those readers who wish to explore these ideas in greater detail are directed to: Paul A. Samuelson, "The Pure Theory of Public Expenditure," *Review of Economics and Statistics* 36, no. 4 (November 1954): 387-89; Julius Margolis, "A Comment on the Pure Theory of Public Expenditure," *ibid.,* 37, no. 4 (November 1955): 347-49; and E. J. Mishan, "The Relationship Between Joint Products, Collective Goods, and External Effects," *Journal of Political Economy* 77, no. 3 (May-June 1969): 329-48. For a treatment of some inherently political aspects of public goods, see Mancur Olson, Jr., *The Logic of Collective Action: Public Goods and the Theory of Groups* (Cambridge: Harvard University Press, 1965).

are borne by those who would prefer a greater investment of the public weal in *alternative* public goods, despite their ability to participate in the present supply of such goods. Second, since the wealth of the collectivity is invested in private as well as public goods, e.g., reduced postal rates for certain consumers, farm subsidies, oil depletion allowances, there are obvious conflicts over which projects receive these monies (not to speak of the issue of whether any such private goods should be endowed at all).

In plural societies, the extent of public goods consumption declines as ethnicity grows in salience. As ethnicity becomes increasingly salient, every political decision favors one community and hinders others. That is, the public goods which result from political decisions become the preserve of the advantaged ethnic community. *Nonexcludability, a defining characteristic of public goods, is violated. Ethnicity serves as a basis for exclusion. And the excluded communities clearly perceive such decisions as "public bads."*

Despres illustrates this consequence of ethnicity in the experience of British Guiana:

> Consider the construction of a new health center by the government. Will the government locate the facility in a predominantly African village such as Ann's Grove, or will it be constructed a short distance away in the Indian village of Clonbrook? Similarly, where will the new school be located? Or, who is to be made chairman of the regional development committee? Who will process applications for loans at the district office of the cooperative savings and loan society? Ultimately, these decisions affect the competitive advantage individuals have with respect to [communal] relations. Although the government may not consider these decisions to be political, they are political from the point of view of the Africans and Indians who are affected by them.[46]

The major implication of the exclusion of specific groups from public goods consumption is a challenge to the very existence of the state. One of the *raisons d'etre* of government is the provision of public goods. States are created to provide collectively what cannot be obtained through private action. Although the "goods" provided may initially take the form of territorial integrity and physical security (hence they might be called "Hobbesian goods"), their scope has expanded considerably in the modern state. The failure of the plural state to insure nonexcludability reinforces communal sentiments; individuals search for alternative sources of public goods — namely, the ethnic community — and, hence, alternative bases for statehood. Thus we see that communalism originally breeds attitudes

---

46. Despres, *op. cit.,* pp. 276-77.

of illegitimacy, which in turn reduce the effectiveness of the state, and further intensify attitudes of illegitimacy.

Finally, we reiterate a point that was theoretically derived earlier: the bankruptcy of moderation. Moderation on the ethnic issue is a viable strategy only if ethnicity is not salient. Once ethnicity becomes salient and, as a consequence, all issues are interpreted in communal terms, the rhetoric of cooperation and mutual trust sounds painfully weak. More importantly, it is strategically vulnerable to flame fanning and the politics of outbidding.

Ceylon and Ulster provide recent examples of the vulnerability of the moderates. In Ceylon, Mrs. Bandaranaike was swept into office in a landslide victory over the moderate incumbent, Dudley Senanayake. Ethnic chauvinism played a part in her campaign. In Ulster, Protestant extremists, led by the Reverend Ian Paisley, have held the governing Unionist party in check, rendering moderation impossible.

Electoral Machinations and Violence. The final feature of politics in the plural society we examine is the eventual breakdown of democratic procedures, often accompanied by physical violence. As the data of part two demonstrate, democracy — the free and open competition for the people's vote — is simply not viable in an environment of intense ethnic preferences. The demand-generating activity of ambitious leaders, the concomitant salience of primordial sentiments, and the politics of outbidding, weaken commitment to national values. "When opinions reach a certain intensity and the cleavages a certain depth, there [emerge] movements demanding total, not shared, control of the state."[47] It is not surprising, then, that a sense of communal self-preservation leads to calculated efforts to manipulate the machinery of the state in order to secure and maintain communal advantage.

Democracy in plural societies is a casualty of communal politics. "The temptation of the majority to strengthen its power by means which are not democratic, and for the minority to rely on such means in order to obtain power, becomes overwhelming."[48] This temptation becomes especially compelling when the dominant group is politically insecure. Thus, in Ulster, "if the Catholics were a smaller proportion of the whole population . . . a better understanding might have been possible. But 35 per cent is an uncomfortably large minority, especially when over 50 per cent of the children under fifteen are Catholic."[49]

The consequences of intensity, insecurity, and the temptation to manipulate the political order take many forms. The most immediate and blatant

47. Herbert Tingsten, *The Problems of Democracy* (New York: Bedminster Press, 1965), p. 47.
48. *Ibid.*, p. 117.
49. *Orange and Green, op. cit.*, p. 4.

is disenfranchisement. The black populations of Rhodesia and South Africa and the Indian Tamils of Ceylon, for example, are constitutionally proscribed from legitimate political participation.

A somewhat less direct technique, with consequences similar to those of disenfranchisement, is the manipulation of voting rules and methods of representation. Majoritarianism is typically favored by a numerically dominant community, whereas proportional or "balanced" representation is preferred by smaller communities. In a similar fashion, the large community prefers *territorial* representation, while the smaller communities, especially if they are territorially dispersed, press for a *communal* basis of representation.

A closely related method of manipulation involves franchise qualifications and vote counting. Under these methods, ordinarily variants of the majority principle, some votes (and voters) are simply more equal than others! Thus, in Ulster, the universal franchise was qualified, until recently, by an additional "business premises vote." On the local government level, there are restrictive property requirements, clearly contrary to Catholic interests, as well as additional votes for Limited Companies (repealed in November 1968). These restrictions are undoubtedly motivated by the fact that "the granting of 'One Man-One Vote' for all over 21 [would] naturally enfranchise Protestants as well as Catholics, but almost certainly more Catholics [would] benefit. . . ."[50]

In Malaysia a somewhat different approach was employed to insure Malay hegemony. Rural constituencies, containing only one-half the electors of urban districts, receive the same representation. Of course Malays are predominantly rural, whereas Chinese are dominant in the urban areas. The result: one man-two votes![51]

The classic manipulative device, known to every student of machine politics, is the gerrymander. Control over the drawing of electoral boundaries allows the dominant political community to perpetuate its hegemony while still retaining the facade of democracy. To insure the effectiveness of the gerrymander, additional control of geographic mobility is often employed. Thus, in Ulster cities local government districts are severely gerrymandered, giving local control to the Unionists (Protestant). The local assemblies they control conveniently have authority over the allocation of housing, which appears to be biased in favor of the Unionist cause. "The main purpose appears to be to maintain the established voting balance, and thus to prevent any challenge to the party controlling the Council."[52]

---

50. *Ibid.* p. 20.
51. See Alvin Rabushka, "The Manipulation of Ethnic Politics in Malaya," *Polity* 2, no. 3 (Spring 1970): 345-56.
52. *Orange and Green, op. cit.,* p. 25.

Other techniques that compromise the democratic character of politics are far less subtle: the jailing of opposition leaders, the deregistration of political parties, forced emigration, militarist interference, and violent intimidation. In short, severe restriction, if not complete elimination, of political competition violates the spirit and practice of democracy.

Plural Societies: Some Variations

To this point we have characterized the plural society by a highly salient ethnic dimension, intense preferences, communal incompatability, and a set of ambitious political entrepreneurs. Jointly, these features imply a number of destabilizing consequences. Although the precise form of these consequences ultimately depends on historical and exogenous circumstances, the plural society invariably loses its democratic flavor.

But democracy depends on numbers. Democratic decision rules are more than procedural guarantees; they provide criteria for determining winners and losers. And this determination depends on *relative coalition size*. In the remaining pages of this chapter, we show that relative community size affects the pattern of democratic instability spelled out above.

Ethnic Configurations.[53] By ethnic configuration we refer to the distribution of the population among ethnic communities with special emphasis on relative community size. Though we do not choose to be quantitatively precise, plural societies may be classified into four configuration categories:

1. balanced competition,
2. dominant majority,
3. dominant minority, and
4. fragmentation.

The first category includes those societies containing a small number of ethnic communities — usually two or three major groups — no one of which possesses clear competitive advantage. Thus, at the outset of independence, no one group can impose its values on the polity, coalitions which overlap ethnic divisions are necessary to govern, and the safeguarding of numerical minorities is enhanced. Guyana, Belgium, Trinidad, and Malaysia fall into this category.

The distinctive features of the balanced configuration include a relatively long-lived multiethnic coalition, its use of ambiguity and demand generation, and the promise of the institutionalization of interethnic cooperation

---

53. See Geertz, *op. cit.,* pp. 117-19.

in a democratic framework. Eventually, however, the seams of this arrangement begin to show. The generation of demand for governmental confrontation with ethnic issues, the fanning of flames of ethnic mistrust and hostility by ambitious, self-serving politicians, and the inability of the multiethnic coalition to defuse these issues lead to ethnic conflict. The ethnic group that comes to power invariably adjusts the electoral machinery to suit its interests. These adjustments vary from the dismantling of local government in Malaysia, to the creation of an overseas electorate in Guyana (which, of course, insured the governing party the votes necessary to retain leadership), to efforts to dismantle the unitary state in Belgium. The final consequence is a set of conditions that inhibits free and open political competition. The other trappings of democracy quickly disappear as well.

The balanced configuration is of interest because, at the outset at least, there is some prospect of the development of viable democratic institutions and practices. This prospect is reinforced by the relative longevity of the multiethnic coalition, as well as by the resiliency of democratic symbols and pronouncements.[54] However, the inability of the coalition to control "political fraud," outbidding, and the consequent necessity of coalition partners to attend to communal concerns signals the demise of intercommunal cooperation and eventually of democratic competition.

Dominance, whether by a majority or a minority, refers to the strategic advantage of one among several communities. In the majority case a single community overwhelms its political competition by virtue of sheer numbers. Coalitional behavior of a multiethnic character is likely to be short-term, if it occurs at all. The role of minority communities — at least their *democratic* role — is politically significant only in the event of major splits in the dominant group. More often they serve as loyal (or not-so-loyal) opposition communities with little promise of political power other than by nondemocratic means. We classify Ceylon, Cyprus, Mauritius, Northern Ireland (Ulster), Rwanda, and Zanzibar in this category.[55]

---

54. In the balanced competition case, democratic symbols survive into the period of ethnic conflict. Even as the electoral machinery is tinkered with, rationales alleged to be consistent with democratic values are given.

55. The reader should carefully take note of the fact that our classification scheme is time-dependent. Thus, Northern Ireland is sixty-five percent Protestant today. Catholics, however, comprise an absolute majority of the school age population, thus suggesting the possible temporary character of Protestant majority dominance. That countries may, over time, cross from one configuration to another is aptly demonstrated in the cases of Rwanda and Zanzibar. Until 1959, Rwandian politics was dominated by the Tutsi community, a group comprising fourteen percent of the population. In 1959 the majority Hutu community came to power and now is a dominant majority. A similar experience occurred in Zanzibar where, until a coup in 1964 by dissident blacks, an Arab minority governed. In both of these cases, which are treated in detail in chapter 5, a formerly dominant minority situation was transformed into a dominant majority situation.

Conflict in the dominant majority configuration occurs at the more fundamental level of constitutional issues than in the balanced case. In the latter there is ordinarily general agreement on matters of constitutional choice and communal protection. Majority rule and a broad-based franchise provide (at the outset, at least) sufficient guarantees for the several ethnic communities. However, where one community is inevitably dominant under democratic rules of the game, the smaller communities are less willing to cooperate. The demands they make — usually an insistence on communal representation and other forms of communal protection against majoritarianism — are, naturally, at the expense of the dominant group. Thus, the conflictual character of politics manifests itself at the constitutional level as well as on individual policy decisions.

The dominant majority configuration, then, is characterized by infrequent ethnic cooperation, immoderate ethnic politics at the expense of minority groups at the constitutional as well as the policy level, and eventual repression of minority political activity. Majoritarianism is the cause of the dominant community and electoral machination is its method of preserving its dominance. Violence is often fostered either by the majority, e.g., Sinhalese rioting during the Ceylonese language crisis, or by the minority, e.g., Catholic rioting and sniper activity in the urban ghettos of Northern Ireland. The end result is the same as in the balanced competition configuration. The symbols of democracy remain; the substance atrophies.

In the case of a dominant minority, democratic pretense is cast aside. A minority community asserts itself, numbers notwithstanding, as a result of some advantage bestowed upon it in the polity's "prenational" period. This is the case in South Africa and Rhodesia where colonial settlers have transformed their prenational dominance into political preponderance. The guise of democratic competition is retained only in the sense that there are splits in the minority community, e.g., competition in South Africa between Afrikaners and Englishmen.[56]

For empirical purposes, then, the dominant minority configuration is characterized by restricted political competition, the absence of democratic safeguards, an overriding fear of the political potential of the dis-

---

56. The dominant minority configuration is, in a sense, out of place in a treatment of *democratic* politics. Although Rhodesia and South Africa are "democratic" in the sense that leaders compete for the votes of citizens, the definition of citizenship is so narrow and contrary to the normative spirit of democracy as to render their democratic designation meaningless. However, we include this configuration for several reasons. First, our model provides some insight into the dilemma faced by members of minority communities who find themselves in a politically dominant position. Second, this configuration underscores our earlier insistence on focusing on outcomes rather than process. And third, the dominant minority configuration provides an opportunity to understand the role primordial sentiments play in inhibiting constitutional change, e.g., franchise expansion, in a "democratic" setting.

enfranchised majority, and the rapid success of extremist politics that serves to eliminate any moderate alternatives.

The final category, fragmentation, includes those plural societies inundated with a large number of ethnic communities, all of which are relatively small and none of which are dominant. The Congo, with some 180 distinct ethnic communities, is the epitome of the fragmentation category. Additional examples include Yugoslavia, Lebanon, Nigeria, and the Sudan.

Politics in fragmented plural societies are chaotic to say the least. The coalition-building skills demanded in such situations are rarely forthcoming in the absence of authoritarian means. The fragmented plural society, then, is marked by a plethora of groups, the scarcity or absence of brokerage institutions, the short supply of coalition-building skills necessary to organize political conflict, the eventual anarchy of unstructured conflict as a result of primordial distrust, and, typically, the initiation of rule by the military who possess a monopoly on organizational and other political skills. Democratic practices are foreclosed under these conditions.

Summary

We began our theoretical analysis of politics in the plural society by describing ethnic preferences. Employing the utility framework developed in chapter 2, we assumed that individual preferences on ethnic issues are intense and thus are characterized by convex utility functions. We supplemented this assumption with a series of additional assumptions concerning:

1. patterns of intra- and inter-communal (dis)agreement (A.1 – A.3), and
2. goals and ambitions of elites.

The consequences of these assumptions provide a set of theoretical expectations that orders and explains the evidence in part two. Specifically, we noted the formation, *ceteris paribus*, of a broad-based multiethnic coalition during the formative period; its survival through the postindependence period, fostered by ambiguous pronouncements on divisive ethnic issues, and the generation of demand for national issues; the emergence of ambitious politicians (political entrepreneurs) whose quest for the perquisites of political office provokes appeals to ethnic passions; the consequent resurrection of ethnicity as the salient dimension of political competition; the development of a politics of outbidding; the disappearance of brokerage institutions and the ethnicization of public goods; the ineffectuality of moderate elements; and, finally, the decline of democratic competition, a result of electoral machinations and political violence.

We then observed that this process of democratic decline often depends on initial conditions: colonial experience, exogenous events, and the ethnic configuration. We emphasized, in particular, the important effects of population distribution among ethnic communities on the style of democratic competition. When the population is distributed rather uniformly among a small number of ethnic groups, politics proceeds on a rather even competitive keel for a short while. On the other hand, if the population is badly skewed in favor of one community or another, the minority is likely to seize power and retain it illegitimately, or the majority legally obtains power and proceeds to insure its dominant position by manipulative or extralegal means. Finally, in the case of a proliferation of ethnic communities, chaos is the typical state of affairs, with the momentarily advantaged (often the military) taking steps to secure that advantage indefinitely.

In this chapter we have presented a paradigm that provides a dynamic account of political change in the plural society. We recognize that some parts of this paradigm are more fully articulated than others: for some we furnish a mathematical representation and nonobvious deductions; for others we rely on theoretically-informed intuition. This paradigm and its attendant insights provide, we believe, a relatively "surprise-free" view of the political world in plural societies.

The paradigm, as it stands, is not complete for two reasons. The first of these concerns those gaps that we have earlier specified. Avenues of additional articulation include:

1. a theory of political entrepreneurship, and
2. a formal treatment of preference formation.

Second, we observe that the force of exogenous events may affect ethnic politics in unpredictable ways. For example, grave economic crises, external aggression, or natural catastrophes may, at times, alter the course of politics in plural societies. These are random shocks and, as such, are inherent limitations in any scientific enterprise.

The logic inherent in the process of democratic competition in plural societies is compelling, we believe. Democracy, at least as it is known in the West, cannot be sustained under conditions of intense, salient preferences because outcomes are valued more than procedural norms. The plural society, constrained by the preferences of its citizens, does not provide fertile soil for democratic values or stability.

PART II

Part one of this book sets forth the theoretical aspects of conflict in the plural society. In part two we turn our attention to the evidence of ethnic politics. Our prime concern is to show that the assumptions and regularities outlined in part one provide theoretically meaningful categories for comparative political analysis.

We adopt a two-fold approach to illustrate the substance of ethnic politics in the plural society. In order to reveal the dynamics of the paradigm, we present several detailed case studies: Belgium and Guyana (chapter 4), Ceylon (chapter 5), and South Africa (chapter 6). We treat the remaining countries in more explicit comparative fashion to point out the common features that apply in each of the respective ethnic configurations. Although this comparative treatment is less detailed than the earlier case studies, we must nonetheless not lose sight of the basic purpose of this book: a theory of democratic instability in the plural society. We are, consequently, more interested in the regularities that politics in the plural society displays, rather than in the separate concatenations of unique features which may condition politics in each of the different countries we discuss in part two.

Our universe does not include all culturally diverse societies. Politics in some of these societies is not primarily ethnic and hence is not accountable in terms of the paradigm. Although we can distinguish those that meet the premises of the paradigm (plural societies) from those that do not (pluralistic societies), until a theory of political entrepreneurship is formulated we cannot provide the mechanism that transforms one into the other. Nevertheless the paradigm identifies trends in pluralistic societies. For example, though the United States and Canada are pluralistic, northern American cities (race) and the province of Quebec (language — culture) suggest a growing salience of the ethnic dimension. More importantly, in already plural societies the paradigm reveals the tenuous and fragile nature of democratic practice. Let us begin, then, our intellectual tour of ethnic politics with the competitive configuration.

CHAPTER 4

The Competitive Configuration

Preference and preference aggregation begins, as we saw in chapter 2, with the individual as the unit of analysis. In the case of plural societies most individuals have intense preferences on those issues that impinge on their ethnic identity. Members in any cultural community learn to share the same values, beliefs and expectations; they thus cohere and act as a single corporate body in the political arena.[1]

In this chapter we explore ethnic politics in those countries that qualify as balanced or competitive configurations. Some scholars argue that the absence of a dominant community creates an environment in which democratic institutions are likely to survive or flourish.[2] We show that this surmise does not always stand up; democratic practices in these non-dominant situations frequently give way to authoritarian forms of government.

The rubric of the competitive configuration includes those societies in which two, or at best three, major ethnic groups monopolize electoral

---

1. We would be naive not to recognize that perfect cohesion is nonexistent or at best rare. Examples of persons who cross ethnic boundaries to participate in multi-ethnic political groups are easily found. We do insist, however, that such defections are rare. Strictly speaking, we assume, for purposes of analysis, that the variance about the mean preference(s) for any given community is small, and can be assigned the value of zero. As a consequence, it makes good empirical and logical sense to reify an ethnic group as an organic entity, an individual with a package of preferences. See Anthony Downs, *An Economic Theory of Democracy* (New York: Harper and Row, 1957), for his treatment of the political party as a "team" of like-minded individuals.

2. Myron Weiner suggests that the most promising prospects for the maintenance of political unity in the presence of cultural diversity are found in such states as Nigeria, India and Malaysia, where no single group dominates. Recent events in Nigeria and Malaysia do not bear out this supposition. See "Political Integration and Political Development," *The Annals of the American Academy of Political and Social Science* 358 (March 1965): 52-64.

politics. A further condition is that no one group is politically dominant at the time competition begins. The process whereby one group comes to dominate politics is outlined in the relatively detailed treatment of racial politics in Guyana. We compare the Guyanese experience with an equally detailed treatment of linguistic politics in Belgium. In a more comparative fashion we extend the treatment to Trinidad and Tobago and Malaya.

Guyana[3]

On January 2, 1969, L.F.S. Burnham appointed the first entirely People's National Congress cabinet in Guyana's history.[4] The People's National Congress (hereafter PNC), almost exclusively representative and comprised of Afro-Guyanese, is a minority party. Guyanese of African and mixed, partially African, descent constitute forty-three percent of the population (see table 4.1). East Indians, on the other hand, make up just over half the population in Guyana, but, as of January 2, 1969, were virtually excluded from Burnham's cabinet. Burnham's appointment of an exclusively PNC cabinet culminates the competition between East Indians and Afro-Guyanese, which dates back to the mid-1950s, at which

---

3. In this section we rely heavily on the excellent study by Leo A. Despres, *Cultural Pluralism and Nationalist Politics in British Guiana* (Chicago: Rand McNally and Company, 1967). For additional treatments, the reader is encouraged to see Raymond T. Smith, *British Guiana* (London: Oxford University Press for the Royal Institute of International Affairs, 1962); "Race and Political Conflict in Guyana," *Race* 12, no. 4 (April 1971): 415-27; Michael Swan, *British Guiana: The Land of Six Peoples* (London: H.M.S.O., 1957); and C. Paul Bradley, "Party Politics in British Guiana," *The Western Political Quarterly* 16, no. 2 (June 1963): 353-70.

R. T. Smith in the preface of his book (p. vi) states "I think it important to emphasize the considerable progress that has been made toward racial harmony and to try to dispel the notions about East Indian communal aggressiveness which some people find it necessary or convenient to cherish." Smith's treatment illustrates precisely the traps into which many students of plural societies have fallen. His analysis of the teamwork between Jagan and Burnham during the 1953 election led him to conclude that Jagan did not consider himself the leader of East Indians as such, even though Jagan's support rested chiefly on his ethnic identification. Smith's expectations and hope for a harmonious racial future (p. 183) did not materialize as this chapter shows. He appears to have generalized from the limited evidence of the cooperative period of Guyanese ethnic politics.

Smith's use of a functionalist perspective also led him to look for the "common cultural equipment" (p. 198) that the whole society shares and that can serve as a basis for unity and future growth, even though "each ethnic group tends to preserve a residue of cultural peculiarities and to exaggerate their importance" (p. 198). Clearly Smith incorrectly emphasized the cohesive forces in Guyanese society instead of the divisive; he was especially unable to identify which forces were politically salient.

4. Guyana became independent on May 26, 1966. Previously, Guyana was governed as the British colony of British Guiana.

time the breakdown of ethnic cooperation in the Guyanese nationalist movement began.

The Origin of Cultural Pluralism in Guyana. The creation of a plural society in Guyana is, in large measure, due to the Dutch West India Company which was engaged in plantation agriculture and sugar cane cultivation in the seventeenth century. The planters brought Negro slaves to work the plantations, but the British, who had obtained Guyana from the Dutch in 1803, created a free Negro peasantry when they abolished slavery in 1833. Most Afro-Guyanese refused to remain on the plantations of their former masters, and moved to the Guyanese coast where they established numerous African villages. Only a small proportion of Africans remained on the sugar estates. Many were lured, however, into the urban areas for

Table 4.1

Ethnic Composition of Guyana in 1966

Ethnic Group	Number	Percent
East Indians	342,190	50.7
African descent	207,870	30.8
Mixed descent	81,400	12.1
Chinese	4,160	0.6
Portuguese	6,120	0.9
Other European	1,480	0.2
Amerindians	31,460	4.7
Total	674,680	100.0

Source: *West Indies and Caribbean Year Book 1970* (London: Thomas Skinner & Co. Publishers, Ltd., 1969), p. 181.

wages by the development of the bauxite and other industries. As evidence of this massive urban migration, the 1960 population census reveals that Guyanese of African descent comprise over seventy percent of the population of Georgetown, Guyana's major city.

The planters sought alternate sources of cheap labor to replace the ex-slaves. They first tried Portuguese and other West Indian immigrants who proved unwilling or unable to survive the hardships of plantation life. They turned next to the recruitment of indentured workers from India and brought over 238,000 to Guyana between 1835 and 1917, at which time the Indian government terminated the indenture system. Most of the Indians who stayed in Guyana after their contract of indenture expired settled in the countryside; today about one-third live on the sugar estates with the balance in rural villages. Because the East Indians migrated as family units, they still maintain much of their traditional culture and live apart from Afro-Guyanese; until recently there has been little or no mingling between Indians and Africans in Guyana.

The Portuguese, Chinese, Europeans, and Amerindians make up the other four of Guyana's six ethnic groups. Each is numerically insignificant in the total composition of Guyana's ethnic political mosaic, and has played, since independence, a relatively minor political role. We focus our attention, therefore, on the political behavior of Africans and East-Indians, Guyana's two most important ethnic political communities.

Political Manifestations of Pluralism. The Afro-Guyanese and East Indian communities are politically organized, respectively, by the People's National Congress and the People's Progressive Party (hereafter PPP). When the PPP was first organized it received widespread support from Guyanese of both communities, thus signifying the formation of a multiracial nationalist movement. Guyanese of both major races felt that it was in their mutual interest to cooperate in order to extract concessions from the British, leading ultimately to independence. As independence appeared imminent, Afro-Guyanese and East Indians began to view each other as potential enemies. One community's gains were now seen as the other's losses. Cooperative behavior is thus a reasonable strategy in the *early stages* of a nationalist movement; it breaks down into interethnic competition with the approach or arrival of independence. In the following pages we explore this transition in greater detail.

Ethnic Cooperation. Shortly after World War II, Cheddi Jagan, an American-trained dentist of East Indian descent, and L.F.S. Burnham of African descent organized a comprehensive nationalist movement in Guyana. They established political cells of the People's Progressive Party in both Indian and African villages and, in effect, put together Guyana's first mass-supported political party in time to contest the first important postwar election of 1953. In that election, the PPP won eighteen of twenty-four elected seats in the House of Assembly, polling fifty-one percent of the vote. Observers of the Guyanese scene used the evidence of this electoral victory to assert that the PPP was an integrated nationalist movement. In actual fact, however, the PPP represented a coalition of ethnic leaders who had cooperated for the purpose of winning an election and thereby moving Guyana closer to independence. The cooperation between Africans and Indians is evident in the slate of candidates put up by the PPP: ten Indians and nine Africans ran as PPP candidates.

In spite of these explicit efforts at ethnic cooperation, most candidates received their primary support from electors of their own race. Several independents were able to poll sizable votes against PPP candidates on the basis of their ethnicity.

Constitutional progress towards independence was momentarily halted when the colonial authorities removed the PPP government from office and suspended the constitution in October 1953. These moves were prompted by reports of communist sympathies and activities among PPP members that led the Colonial Office to appoint an interim government until such time as the constitution could be revised and new elections scheduled.

Before the British could schedule new elections, Jagan and Burnham had a falling out in 1955. The Jaganites disliked Burnham's reserved ideological views, doubting the sincerity of his Marxist convictions. They suspected that he would betray the Marxist revolution and ultimately join forces with anti-Marxist middle-class African intellectuals, thus making ideological differences coincidental with racial distinctions. (The involvement of the CIA and AID in Guyanese affairs seems to confirm those suspicions.)[5] Furthermore, they differed on the issue of entrance into the Caribbean Federation, which was favored by Burnham. Although Jagan opposed Burnham on the grounds that Federation implied a "capitalist" takeover of the PPP working-class movement, he pragmatically also knew that federation membership would mean black domination and loss of his Indian support.

In a series of clever party maneuvers, Jagan and his associates forced Burnham out of the party; in reply, Burnham established his own branch of the PPP. By this time (1957) the British had scheduled new elections under a revised constitution which provided for fourteen elected seats. Jagan's faction of the PPP won nine seats with 47.5 percent of the vote, whereas, Burnham's faction was able to garner only three seats, all in Georgetown constituencies which are heavily populated by working-class Africans.

Thus, the year before the elections, the nationalist forces had crystallized into rival sectional groups. During that year three influential Africans resigned and withdrew their support from Jagan's PPP in the belief that Jagan's policies and views represented and depended upon East Indian racialism. Meanwhile, the political arm of the African middle class, the United Democratic Party, dissolved and merged with Burnham's faction of the PPP to form the People's National Congress (PNC). Two mass-based parties, one Afro-Guyanese and the other East Indian, thus grew out of the ethnic pressures which split the comprehensive nationalist movement of the early fifties. Nationalist politicians came increasingly to associate their political survival with the fortunes of their respective ethnic groups and the rewards they could obtain from them in the political arena. The growing salience of race could not be masked by ambiguous allusions to socialist ideology.

5. *The New York Times,* February 22, 1967, p. 1.

The British introduced a new constitution in 1961 which expanded the Legislative Assembly to thirty-five members. Three parties, the PPP, the PNC, and the United Force, a new party comprised chiefly of Europeans and other business interests, contested these seats. The PPP won twenty seats, all in rural constituencies with East Indian majorities; the UF won four, three in populous Portuguese constituencies in Georgetown; and the PNC the remaining eleven, again in African-majority urban areas. Close races occurred only in constituencies where Africans and Indians were nearly equal in number. Overall the PPP received 46.7 percent of the vote and the PNC 44.7 percent, a division that represents their approximate distributions in the population (when the "mixed" are counted as Africans). We thus infer almost perfect racial voting.[6]

The process of constitutional advancement in Guyana entailed the development of widespread participation, universal suffrage, and parliamentary democracy. Party victories, as a result, came to depend upon mass electoral support. In the early fifties appeals for joint action against colonial domination were possible. However, following the Jagan-Burnham split, *the only remaining source of mass support were the Afro-Guyanese and East Indian cultural communities*; these represented the natural bases for building organized, mass political movements. A detailed examination of the campaign tactics employed by the major parties sheds light on the process by which the separate communities were mobilized into politically competitive, opposing groups.

Ethnic Competition: the 1961 Election. During the 1961 election campaign, Jagan and the PPP invoked the principle of "apanjaht," which in Hindi means "vote for your own kind." This slogan constitutes an appeal to the Indian sense of cultural identity; its underlying assumption is that "one's own kind of people are more likely to keep one's own interest in heart."[7] To gain widespread support from the East Indian community, Jagan *actively stimulated* the consciousness of Indian nationalism, i.e., he fanned the flames of ethnic extremism. By so doing he generated demand for the politics of racial extremism.

---

6. We recognize that the "ecological fallacy" renders this inference problematical. Judgments about the way individuals vote cannot be directly made from an analysis of aggregate voting results. To say that PPP candidates received 46.7 percent of the vote and, therefore, that all Indians voted for PPP candidates may be incorrect. Any given Indian may have voted for a PNC candidate, but this ballot can be offset in the total vote if a corresponding Afro-Guyanese crossed racial lines to vote for an Indian candidate. Hard survey data from which we could decipher the precise extent of racial voting in the 1961 elections do not exist. However, the character of the election, e.g., party campaigns, ethnic appeals, etc., suggests that we need not be overly concerned with the "ecological fallacy" and that racial voting dominated the 1961 elections.

7. Leo A. Despres, *op. cit.*, p. 229.

Jagan began his pursuit of the East Indian business community immediately following the 1957 elections, when, as Minister of Trade and Industry, he liberalized Guyana's trade policy which allowed Indian merchants to profit from their control of the import and distribution trade. In addition, he extended political recognition to the Indian-dominated Junior Chamber of Commerce, which increased the political influence of the Indian business community, and in turn Jagan's power. These policies gave the PPP the financial and political support of most Indian businessmen in the 1961 election.

Indian professionals, mainly teachers, were also brought under the influence of "apanjaht" politics. Indian teachers complained of racial discrimination in promotions, especially in church-run denominational schools headed by Africans. When a number of Indian teachers threatened to quit the PPP and join Peter D'Aguiar's United Force party, Jagan responded by announcing that his government had decided to assume control of all publicly built denominational schools. The Indian teachers were quietly informed that a teacher's service commission would be created and that it would divest African head teachers and Christian schoolboards of their power. The introduction of this Education Bill in the election year of 1961 gained the support of Indian teachers for Jagan.

Jagan concentrated his major efforts, however, upon the East Indian peasants, principally the sugar workers and rice farmers who formed the vast majority of the Indian population. To obtain the support of the sugar workers he tried to discredit the Man Power Citizen's Association, the union which the Sugar Producer's Association currently recognized. To accomplish that end, Jagan encouraged and helped finance the Sugar Estates Clerks Association to strike and hold out until all their demands had been met. He tried throughout the campaign to link the PNC directly with the sugar industry, hinting that a PNC victory meant "black domination." As expected, Jagan's efforts secured the support of Indian sugar workers for the PPP.

Jagan employed a different approach to mobilize the geographically more dispersed Indian rice farmers. He concentrated the resources of Guyana's economic development program, what are normally thought of as public funds, into the expansion of the chiefly Indian rice industry and neglected the economic interests of the Afro-Guyanese. These steps entailed giving Indian peasants new land and extensive agricultural credit at public expense. These measures effectively doubled rice output and rural Indian profits, and thereby obtained Indian peasant support for Jagan's PPP.

Jagan had thus appealed to nearly every East Indian: economic power for businessmen, access to the civil service for teachers, and greater profits for Indian peasants. In addition, higher fertility rates among Indians implied a growing Indian majority in Guyana. Thus apanjaht politics, the politics of racial extremism, seemed tailor-made as a strategy to insure permanent Indian rule.

Burnham responded to apanjaht politics by forming the PNC. He hoped to aggregate the rural Afro-Guyanese, whose support he had retained after the 1955 split with Jagan, the conservative, middle-class Africans in Georgetown who had formed their own party (the United Democratic Party), and the Portuguese and Amerindians whose leaders opposed the communist ideology of the PPP. Together, these groups make up nearly half of Guyana's population.

Burnham adopted a defensive strategy: he invoked the theme of racial politics among rural Afro-Guyanese. "This fight is for survival and the Afro-Guyanese must stick together or lose the country to the Indians and the Communists."[8] In the cities, though, African racial extremism would divide the African and Portuguese coalition. Burnham thus adopted an *ambiguous* position in the cities and appealed for party unity by emphasizing the PPP as a common enemy.

Burnham's united front strategy dissolved when the Portuguese broke away to form their own party, the United Force, after Burnham had spurned an attempt by D'Aguiar and his associates to buy control of the PNC. D'Aguiar had offered an announcement of public membership and financial backing in exchange for nine of the fifteen seats on the PNC's Executive Committee. The formation of the UF meant that Burnham was now opposed by the white Portuguese community in the urban areas.

Nothing remained to moderate Burnham's racial stance. The PNC turned exclusively to racial politics and warned the Africans of possible East Indian domination. They stressed Indian agricultural expansion in the rural areas, Indian domination of the civil service to middle-class Africans, and also pulled African labor unions into the PNC camp. Burnham's reverse racialism produced 89,000 votes for the PNC, just 3,000 under the total vote of the PPP, although the heavy concentration of African voters in urban constituencies netted his party only eleven seats. Because the Indian population is more widely scattered than the African, the majority of seats went to Jagan's party and thus the PPP formed the postelection government.

Postelection Conflict. The 1961 election campaign polarized the African and Indian communities and virtually destroyed any basis for future bargaining or compromise. The latter stages of the campaign were charac-

---

8. *Ibid.*, p. 256.

terized by heightened racial tension, threats of intimidation, and sporadic violence. Jagan's victory further intensified fears of future racial violence.

Shortly after the 1961 elections, the opposition parties sought the downfall of Jagan's government. D'Aguiar and Burnham led a protest march against a ban on public gatherings in the vicinity of public buildings that immediately developed into a riot. The 150-man police force was unable to control the mob, which gutted nearly every East Indian shop in Georgetown's business district. The riot was controlled only upon the arrival and deployment of British troops.

During 1962 and 1963 the opposition parties pressed the British Colonial Office for various constitutional reforms, including proportional representation. The Colonial Office accepted these demands in spite of the bitter protests lodged by Jagan and the PPP. Given that the East Indians comprised slightly less than half of all Guyanese and contained a proportionately greater number of young people under voting age, the implementation of proportional representation denied to the Indian community the possibility of forming a majority government by itself. Jagan's demand that the voting age be lowered to eighteen was denied by the Colonial Office, perhaps out of deference to the American government's interest in seeing a friendly, noncommunist government in Guyana.

The Colonial Office scheduled new elections in December 1964 which British troops policed to insure law and order. The PPP was proportionally awarded 24 seats having polled 45.8 percent of the vote. The PNC was given 22 seats (40.5 percent) and the United Force received the remaining seven seats. As expected the anticommunist sentiments of the Portuguese business community facilitated a PNC-UF coalition government. Thus a change in the rules of the electoral game transformed Jagan and the PPP into a minority, opposition party even though they again polled the greatest number of votes.

A Guyanese professor confirms the changes that had taken place in Guyanese politics.

> By early 1964 it was clear that "communalism" much more than "communism" was the obstacle to independence. . . . Dr. Jagan's party had by now changed, in fact if not in rhetoric, from an anticolonial radical front into an Indian organization. It received practically the same number of votes as there were Indian names on the register. Likewise, Mr. Burnham's People's National Congress reflected not so much its leader's modified socialism as defensive African opinion, and secured the Negro vote. . . . [The election results] confirmed that racialism had become the major element in Guianese politics.[9]

---

9. B.A.N. Collins, "The End of a Colony—II," *The Political Quarterly* 36, no. 4 (October-December 1965): 406-16 (quotation at p. 409).

Independence: The Politics of Ethnic Manipulation. On May 26, 1966, Guyana was granted independence. Burnham, as expected, was sworn in as Prime Minister. Jagan claimed that Guyana's constitution was designed to permit minority rule and that its provisions for "emergency powers" were intended to enable the government to suppress his party.

His fears materialized quickly. In December 1966 a National Security Bill was passed in Guyana's parliament. This bill provides for: (1) preventive detention up to eighteen months, (2) flogging or life imprisonment for illegal possession of arms, (3) deportation of undesirables, and (4) police powers of search and arrest. (An International Commission of Jurists visiting Guyana in 1968 found that 73.5 percent of its police force was of African descent and only 19.9 percent of Indian background.) The PPP walked out of Parliament in protest of this measure.

By late October 1968 the Guyanese government completed a series of major electoral changes that drastically altered the rules of the political game (much like the adoption of proportional representation in 1964).[10] These changes provided that (1) the party leader can choose from the election list those candidates who fill the seats his party wins, thus insuring party loyalty, (2) the government rather than a bipartisan commission controls voter registration, and (3) overseas electors are eligible to vote in Guyanese elections. An overseas electors list of 66,000 names was drawn up representing approximately 22 percent of the total electorate. The overwhelming majority of these new electors were African.

How was Burnham able to accomplish these changes, especially since four members of the United Force, partners in Burnham's coalition government, crossed over to the opposition? Burnham succeeded in forming a minimum winning coalition of twenty-seven votes by obtaining the support of the three remaining UF members, two disillusioned Jaganites and all twenty-two members of the PNC. The current whereabouts of these five non-Africans were not reported in the *New York Times!*

Jagan charged fraud, and perhaps rightly so. Grenada Television checked 650 alleged Guyanese residents in Britain and found, on the average, only one name in twenty on the registration list.[11] In a similar fashion, the overseas list for New York City of 11,700 contained many fictitious names.[12] Moreover, the East Indian population had increased by 1968 to total 51 percent of the resident population in Guyana which meant that the majority community occupied a minority political position in a representative democracy.

The 1968 general election results were reported in full on December 21, 1968.[13] The PNC polled 174,214 votes and thereby secured an absolute

10. *The New York Times,* October 27, 1968, p. 27.
11. *Ibid.,* December 13, 1968, p. 15.
12. *Ibid.,* December 16, 1968, p. 14.
13. *Ibid.,* December 21, 1968, p. 55.

majority of 30 seats in the new parliament. The PPP obtained 113,861 votes, the UF 23,161, and a new minority party, the Guyana Muslims, 889. Burnham received 93 percent of the overseas vote. If the 60-odd thousand votes Burnham received from the overseas electors are subtracted from the PNC total, we find that the PNC and PPP did equally well among resident Guyanese, but that neither party would have been able to form a government by itself. The changes in the electoral laws have now rendered the support of the United Force superfluous for the PNC. And so, we come full circle and, as we saw at the outset, Burnham was able to appoint the first entirely PNC cabinet in 1969.

Politics in Guyana: Lessons from the Competitive Configuration. Our substantive exploration of ethnic politics in Guyana renders a complex political process relatively surprise-free. A series of distinct features, as specified in the paradigm of chapter 3, emerges from this explanation. We draw upon the analytical distinctions of the paradigm to summarize Guyanese politics:

1. *Members of different ethnic communities cooperate in the early stages of their nationalist movement against the common colonial enemy, but separate into rival ethnic factions upon independence or its imminent approach.* Independence changes the rewards of the political game. No longer do all indigenous peoples gain by extracting concessions from the colonial power, but rather by obtaining a disproportionate share of the available resources after the colonial power departs. Both Jagan and Burnham employed ambiguous socialist ideology in a common effort to downgrade the racial question, but in the long run a class-based ideology failed to control the pressures of ethnic politics.

2. *As the cooperative movement disintegrates, ethnic communities provide a natural source of political support.* Ethnic communities represent institutionalized groupings that can be mobilized or tapped for political support by astute entrepreneurs. Members of an ethnic community view the world in the same light (intracommunal consensus — A.1). All communities perceive most political issues in ethnic terms (perceptual consensus — A.3). The importance of self-preservation, of opportunities for gain, and of ethnic identity correspondingly increase. Thus direct political competition among ethnic groups on such explicit ethnic questions as jobs, language, religion, etc., reinforces the natural divisions between the communities (intercommunal conflict — A.2). Apanjaht politics is thus a natural strategy for two reasons. (1) From the standpoint of a political leader, ethnic groups provide a ready-made source of support that can be activated by appeals to their primordial sentiments. Thus Jagan mobilized the entire East Indian community, and Burnham retaliated by relying upon

"his own" Afro-Guyanese. The result: politics in Guyana is synonymous with race. (2) The masses of any community hold the view that their share of the symbolic and material rewards that accrue from control over government and the public sector ought, as a matter of course, to increase — "leaders of one's own kind are more likely to keep one's interests in heart." Put another way, entrepreneurs sensitized the electorate to the importance of ethnicity — they made ethnicity *salient* — and a communal electorate with intense ethnic preferences responded favorably.

3. *The politics of moderation is replaced by the politics of outbidding.* During the 1961 election the implicit PNC – UF coalition dictated an ambiguous racial posture in the urban centers. However, Burnham refused D'Aguiar's offer to join with the PNC perhaps because he feared that a more extreme Afro-Guyanese politican would charge him with selling out the interests of the Africans. Burnham stayed on as the uncompromising leader of the Afro-Guyanese, speaking enthusiastically on their behalf and actively fanning the flames of fear of Indian domination.[14]

4. *Ethnic politicians manipulate the rules of the game to obtain or maintain partisan advantage.* Once in control, Burnham created a list of overseas electors, predominantly African, which eliminated the need for cooperation with any other section of Guyanese. The legality of this procedure is questionable, since independent inquiry showed that many of these overseas electors could not be located.

5. *In the context of plural politics, there are incentives for disadvantaged political communities to resort to extra-constitutional methods.* Shortly after Jagan's 1961 victory, both Burnham and D'Aguiar resorted to strikes, protests, riots, and massive anti-Indian mob violence. British troops restored order but new negotiations between the British and Guyanese changed the electoral rules. Jagan was not permitted to lead Guyana to independence even though the PPP had won the 1961 election.

Belgium

On Wednesday, February 7th, 1968, Mr. Paul Van den Boeynants handed in his resignation of his Government to the King of the Belgians. This marked the end of an era in Belgian politics. Since the last world war, at least, the three traditional parties—the Christian Social Party, the Socialists, and the Liberals — have provided Belgium with relatively stable government, but *only by largely*

---

14. The reader should recall figures 3.8 and 3.9 where it is shown that only extreme positions on the ethnic issue can defeat an otherwise more ambiguous stance (i.e. a lottery).

evading the issue which divides the country most deeply—namely,
the conflict between the French-speaking and Flemish communities.
The next government will have no alternative but to face that issue
head on. The fall of the Van den Boeynants coalition (of Christian
Socialists and Liberals) will also force political observers to re-
consider their conventional analysis of the Belgian political system.
Up to now that system has been celebrated as a case where a highly
particularistic and diffuse political culture sustained a more-or-less
stable and effective national government. The key to this interesting
combination *has been the ability of the three traditional parties to*
appeal to both linguistic communities more-or-less equally, and to
maintain internal discipline, thus counteracting the powerful cen-
trifugal tendencies in Belgian society.[15]

The Origins of Cultural Pluralism in Belgium. The present language conflict between Flemings (Dutch-speakers) and Walloons (French-speakers)
dates from the founding of Belgium in 1830, although the origin of the traditional language frontier is found in the latter days of the Roman Empire.[16] As the legions withdrew from northern Roman territories to defend
Rome against possible Goth invasions, Franks crossed the Rhine and eventually settled in Belgium territory north of the line (see map) that today
legally separates the French-speaking (Wallonia) and Flemish-speaking
(Flanders) regions of Belgium. The customs and language of the Germanic
peoples became firmly established north of the line, while south of the
line French-speaking Gauls predominated.

No attempts were made to match linguistic with political boundaries
when Charlemagne's empire was partitioned in 843 by the Treaty of
Verdun. Instead, Belgium became a buffer state between the French and
German blocs that the treaty designated. But language was politically
unimportant to the Belgians of that period since the official written language was Latin. Although French flourished and gained prestige — most
of the Flemish bourgeoisie spoke French — Flemish survived and was
regularly used as a local administrative language. Language in early
Belgium did not constitute a rallypost for political movements.

Prior to the unification of Belgium and the Netherlands by Charles V
in 1543, commercial activities in such cities as Ypres, Bruges, and Ghent,
which continually struggled to maintain their independence from either
encroaching French or German authority, dominated Belgian history.

---

15. David Coombs and Richard Norton-Taylor, "Renewal in Belgian Politics: The
Elections of March 1968," *Parliamentary Affairs* 22, no. 1 (Winter 1968-69): 62-72
(quotation at p. 62—emphasis added).
16. This discussion follows Vernon Mallinson, *Belgium* (New York: Praeger,
1970), chapter 13.

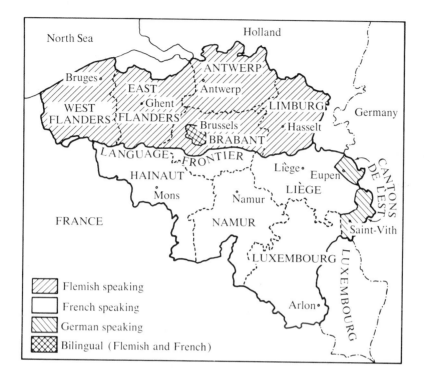

The Languages of Belgium

However, the influence of the merchant bourgeoisie and the political power of the Belgian principalities virtually disappeared following the unification. Twelve years later (1555), Charles V abdicated his responsibilities and Philip II, his nephew, inherited the Spanish throne and the seventeen provinces comprising most of Belgium and the Netherlands. Philip's rule was harsh and native dissent culminated in a war of liberation: as a result, the Dutch secured their independence in the United Provinces in the north (Holland) and the King of Spain retained his authority in the Catholic Lowlands of the south (Belgium). Philip, both ill and wearied, transferred the troublesome territories to his daughter, the wife of an Austrian Archduke.

During the period of Spanish rule, French was used as an administrative and legal language for all-Belgian affairs, although Flemish was normally employed for local level administration. French became the predominant language in Belgium during the eighteenth century as French language and culture grew in prominence: the Flemish bourgeoisie usually sent their children to school in France or in the French-speaking cities of Wallonia.

Austrian rule ended when French revolutionary armies invaded Belgium. Belgium was subsequently annexed to France as a French department by 1794. Following annexation, the French forcibly introduced their language throughout the Flemish provinces. This process of Frenchification was halted, however, with Napoleon's defeat in 1815 and William of Holland seized the opportunity to declare himself King of the low countries, a union made up of the Netherlands and Belgium.

William's union was not the result of natural political and social pressures within the two countries: the Northern Provinces (Holland) were largely Protestant whereas the Southern Provinces (Belgium) were almost entirely Catholic. (Catholicism in Belgium is strongest in Flemish areas.) Although this political union was sanctioned by the major European powers, the Belgians viewed the Dutch as conquerors. This ill-liked union, which ended with the revolution of 1830, did, however, arouse new interest in Flemish culture. King William had created new state secondary schools that used Dutch as their medium of instruction in Flemish areas, and now, as a result of William's union, courses in the Dutch language and literature were taught in three new universities he created for Belgium.

The Revolution of 1830: Flemish-French Cooperation. The union with Holland was short-lived, in part because the Flemish bourgeoisie admired French culture and despised the Netherlands and Protestantism. They joined with the French-speaking Walloons in throwing off Dutch rule and created the new kingdom of Belgium in 1830. This new state displayed a pronounced French bias — all new laws and regulations were published in French, although translations were provided in Flemish-speaking areas.

Social Cleavages and Language in Modern Belgium. Belgium is described as a society with three sharply-defined cleavages: religion, class, and language.[17] These three cleavages have each assumed primary importance during various periods in Belgian political history. Although both religion and class cut across regional and language boundaries, it certainly does

---

17. Val R. Lorwin, "Belgium: Religion, Class and Language in National Politics," in Robert A. Dahl, ed., *Political Opposition in Western Democracies* (New Haven: Yale University Press, 1966), pp. 147-87. On the same theme see also Derek W. Urwin, "Social Cleavages and Political Parties in Belgium: Problems of Institutionalization," *Political Studies* 18, no. 3 (September 1970): 320-40; Mieke Claeys-van Haegendoren, "Party and Opposition Formation in Belgium," *Res Publica* 9, no. 3 (1967): 413-35; André Philippart, "Belgium: Language and Class Opposition," *Government and Opposition* 2, no. 1 (November 1966): 63-82; and James A. Dunn, Jr., *Social Cleavage, Party Systems and Political Integration: A Comparison of the Belgian and Swiss Experiences* (unpublished Ph.D. dissertation, Pennsylvania, 1970).

not follow that they automatically offset the destabilizing effects of linguistic politics. Most experts of the Belgian scene concede the primacy of language in contemporary Belgian politics. Lorwin, for instance, observes that "the linguistic-regional conflict appears more intractable than class-conflict or the religious-ideological conflict."[18] Dunn, also, echoes Lorwin's conclusion. "Since 1961 the Belgian political system has been dominated by the linguistic-cultural conflict."[19] And, finally, we find that Urwin agrees with this analysis of modern Belgian politics.[20] Although the study of Belgian politics appears ripe for the application of the cross-cutting cleavage hypothesis, especially as it relates to democratic stability, we find, nevertheless, that the *overwhelming salience* of language renders that hypothesis inadmissable. Indiscriminate counting of cross-cutting cleavages is likely to yield a less satisfactory analysis of Belgian politics than is an assessment of their relative salience.

Why is language more salient in contemporary Belgian politics than either religious or class distinctions? To answer that question we shall investigate two aspects of Belgian political history: (1) the period from 1830 to 1958 during which religion first, and then class distinctions, took on primary relevance, and (2) party politics since 1958, when language became the overriding political issue for Belgians.

Politics in Belgium from 1830 to 1958: the Salience of Religion and Class. Modern Belgium came into existence, as we have seen, by joint Flemish-French cooperation against Dutch rule. Although Belgians were divided over the issue of church-state relations, as evidenced in the existence of separate Catholic and Liberal political factions, both sides pursued a policy of unionism to protect the independence of the new Belgian state from Dutch authority. But the danger of foreign intervention disappeared by the mid-1840s and with its disappearance came the rise of a two-party system. The election of 1847 disclosed an unambiguous bipolar electorate: Liberals, on the one hand, supported the goals of secularization, while Catholics, on the other hand, stood for the primacy of the Church in Belgian political life.[21] The principal issue over which Catholics and Liberals fought for virtually an entire century was education. Liberals sought to eliminate Church influence on education, while Catholics, conversely, sought maximum Church influence. At various times each side held political authority and used it in pursuit of its goals. Thus, this early period

---

18. *Op. cit.*, p. 174.
19. *Op. cit.*, p. 112.
20. *Op. cit.*, p. 333.
21. An excellent treatment of this entire topic is found in Urwin, *op. cit.*, pp. 322-30.

of modern Belgian history is characterized by "the institutionalization of the Church-State division, with the consolidation of two well-defined camps in Parliament, both of which sought to strengthen their position through increased efforts at electoral mobilization."[22]

The emergence of the Workers Party and a concern with different types of issues led to accommodation and a toleration of the *status quo* between Catholics and Liberals. The new issues that arose emphasized class problems and worker demands for social legislation. The first Worker's organizations appeared in 1886 as an economic crisis developed in Wallonia, and almost immediately made the Belgian Workers Party the beneficiary of massive working-class support. A strike in 1886 led to the adoption of a number of social laws designed to improve the conditions of workers, and a peaceful general strike seven years later extended the franchise to all Belgian males.

The new class party was almost immediately integrated into the party system. Extension of the franchise enabled the Workers Party to achieve some immediate measure of success in the Belgian House of Representatives: they gained twenty-eight seats in their first try in 1894, all in Wallonia.[23] Meanwhile, the established elites displayed a willingness to tolerate the new party, especially as the possibility of a general strike, threatened four times before 1914 by the Workers Party, might seriously disrupt the Belgian economy and, with it, both the position of the Church and the economic elites. The Workers Party initially agreed to play the parliamentary game, rather than try to stage a Socialist revolution, on the belief that they would ultimately get a parliamentary majority through further industrialization and greater extension of the franchise.

World War I unified the various factions in the national government that included, for the first time, the Workers Party. With the introduction of proportional representation by the Catholic government in 1900, each of the three parties was able to maintain its political support — the Liberals were, therefore, not eliminated by the replacement of religious with economic issues. Proportional representation also implied the need for post-1918 coalition governments: given the distribution of electoral cleavages at that time, no party could win an absolute majority. This situation meant that the leaders of the Workers Party could expect to participate in government decision making, and thereby extract rewards for its followers, on a more regular basis than in prewar Belgium. "By the 1930's the three

---

22. *Ibid.*, p. 324. Incidentally, the "censitaire" suffrage system, i.e., voting on the basis of taxes paid, which was in effect during this period, was restricted to a very small and affluent minority of Belgian citizens. Most qualified electors in Flanders were thus the French-speaking Flemish bourgeoisie.

23. Dunn, *op. cit.*, p. 82.

major parties [Catholics, Liberals, Workers] had institutionalized the religious and class divisions."[24]

What accounts for the absence of language as a relevant factor in Belgian political life during this period? Claeys-van Haegendoren offers the following reasons.

1. Until 1894, the franchise was restricted to a small, affluent French-speaking Flemish bourgeoisie. Hence, votes could not be garnered by appeals to the linguistic sentiments of the nonfranchised; as well, the Flemish elite was unlikely to respond to linguistic appeals since its privileged position in Flanders rested, in part, on its monopolistic ability to speak French.

2. The Flemish movement, when it first materialized after 1830, was essentially a romantic-literary movement. Political objectives, at first, were only secondary aims, especially in view of the "censitaire" suffrage system then in effect.

3. The first "flamingants" did not question the principle of French as the official language. They only sought some recognition for Dutch.[25]

When the Flemish movement finally took on political overtones, it was subordinated first to the clerical-anticlerical controversies, and second to the class issues that had led the Belgian Workers Party to mobilize the masses. Parenthetically, Flemish political nationalism was most successful where the traditional parties and trade unions had not yet obtained a foothold by 1918.[26] In addition, the absence of a specific Flemish elite — the upper classes in Flanders spoke French — hindered the political development of the Flemish nationalist movement.

Now we turn the coin around and ask the converse question: what enabled language to become the primary factor in Belgian political life? André Philippart suggests three important possibilities.

1. The "Pact Scolaire," which granted parity for religious and public schools and involved the Church ceding certain of its privileges, was passed into law on May 29, 1959. As a consequence, Catholics and their adversaries were deprived of a main bone of contention. This pact has effectively reduced the saliency of the religious cleavage and opened the way for other issues to emerge and capture political attention.

2. As a result of urbanization, the Church has seen its overall political influence diminish significantly.

3. The Socialist Party had evolved into a major participant in Belgian politics after World War I, seeking principally to distribute rewards to its followers. The revolutionary appeal of socialism was no longer an effective political strategy for its leaders to employ as the basic grievances of the

---

24. Urwin, *op. cit.*, p. 329.
25. *Op. cit.*, p. 419.
26. *Ibid.*, p. 428.

working class, e.g., the franchise, social welfare legislation, had already been implemented.[27] Thus, the cleavages of religion and class had lost much of their political relevance by 1959, the date of the "Pact Scolaire."

At this point, as promised, we turn our attention to an examination of party politics in Belgium since 1958 to illustrate the concepts of demand generation, ambiguity, outbidding, and democratic instability in another competitive configuration.

Party Politics in Belgium Since 1958: the Salience of Language.[28] Modern Belgium has three national or "traditional" parties that represent, respectively, the ideological concerns usually voiced by the left, the center and conservatives. Since 1920, most Belgian governments have been comprised of coalitions that usually combined the center with either the left or conservative parties. Thus the policies of government have often shifted as the center party forms its coalition with either the left or right. Frequent participation in government by all three parties has led each to accord the system legitimacy. "With the exception of the linguistic extremist parties, Belgian parties have a vested interest in the maintenance of the political system."[29]

The largest political party in Belgium is the Christian Social Party, which derives its main support from its pro-Catholic outlook; it is the successor of the prewar Catholic party. The party is naturally strongest in Flemish areas where Catholic convictions are intensely held. Electors equate the Social Christians with Catholic tradition and social stability; they do not see it as a party that is defined by a distinct ideology or package of policies. The party possesses a *relatively vague program* on most issues and relies on the appeal of its leaders to capture widespread support from both linguistic communities. For example, Paul van den Boeynants, a popular bilingual Brussels politician, often stresses the need for economic development and deemphasizes language in his political campaigns. Boeynants is his party's top electoral attraction (even though his government was forced to resign when the Christian Socials split into separate Flemish and French wings).[30]

The Belgian Socialist Party is the second largest party in Belgium and is a direct successor of the Belgian Workers Party, discussed earlier. Its support comes chiefly from those Belgian workers, especially in Wallonia,

27. *Op. cit.*, pp. 78-79.
28. Gordon L. Weil provides an excellent summary of contemporary parties in modern Belgium. See *The Benelux Nations: The Politics of Small-Country Democracies* (New York: Holt, Rinehart and Winston, Inc., 1970), chapter 4.
29. *Ibid.*, p. 100.
30. Coombes and Norton-Taylor, *op. cit.*, p. 62.

who are disenchanted with the Catholic Church. (We may recall that Catholicism is more firmly entrenched in Flanders.) The Socialists typically favor strengthening the public sector of the economy, but do not oppose free enterprise or Belgian membership in NATO. In actual electoral situations, the party displays an ambivalence toward ideology and concentrates on getting votes.

The party's organization resembles that of the Christian Socials with separate party congresses at both the regional-linguistic and national levels. As a consequence, the linguistic difference is institutionalized within the party. Although the party tries to downgrade language by emphasizing leadership and good discipline, some Flemish party members seem disturbed by the Socialists' preoccupation with Wallonia; Weil hints that party unity is fragile and susceptible to collapse.[31]

The Liberals (The Party for Liberty and Progress) represent the third major party. They are Belgium's conservatives and appeal chiefly to the Belgian business community and other middle-class voters. Their strength is concentrated in the areas of Brussels and Wallonia.

The Liberals do not possess two separate linguistic wings, as is the case in the two other major parties. They focus mainly upon economic issues and try to subordinate language to a secondary position, deliberately appealing to a broader Belgian consciousness. Weil believes that this stand is Belgium's most progressive party outlook, although it "will have only a limited appeal,"[32] and, he notes, the Liberals are overly dependent on the personal popularity of their president.

These three major parties since 1958 have experienced a steadily growing measure of competition from more extremist parties, all of which, except the decreasingly important Communist Party, are linked to the language question. The largest of these is the Volksunie, which draws all of its support from Flemish areas. It takes a purely Flemish stand on all aspects of the language question and advocates the creation of an independent Flemish state within a Belgian federation. The growing success of the Volksunie—five seats in 1961, twelve seats in 1965, and twenty seats in 1968—has in turn stimulated the development of two French-language parties: the French-speaking Democratic Front (Front démocratique des Francophones) in Brussels, which has cut into the Liberals' strength, and the Rassemblement Walloon, which has taken hold in Wallonia and has, since 1965, developed ties with its counterpart in Brussels. These French-speaking parties also favor federalism and advocate the linkage of Brussels with Wallonia, a move bitterly opposed by

---

31. Weil, *op. cit.*, p. 104.
32. *Ibid.*, p. 106.

Flemish-speakers in whose territory Brussels is located. Their combined representation in the 212 seat Chamber (House) of Representatives has grown from one seat in 1961, to five in 1965, to twelve in 1968. Together the three extremist parties have increased their representation from six seats in 1961 to thirty-two seats in 1968 and have also caused splits in the major parties along language lines. These results are summarized in table 4.2.

Table 4.2

Chamber of Representatives: Distribution of Seats by Party

	1946	1949a	1950	1954	1958	1961	1965	1968
Christian Social (PSC/CVP)	92	105	108	95	104	96	77	69
Socialist (PSB/BSP)	69	66	77	86	84	84	64	59
Liberal or PLP/PVV	17	29	20	25	21	20	48	47
Communist	23	12	7	4	2	5	6	5
Volksunie		0		1	1	5	12	20
French-speaking and Walloon						1	5	12
Other	1	0	0	1	0	1	0	

aIn 1949 the vote for women was introduced.
Source: Gordon L. Weil, *The Benelux Nations* (New York: Holt, Rinehart and Winston, Inc., 1970), p. 111.

The language question now exerts profound impact on contemporary politics. To see how this situation has come about, we present a detailed analysis of recent electoral history.

The Start of Linguistic Politics in Belgium: Post-1958 Election Developments. A coalition of Social Christians and Liberals was formed directly after the 1958 election. Their most important policy was the implementation of a general austerity program caused by a worldwide recession and the economic dislocations that were produced by the granting of independence to the Congo. Two days after the austerity measure was passed into law, the predominantly Walloon Socialist Trade Union ordered a general strike; its leader charged that workers were being forced to bear the unreasonable new costs of higher taxes and reduced social benefits. Its Flemish counterpart, the Catholic Trade Union, refused to strike. (Flemish trade union membership numbered about 800,000 compared to

700,000 for Walloons.) As a result, the strike was effective only in Wallonia. A compromise solution was not reached until after some rioting had erupted that caused injuries and one death. The important lesson of this strike for Belgian politics must not be lost; "it highlighted for the first time the divisive nature of Walloon and Flemish aspirations."[33] A delegation of Walloon Socialist deputies petitioned the King to intervene in the strike on the grounds that the Belgian government was systematically advantaging the Flemish north by establishing newer and more industrial plants there.[34] The Flemings, conscious of their numerical superiority, seem determined to hold onto and extend, where possible, their gains. Thus, disagreements about the Austerity Law forced the Liberals to withdraw their support from the government and a new election was called for March 26, 1961. The politics of language had made its first significant postwar appearance.

The 1961 Election: Language Legislation. Following the 1961 election, the Social Christians and Socialists formed a coalition that was able to bring about some degree of language reform. First, they legally stabilized the language boundaries between Wallonia and Flemish areas in February 1962, which had been a major bone of contention, and nine months later passed another bill that declared Brussels bilingual, required all schools in Flemish areas to teach in Flemish, and provided for an adequate supply of Flemish schools in Brussels.

Subsequent legislation in 1963 readjusted the frontiers of the nine Belgian provinces. Meanwhile, the government went ahead with plans to increase the Brussels community, which is situated entirely in Flemish territory, from nineteen administrative communes to twenty-five. Their plans called for the predominantly Flemish-speaking communes to be administered in Flemish, though the French-speaking minorities could demand to have their documents presented to them in French. This decision

---

33. Mallinson, *op. cit.*, p. 165.
34. According to the laws of 1932, a language census must be taken every ten years. The *first and only* such census took place in 1947 amid chaos resulting from disputes about which villages along the language border should be considered Flemish or French-speaking. The census results revealed 51.3 percent Dutch-speaking, 32.9 percent French-speaking, and 15.7 percent Flemish and French in Brussels. (For details, see Dunn, *op. cit.*, pp. 18-19). These results coincide with a transfer of relative economic power from Wallonia, where the first industrial development of the coal and steel industry occurred, to the Flemish north which has undergone the development of new technological projects, massive foreign investment, and the revivification of the port of Antwerp since World War II. Thus, the Flemish numerical and political power is being increasingly enhanced by economic power. Competition for public works expenditures and tax incentives for investment, i.e., public goods, exacerbates the regional rivalry.

created a storm of protest among the Bruxellois and the Prime Minister threatened to resign. A compromise solution was reached that guaranteed the full rights of the French-speaking minorities in any of the disputed Flemish communes, dissolved schools with parallel classes in Flemish and French, and instituted a dual ministry of education with French- and Flemish-speaking counterparts to provide for unilingual schools for the two communities.

The decision to make Brussels bilingual outraged the Flemish who abhored the presence of a predominantly French-speaking city in Flemish territory. Flemings fear that the French-speaking population wants to expand the boundaries of Brussels until contact is made with Wallonia, thus increasing the strength of the French-speakers in central Belgium. (These fears subsequently materialized in the platforms of the French linguistic parties.) In addition, they are disturbed by the fact that of the Flemings who move to Brussels, many choose to educate their children in French either because Flemish educational facilities are inadequate or because of the social prestige and economic advantage of French in Brussels.

The 1965 Election: The Emergence of Extremist Linguistic Parties. As a result of its mishandling of the lingustic problem, the Social Christians lost heavily to the Volksunie in Flemish areas, to French-speaking independents in Brussels, and to Liberals everywhere in the general election of May 23, 1965.[35] As shown in table 4.2, the Flemish nationalists won twelve seats and the two French parties five. The popular vote totals revealed a dramatic gain of nearly one hundred percent for the Flemish nationalist parties: they obtained 354,843 votes on May 23, 1965, compared with only 182,407 in the 1961 election. The purely French parties obtained 76,507 votes in their first major outing. After analyzing these results Philippart concludes that

> [By 1965] a process of radicalization has occurred within the two linguistic communities: certain voters voted for those who appeared to be defending their language above all else . . . . the language question was the main factor in the electoral success of the opposition in the elections of 23 May 1965.[36]

The new Prime Minister, Pierre Harmel, felt compelled to announce a program that conceded cultural autonomy to the regions and to establish commissions designed to improve relations between Wallonia, Brus-

---

35. Though the Liberal Party attracted substantial bicultural support in 1965 on an explicit national platform, it, too, felt the pressure of linguistic politics. In 1968 it split into separate linguistic wings.

36. *Op. cit.*, pp. 72, 81.

sels and the Flemish north. However, he made the mistake of placing fourteen French-speakers and only thirteen Flemings in his cabinet. Flemings, comprising a clear majority of the population, objected to disproportionate French representation in the cabinet. This issue and others, particularly the government's inability to cope with a threatened doctor's strike, forced Harmel's resignation and Paul van den Boeynants assumed office on March 19, 1966.

Boeynants immediately corrected Harmel's misjudgment and balanced his cabinet on a regional/linguistic basis by appointing twelve Flemings, six Walloons and five persons from the Brussels area. In spite of these efforts to improve regional relations, the linguistic situation steadily deteriorated. A crisis erupted at the University of Louvain when eight Flemish Social Christian members of the cabinet resigned in protest over the government's refusal to commit itself to a transfer of the French-language facilities to French-speaking territory. (The facilities of the University of Louvain are entirely in Flemish territory.) Boeynants had no alternative but to tender his resignation to the King. This "was the first time in Belgium's history that a government had fallen over the language issue."[37] As a consequence, Belgians again went to the polls to elect a new government on March 31, 1968.

The 1968 Election: The Triumph of Linguistic Extremism.[38] The downfall of Van den Boeynants's government is directly traceable to the problems of Louvain and Brussels; we have already reviewed the latter problem. The former, the issue at Louvain, concerned the future of the French-speaking sections of the university that are entirely located in Flemish territory. The University of Louvain is essentially divided into separate Flemish and French faculties. In May 1966 the seven Catholic bishops of Belgium, who hold ultimate responsibility for the University, refused to accede to Flemish demands—one manifestation of a growing Flemish political consciousness—to transfer the French-speaking section of the University of Wallonia. As if these demands did not comprise a warning of impending trouble, the publication of the future expansion plans of the French-speaking sections in Louvain led immediately to widespread rioting throughout northern Belgium. Most Flemish leaders, including the bishop of Bruges, opposed the government and forced its resignation.

The election of March 1968 displays all the characteristics of extremist ethnic politics: the overwhelming salience of language, the rise of the political entrepreneur, the politics of outbidding, the demise of modera-

---

37. Mallinson, *op. cit.*, p. 173.
38. Coombs and Norton-Taylor, *op. cit.*, provide an excellent discussion of the 1968 election.

tion, etc. During the campaign the Socialists stressed general social and economic policy in a conscious effort to minimize the language issue; their strategy failed when their Flemish wing broke free to contest the election on its own in Brussels just before the election. The Liberals also tried to deemphasize the language issue, which had been responsible for Boeynants's resignation; they advertised themselves as the only party opposing regional autonomy. The party, however, separated into French and Flemish wings before the election and campaigned only in their respective regions of Wallonia and Flemish areas. Boeynants himself headed up a distinct list of Social Christian candidates and campaigned only in the region of Brussels, invoking the theme of national unity. He hoped to emerge as the only suitable national leader after the election.

The Social Christian split was crucial for now its Walloon wing resembled the extremist French parties, the French-speaking Democratic Front of Brussels (FDF) and the Rassemblement Wallon. The Rassemblement Wallon campaigned for recognition of a separate Walloon community with its own directly elected assembly responsible for internal Walloon affairs. Both it and the FDF played upon fears of "Flemish imperialism," complained of neglect in the southern industrial areas, and exclaimed the virtues and international character of French language and culture. Its Flemish nationalist counterpart, the Volksunie, appealed exclusively to the linguistic sentiments of Flemings. They spoke out in behalf of an independent Flemish state in a Belgian federation.

The election results disclosed marked losses for the major parties that had always managed in previous postwar elections to maintain a national organization and present an image of national unity. Linguistic splits within the major parties, however, proved disastrous. As the extremist parties successfully generated a demand for the issue of language, the moderate stance usually embodied in the platforms of the "traditional" national parties gave way to an attempt to combat fire with fire. *But the separatist wings of the major parties were not successful. Their position was not credible to voters whose principal concern was with the linguistic-cultural question.* Consequently, the Walloon wing of the Social Christians lost heavily to the Rassemblement Wallon in the South; the Volksunie, correspondingly, registered dramatic gains in the North. The full extent of the linguistic vote and the way in which the electorate was becoming increasingly polarized over the issue of language is evident in the combined votes received by the Walloon Social Christians, the Volksunie, the FDF, and the Rassemblement Wallon. *Together they obtained nearly thirty percent of the votes and caused serious internal divisions over language in the hitherto "national" parties.*

Following the election, the King called on Boeynants to form a coalition. Boeynants tried to incorporate members of the three major parties in his government, but this attempt backfired when the Liberals split into separate Flemish and French wings, as had the Social Christians and Socialists before the election. A government that combined mainly Flemish Social Christians and Socialists was finally formed without Boeynants. It was headed by the former Catholic leader, Gaston Eyskens, and consisted of a coalition of fourteen Flemish and fourteen Walloon ministers. Eyskens has since set up separate Ministries of Education, Culture, and Regional Economic Development in order to satisfy growing pressure for more Flemish and Walloon autonomy.

In July 1970 Eyskens's government failed in its efforts to amend the constitution and thus provide cultural and economic councils giving the two regions a degree of autonomy.[39] The defeat was due primarily to the French-speaking Brussels representatives who insisted that the capital should be allowed to find its natural limits, and that its territory should not be restricted to the nineteen communes that now comprise the metropolitan area. On December 10, 1970, however, Belgium's lower house of Parliament approved a controversial plan that gives the two regions cultural autonomy and economic decentralization, while stopping short of what extremists on both sides want — outright federalism. The new plan, in effect, recognizes the existence of *three* national communities.[40]

Members of Belgium's coalition government must have concluded that the future for stable democracy in a unitary state was bleak. Whether this action stems the growth of linguistic chauvinism will become apparent only after the next major election.

Belgium: A Theoretical Appraisal. The Belgian case, like Guyana, is a concrete illustration of the paradigm. Each of the two cultural communities, the Flemish and the Walloon, views the political world from a communal perspective (A.3) and perceives the other's preferences as antagonistic to its own (A.2). The growing success of the extremist parties, and the accompanying breakup of the traditional national parties along regional lines, reveals a communally segregated electorate with intense cultural preferences (A.1). Until their breakup, the three traditional parties tended to downgrade the language issue by generating demand for national issues, e.g., economic growth, Belgian national consciousness, etc., thus rendering their position on language ambiguous. Linguistic entrepreneurs, however,

---

39. *The New York Times,* July 5, 1970, p. 11
40. *Race Today* 3, no. 1 (January 1971): 32.

had succeeded by 1968 in making language the salient issue in Belgian politics. The growing success throughout the 1960s of linguistic extremism ultimately forced the traditional parties to confront the language issue directly. As a result, they separated into their respective ethnic wings. The policies of the new government, increased cultural autonomy and economic decentralization, appear to be a direct consequence of regional pressures.

With the paradigm in mind, we now turn to a comparative analysis of ethnic politics in Trinidad and Malaya; our dimensions of comparison are those that have already been used to explain politics in Guyana and Belgium.*

Ethnic Politics in Trinidad and Malaya

Ethnic Cooperation in Preindependent Trinidad.[41] The demography of Trinidad places Negroes or Africans in a more advantageous position when they are compared with their counterparts in Guyana. Table 4.3 discloses that they are the largest minority in Trinidad. Their numerical

---

* As this book goes to press, the results of the November 7, 1971, Belgian elections are becoming available. As our theory predicts, the major "parties tried to campaign on the theme that the [linguistic-cultural] quarrel was part of the past and that the country had to think of more important national and international problems" (*New York Times,* November 9, 1971, p. 5). That is, the major parties attempted to *generate demand* for national issues in order to outflank the linguistic extremist parties. However, as also predicted, the extremist parties harped on the language issue. And the electorate spoke: the election "showed that Belgium's internal divisions were still very much alive," *ibid.* Premier Gaston Eyskens has resigned and a new cabinet will be formed by the old coalition partners, the Social Christians and the Socialists, "since both just managed to retain their strength in the 212-seat House of Representatives," *ibid.*

Ironically the *New York Times* (November 8, 1971, p. 30) earlier reported a quiet election—"the first postwar election campaign here not dominated by language issues." Yet, as the early returns suggest, the linguistic parties, especially in Brussels and Wallonia, enjoyed a very successful campaign, mostly at the expense of the Liberals. In Brussels, "the extremist, anti-Flemish, French-speaking Democratic Front doubled its strength and, with close to 40 percent of the vote, emerged as the strongest group in the city. In Wallonia, the allied Walloon Union party also doubled its vote to 20 percent." Athough the complete returns, especially in Flanders, are unavailable at this time, the conclusion drawn by the *New York Times* reporter is telling: "As a result [of the election] a much more radical opposition, favoring a federal system for Belgium, is now in the House of Representatives and in the Senate, and the majority parties will find it much more difficult to get enabling acts through Parliament."

41. An excellent treatment of ethnic politics in Trinidad is contained in Ivar Oxaal, *Black Intellectuals Come to Power* (Cambridge, Massachusetts: Schenkman Publishing Company, Inc., 1968). We follow standard practice and refer to Trinidad and Tobago as Trinidad.

position is enhanced even more since most persons falling into the mixed category have some Negro ancestry.

Table 4.3

Ethnic Communities in Trinidad

Race	Number	Percent
Negro	358,588	43.3
East Indian	301,946	36.5
Mixed	134,749	16.3
White	15,718	1.9
Chinese	8,361	1.0
Others	8,595	1.0
Totals	827,957	100.0

Source: *1960 Census of Trinidad and Tobago* (Bulletin Nos. 1 and 2).

Political developments in Trinidad after World War I, when major changes were taking place throughout the British empire, involved the formation of nationalist political parties.[42] Trinidad's Captain Andrew Cipriani of French Creole extraction, who had successfully commanded West Indian soldiers in the Middle East during World War I, returned to Trinidad where he undertook the leadership of the budding working-class political movement — the Trinidad Workingmen's Association. He later formed the Trinidad Labor Party, an attempt at a class-based, explicitly multiracial nationalist movement; the party had associated with it a number of prominent East Indians. As a political movement the party stressed the need for unity between Negroes and Indians and tried to focus on class and economic issues. Hughes observes, however, that the party never developed a solid organization.[43]

Next in line came the British Empire Workers and Citizens Home Rule Party. Led by Uriah Butler, who had become famous because of his prominence in the 1937 labor riots, the party operated on an interracial basis, but declined shortly after Butler's retirement from politics.

Several other minor parties, all obstensibly nonracial, also appeared on the Trinidad political scene. Among them one can find the Party of Political Progress Groups (1953), formerly known as the Taxpayers Association (1941); the Caribbean National Labor Party (1956), which had its origins in the Oilfield Workers' Union; the West Indian Nationalist Party

42. For a first-rate treatment of the period of multiethnic parties in Trinidad, see Colin A. Hughes, "Adult Suffrage and the Party System in Trinidad," *Parliamentary Affairs* 10, no. 1 (Winter 1956/57): 15-26.
43. *Ibid.*, p. 18.

(1943) of Dr. David Pitt; and, finally, the United Front (1945). None of these parties, however, had been able to garner mass support or significant representation in the Legislative Council.

Part of the problem, at least until the introduction of universal adult suffrage in 1945, followed from the absence of a broad-based electorate. In 1925, the list of eligibles was restricted to 22,000 voters who could meet certain property requirements. By 1938, the list had grown to only 31,000 voters, but with the introduction of universal adult suffrage in 1945, the list of qualified voters shot up rapidly to include 259,000 by the following year. A mass basis for electoral politics was now available.[44]

The presence of numerous popular candidates who ran as independents, and the general lack of appeal of the existing parties, produced a rather uneventful post-World War II political history in Trinidad until 1953, when the first definitely racial party was established — the People's Democratic Party formed with solid Indian backing and led by B. S. Maraj. In addition, the recognition that world public opinion after World War II opposed colonial rule and favored the earliest possible granting of independence to most colonies spurred the creation of the People's National Movement, a predominantly Negro Party led by the former historian Dr. Eric Williams. With the impending arrival of independence in Trinidad, the multiracial nationalist movement dissolved into competitive communal factions, leading, in the 1956 elections, to the emergence of racial voting. Table 4.4 displays this development convincingly.

Table 4.4

Election Results in Trinidad in 1950 and 1956, by Percentages

	1950	1956
Trinidad Labor Party	7.5	5.0
Butler Party	21.5	10.0
P.O.P.P.G.	4.0	5.0
Carribean Socialist Party	12.5	——
Trade Union Congress	4.5	——
C.N.L.P.	——	1.0
P.N.M.	——	38.5[a]
P.D.P.	——	20.0[a]
Independents	50.0	20.5

[a]Predominantly racial voting.
Source: Colin A. Hughes, "Adult Suffrage and the Party System in Trinidad," *Parliamentary Affairs* 10, no. 1 (Winter 1956/57): 23.

44. The reader should recall that a similar restriction on the franchise, the "censitaire" system, delayed the rise of a Flemish nationalist political movement in Belgium for a considerabe period of time.

Thus democratic politics in Trinidad began after World War I with the rise of several multiracial parties that stressed class and economic issues. These issues continued to dominate Trinidad electoral politics well after the franchise became universal. However, since the arrival of the two racial parties in the early 1950s, the multiethnic class-based parties have almost completely disappeared.

Ethnic Cooperation in Malaya.[45] Three distinct communities make up the population of Malaya: Malays comprise about fifty percent, Chinese thirty-seven percent, and Indians and other minorities the remaining thirteen percent. Prior to World War II, nationalist politics in Malaya did not involve the Chinese and Indian communities; their attention lay in watching events in their respective mother countries. Only Malays engaged in any serious expression of communal feelings or in the creation of organizations of a potentially nationalist nature.[46]

The British tried to alter the traditional political character of the Malay States after World War II by replacing the federal form that existed under prewar colonial rule with a unitary form of government, known as the Malayan Union. As a response to this threat to traditional Malay political supremacy, the United Malays National Organization (UMNO) was formed. This first mass-based political party in Malaya successfully fought the Malayan Union, which would have eliminated in large measure the traditional privileges of the Malays.

The British, however, insisted on withholding independence until a national, responsible party that commanded broad support emerged. The Alliance party, which consists of three distinct communal parties — UMNO, the Malayan Chinese Association (MCA) and the Malayan Indian Congress (MIC) — was formed and successfully met the stipulations of the Colonial Office. They contested the 1955 Legislative Council election and won fifty-one of fifty-two elective seats. Independence day arrived in August 1957 and Malaya seemed, for the moment, to provide evidence that peaceful racial coexistence was possible in a competitive plural setting.[47]

---

45. Malaya refers to the territory of the Federation of Malaya that in the state of Malaysia is called West Malaysia. Our discussion excludes developments in the Borneo States of Sarawak and Sabah, now East Malaysia.

46. See William R. Roff, *The Origins of Malay Nationalism* (New Haven: Yale University Press, 1967).

47. For a detailed analysis of the 1955 and 1959 elections see K.J. Ratnam, *Communalism and the Political Process in Malaya* (Kuala Lumpur: University of Malaya Press, 1965).

Ethnic Competition: The Politics of Demand Generation
and the Bankruptcy of Moderation

Trinidad. The election of 1956 was fought between the parties of the two
major communities: Eric Williams's PNM polled thirty-nine percent of
the vote and won thirteen of the twenty-five elective seats. The Indian-
supported PDP obtained five seats with twenty percent. PNM victories
occurred chiefly in the predominantly Negro urban areas of Port of Spain
and San Fernando whereas the Indian party of Bhadase Maraj prospered
in the East Indian sugar belt. Because the PNM emerged as the strongest
party after the election, the Colonial Office allowed it to name two of the
four nominated members to the Legislative Council, thus conferring on
the party a clear majority — fifteen of the twenty-nine seats. During the
next year the Democratic Labor Party (DLP) was formed and replaced
PDP. As the 1961 election approached, political divisions in Trinidad
crystallized almost exclusively along ethnic lines; this was a radical departure from the multiracial movements of Cipriani and Butler.

> With one "doctor" leading the predominantly Creole political party
> and another "doctor" [Rudranath Capildeo] rallying East Indian sup-
> port for the politicians who chiefly represented that ethnic minority,
> the Trinidad two-party system emerged in a form which strongly
> tended to parallel the island's ethnic structure.[48]

The East Indian leaders charged that the PNM had ruled fraudulently
as a majority party since 1956 because it had obtained just under forty percent of the vote. In the 1961 election the PNM received fifty-seven percent of the vote, enough for majority rule, but again the Indian leaders
charged fraud: they accused the PNM of having introduced voting ma-
chines to confuse the Indian voter. The DLP obtained only forty-two percent of the vote and did no better in the subsequent election in 1966:
Negroes again won two-thirds of the seats and the Indian party the remaining one-third. C.L.R. James and his Worker's and Farmer's Party,
a proposed middle-class intellectual organization, did very poorly and all
the candidates of this party lost their deposits (a fixed number of votes
must be received or the deposit is forfeited).

Oxaal neatly summarizes the changing character of Trinidad politics.

> The rise of East Indian militancy after World War II, and the
> emergence of the Hindu community as a fairly solid bloc in the

---

48. Oxaal, *op. cit.*, p. 155.

era of universal suffrage, created a new political situation from that which had been envisaged by the earlier middle class radicals like Cipriani. In place of class struggle against the white employers and political directorate, a movement which Uriah Butler brought to a climax in the late Thirties, there developed an increasing tendency to vote on the basis of ethnicity. . . . The process of greater ethnic polarization between East Indian and Negro was thus aggravated as the latter became aware of the political strength of the former arising from the Indians' sense of ethnic solidarity.[49]

More recently (1970), Trinidad has experienced the massive racial violence to which the Guyanese have become accustomed. Those disorders have materialized under the rubric of "black power." Black extremists led several marches to protest the control of Trinidad's economy by expatriates and overseas white business interests, e.g., Texaco's ownership of Trinidad's refinery. They invoked the issue of race, charging that the PNM had sold out the interests of the working classes of Trinidad to the wealthy white minority.[50] Williams's government in turn claimed that the black power demonstrations were engineered by communist agitators trained and paid by Cuba's Fidel Castro. Rioting and burning erupted: a young black power supporter was shot and killed by a policeman; simultaneously, a part of Trinidad's small armed forces rebelled. The insurrection was quickly put down and political order was restored. But Williams is likely to be confronted head on with the racial issue for the indefinite future. His position as a black moderate, especially on economic issues, is likely to be contested by extremists within his own community.

Why did politics shift solely to an ethnic dimension? Oxaal suggests that with the departure of the colonial authorities (independence day was August 31, 1962) "politics suddenly became a rather more serious undertaking because power finally had become local."[51] Put another way, gains and losses no longer came at the expense of the colonial authority but from whichever community lost the capacity and authority to make political decisions.

Malaya. The Alliance party dominated Malayan electoral politics until the 1969 general election. Following their victory in the 1955 Legislative Council election, they easily were the major victors in the 1959 election

---

49. *Ibid.,* p. 180.
50. For details about the 1970 riots, see David G. Nicholls, "East Indians and Black Power in Trinidad," *Race* 12, no. 4 (April 1971): 443-59. Nicholls notes that ninety-nine percent of the marchers were black (p. 447).
51. Oxall, *op. cit.*

winning 74 of the 104 contested parliamentary seats and 207 of the 282 total seats in the eleven state assemblies. Deemphasis of the racial issue and programs for national economic development constituted their public position.

Opposition parties, which include such Malay extremists as the theocratically oriented Pan Malayan Islamic Party (PMIP), and such Chinese and Indian (non-Malay) extremists as the Labor Party, the Democratic Action Party, and so forth, tried to fan the flames of ethnic animosity. The PMIP accused UMNO of selling out Malay interests; extremist Chinese spoke of discrimination of Chinese by the Malay-dominated Alliance party. The opposition strategy failed dismally in 1964: the Alliance won 89 seats in parliament and increased their representation in the eleven state assemblies to 240 seats. The Alliance continually pointed to the external threat posed by Indonesian "confrontation" and labeled as traitors those who failed to support the government, *viz.*, the opposition. Military landings on Malayan soil by Indonesians proved that confrontation was a credible threat and verified the Alliance warnings. Demand generation for national issues was clearly successful in this case.

Flames of ethnic animosity were again fanned by the opposition in 1969. This time no credible external threat existed. Emphasis upon economic issues coupled with ambiguity on the racial issue cost the Alliance heavily. For the first time in postindependence history, UMNO was unable to form a working coalition in parliament; the conservative MCA, the party of the Chinese business community, felt unable to enter into a coalition with UMNO due to their poor performance in the election. They failed to defeat the political appeal of extremist Chinese parties and were beaten in 20 of 33 parliamentary contests. Altogether the Alliance won only 66 of 103 contested parliamentary seats given to representatives of Malayan States. To make matters worse, opposition parties for the first time controlled the state assemblies in Penang, Perak, and Kelantan, and were deadlocked with the Alliance in Selangor.[52]

The politics of moderation and ambiguity thus gave way to the politics of extremism and demand generation. Several days after the election, Chinese-Malay rioting broke out. The rioting can be traced to Chinese

---

52. For a detailed treatment of the 1964 election see K.J. Ratnam and R.S. Milne, *The Malayan Parliamentary Election of 1964* (Singapore: University of Malaya Press, 1967). For detailed analysis of the 1969 general election see K.J. Ratnam and R.S. Milne, "The 1969 Parliamentary Election in West Malaysia," *Pacific Affairs* 43, no. 2 (Summer 1970): 203-26; Martin Rudner, "The Malaysian General Election of 1969: A Political Analysis," *Modern Asian Studies* 4, no. 1 (January 1970): 1-21; and Stuart Drummond and David Hawkins, "The Malaysian Elections of 1969: An Analysis of the Campaign and the Results," *Asian Survey* 10, no. 4 (April 1970): 320-35. For a chronological review of the effect of race in local Malayan politics see Alvin Rabushka, "The Manipulation of Ethnic Politics in Malaya," *Polity* 2, no. 3 (Spring 1970): 345-56.

taunts of Malays following Malay electoral gains. Malays fearing Chinese encroachment upon their privileges responded with violence. Racial disorder was halted by the declaration of an emergency that suspended Parliament and established a National Operations Council to run the country.

Ethnic Advantage: The Manipulation of Electoral Rules

Malaya. The Chinese have been the victims of extensive manipulation.[53] To protect a position of advantage, in 1962 the Malays in Parliament implemented a constituencies amendment that permits rural constituencies to contain as few as one-half the number of electors as urban constituencies on the grounds that rural constituencies are more dispersed. It is not uncoincidental that Malays are overwhelmingly rural dwellers while Chinese, on the other hand, tend to concentrate in cities.

The Chinese have also been the victims of discrimination in local elections. Chinese and Indian-based parties have exercised control of the municipal councils of Georgetown (Penang), Malacca, Seremban (Negri Sembilan), and Ipoh (Perak); in 1965 these local councils and the elections for their members except in Ipoh were suspended by the Malay-dominated national government on grounds of corruption and malpractice. A Royal Commission Enquiry on Local Government was created and made its report to Parliament, which has since led the government to abolish elected local councils. The coincidence between charges of city council malpractice and the growth of urban Chinese political power cannot be overlooked. Thus Chinese are disadvantaged by gerrymandering in state and parliamentary elections, and have been barred from municipal council positions by legislative fiat.[54]

The Paradigm and Surinam: A Prognosis[55]

Surinam is Guyana's immediate neighbor and contains a somewhat comparable ethnic mosaic: East Indians make up about two-fifths of the

---

53. See Rabushka, *op. cit.*
54. Machinations in Trinidad are less blatant than in Malaysia. The only threat to black rule comes from extremists within its own ranks. Williams, the Prime Minister, has taken steps to restrict extremist political activity by unreasonably harassing their organizations.
55. This material is taken from Philip Mason, *Patterns of Dominance* (London: Oxford University Press for the Institute of Race Relations, 1970) pp. 300-301. For a somewhat different view see Peter Dodge, "Ethnic Fragmentation and Politics: The Case of Surinam," *Political Science Quarterly* 81, no. 4 (December 1966): 593-601.

population, Creoles another two-fifths, and Javanese (from Indonesia) the remaining one-fifth. Although political parties exclusively follow ethnic lines, there is less political tension. Two factors seem to account for this relative ethnic tranquility. First, political awareness is at an earlier stage of development than in Guyana, or Trinidad for that matter, due in part to the fact that Surinam is ruled as an integral part of the Tripartite Kingdom of the Netherlands. Thus the measure of self-rule that the Surinamese possess is not equivalent to fully independent, decision-making authority. Second, there exist sharp, somewhat salient, divisions within each ethnic group.

But Mason is no wishful optimist with regard to these intraethnic distinctions foretelling a future era of racial harmony. He suggests, instead, that

> it seems probable that as the possibilities open to political parties become more widely understood, the internal differences will recede and the main ethnic groups will harden into parties sharply opposed.[56]

We suggest that part one and the evidence of this chapter lend credibility to Mason's predictions.

---

56. *Op. cit.*, p. 301.

CHAPTER **5**

Majority Domination

We turn in this chapter to an analysis of ethnic politics in dominant majority configurations. A major theme that emerges from this analysis is the denial by majorities of political freedoms to minorities as well as access to a proportional share of the public sector. First we explore ethnic politics in Ceylon to illustrate how a dominant Sinhalese majority deals with an important Tamil minority; second, we extend the empirical coverage with a comparative treatment of majority domination in Northern Ireland, Cyprus, Mauritius, Rwanda, and Zanzibar (now part of Tanzania).

Ceylon

The most important source of division and disruption in Ceylonese politics and the greatest impediment to integrative trends has been the persistence of sentiments of identification and solidarity with broader primordial groups generally referred to as communities.[1]

The Sinhalese, constituting about seventy percent of the population, is the majority community in Ceylon. The remaining minorities consist of Ceylon Tamils who arrived from India between the fourth and twelfth centuries, eleven percent; Indian Tamils who arrived in the nineteenth and twentieth centuries to work on the tea estates, twelve percent; Moors

---

1. Robert N. Kearney, *Communalism and Language in the Politics of Ceylon* (Durham, North Carolina: Duke University Press, 1967), p. 4. We rely heavily upon the evidence Kearney provides of Sinhalese politics. See also W. Howard Wriggins, *Ceylon: Dilemmas of a New Nation* (Princeton: Princeton University Press, 1960); Calvin A. Woodward, *The Growth of a Party System in Ceylon* (Providence: Brown University Press, 1969); and I. D. S. Weerawardana, *Ceylon General Election 1956* (Colombo: M. D. Gunasena & Co., Ltd., 1960).

who are Islamic descendents of Arab traders, six percent; and very insignificant minorities of Burghers, Eurasians, Malays, and others. These communities also tend to be regionally concentrated: Tamils reside in the northern and eastern portions of the island in numbers large enough to insure Tamil constituency pressures in those regions, while Sinhalese generally predominate elsewhere. In particular, more than ninety-five percent of the residents in Jaffna are Tamils, whereas Sinhalese form eighty percent or more of the population in much of the west and south.[2]

Ceylon

Ethnic Cooperation. Modern Ceylonese nationalism materialized in the early part of the twentieth century. Since 1798, when they obtained Ceylon from the Dutch, British colonial rule had been very autocratic. Authority was concentrated in the hands of the colonial officials while the native Ceylonese were almost entirely excluded from participation in the government. It was the growth of an English-educated middle class that stimulated a demand for Ceylonese participation in government.

By 1900 many Ceylonese had entered middle-class professions. Christian missionary schools, disproportionately concentrated in the Tamil north, expanded literacy in English thereby encouraging social mobility. On this

2. Kearney, *op. cit.*, p. 12.

point Woodward observes that "a small class of wealthy Ceylonese emerged, and, more important, a large indigeneous middle class developed that sought entry into the professional, commercial, and public service career systems."[3] British mishandling of the Sinhalese-Muslim riots in 1915 accompanied by overly harsh punishment of the rioters hastened the internal desire for political reform. In response to nationalist pressures, the British allowed the formation of representative institutions and Ceylonese participation in government.

The Ceylon National Congress (CNC), the attempt of some Ceylonese to copy the Indian Congress Party, was the first major nationalist organization that played a role in bringing about British reforms. The movement was entirely middle class and tied together Tamils and Sinhalese with Western outlooks. It was hoped and expected by some "that the struggle for Ceylonese self-government would unify the Sinhalese and Tamils in a common cause."[4] The CNC sought and obtained an enlarged Legislative Council, which provided for nineteen elected members; they also appealed for the abolition of communal electorates, then reflected in the stipulation that eleven of the elected Councillors must represent specific sections of the country. CNC leaders asked for a territory-wide elected majority, with executive responsibility residing in its hands. This request strained Sinhalese-Tamil cooperation, which had appeared at the very onset of the movement.

> The Tamil leadership considered the attempt of the CNC to obtain such a system a betrayal of the tacit agreement between the two communities to maintain balanced representation. Consequently, the Tamils withdrew from the congress and, together with other minority groups in the Council, formulated their own communally oriented proposal for reform of the Council.[5]

Woodward observes here that some twenty-seven years before independence "the communal rift between the Tamil and Sinhalese elites ended the operation of the CNC as a comprehensive and inclusive nationalist organization."[6] In reference to this extremely short-lived coalition of two years, Kearney records that

> the split was a triumph of primordial identification and loyalty over the new identifications based on class, urbanization and Westerniza-

---

3. *Op. Cit.*, p. 26
4. Kearney, *op. cit.*, p. 27.
5. Woodward, *op. cit.*, pp. 31-32.
6. *Ibid.*

tion. The Tamil departure from the Congress marked the beginning
of the rivalry between Sinhalese and Tamils which, although seldom
bitter and never violent [before independence] became a persistent
feature of the transition to independence.[7]

The CNC lost its cooperative character and developed into an exclusively
Sinhalese movement. As of 1921, Tamils expressed nationalist sentiments
in their own communal organizations.

Ethnic Conflict. At the outset, the nationalist movement fostered some
Sinhalese-Tamil unity, though short-lived, in opposition to the common
colonial enemy. With the breakup of the CNC, the rivalry between the
Sinhalese and Tamils steadily increased. These disputes were initially limited to constitutional issues. Ceylon had its constitution replaced with a
new one in 1920, 1924, 1931, and 1946, the latter being converted, with
some modification, into the constitution of independent Ceylon.

The constitutional debate revolved chiefly around the problem of representation. It was clear that universal suffrage favored the Sinhalese majority. As an alternative the Tamil Congress proposed a "fifty-fifty" scheme
in which half the seats in the Ceylon legislature would be reserved for the
minority communities. In addition, no more than half of the Cabinet
could be appointed from any one community. This scheme, Tamils believed, would preclude any one community from imposing its will on the
others.

The Soulbury Commission, which arrived in Ceylon in 1944 to implement constitutional reform, rejected the Tamil "fifty-fifty" scheme on the
grounds that it furthered communal representation. The Commission knew
that majority rule implied Sinhalese domination, but believed that constitutional safeguards would forestall minority persecution. They expected
that D. S. Senanayake would become Ceylon's first Prime Minister and
that he would be a man of good will toward the minority communities.
With the approval of the constitutional draft by the State Council of
Ceylon, the period of postindependence politics began.

The 1947 election, held one year before independence, already foretold
the communal character of Ceylon electoral politics. Most successful candidates were of the same ethnic group as the majority of their constituents.
Furthermore, no multiethnic party won a seat in the Tamil North. The
United National Party (UNP), formed by the leaders of the CNC and the
Sinhalese-dominated Council, easily won the election. With the departure
of the British the new government turned its attention to internal matters,
and "the existing sense of communal identification and loyalty dictated

7. *Op. cit.*, p. 29.

that communal interests and aspirations be protected and promoted in the political sphere."[8]

Language and Nationalist Politics. Immediately upon independence most Indian Tamils were excluded from Ceylonese citizenship and the franchise. The Citizenship Act, passed in 1948 and liberalized somewhat in 1949, possessed requirements that the majority of Indian estate laborers could not satisfy.[9] By legislative enactment, the Sinhalese had cut Tamil political strength in half: only the Ceylon Tamils qualified for citizenship and the franchise.

Since independence the language issue has governed Ceylonese politics. The prime political issue has been whether Sinhalese is to be the sole official language of Ceylon or whether Tamil is also to be recognized.

Under British rule, knowledge of English was a prerequisite for employment in the public service. Consquently, English-language education spread rapidly during the period of British rule. By 1953, the number of English literates made up one-seventh of all literate Ceylonese, and this English trained elite was disproportionately Tamil in composition. This dual system of education separated the English-educated from those who were educated in vernacular languages and gave the former a monopoly over the major positions in the public service, the legal profession, and in education.

Vernacular-speaking Ceylonese began to oppose the influence and power of the English-educated. They started a movement, known as "swabhasha," demanding the use of the vernacular languages in government. " 'Swabhasha' [was] a marvelously *ambiguous* slogan for rallying political support."[10] To the majority Sinhalese community, the term could mean Sinhalese and to the Tamils it could mean Sinhalese and Tamil, the languages of the Ceylonese people. Though the movement was led for the most part by Sinhalese, since the English-educated Tamils had gained admission to the professions and the clerical and administrative grades of the public service disproportionate to their numbers, the ambiguous goals implied in the slogan "swabhasha" attracted some Tamil support.

The swabhasha campaign combined up-country Sinhalese and other vernacular speakers in a joint struggle against the small and exclusive English-educated elite. The demand for swabhasha among the Sinhalese majority was soon transformed, however, into insistence on Sinhalese as the sole official language, and the consequent intensification of communal

---

8. *Ibid.*, p. 40.
9. I. D. S. Weerawardana, *op. cit.*, p. 83.
10. Kearney, *op. cit.*, p. 68 (emphasis added).

rivalry.[11] Increased Sinhalese demands for Sinhalese-only grew from resentment of Tamil visibility in the Civil Service. Tamils had secured about thirty percent of the bureaucratic positions although Sinhalese are six times more numerous in the population. Furthermore, the Sinhalese believed themselves to be a numerical minority and hence opposed parity for the Tamil language. Weerawardana notes that there are only five to six million people in the world who speak Sinhalese, all in Ceylon, whereas forty to fifty million speak Tamil, most living in South India across the narrow Palk Strait.[12] The Sinhalese-only advocates insisted that the minority size of the Tamil community could not justify equal treatment for their language.

Politics until 1956 remained calm and free of intense linguistic pressures. In 1952 D. S. Senanayake, one of the early leaders of the United National Party, died and was succeeded by his son, Dudley Senanayake. Although swabhasha was endorsed by all the major parties, it did not dominate the 1952 campaign, and the election produced a solid UNP triumph. Shortly thereafter, Dudley Senanayake stressed to an annual UNP conference the continued commitment of his party to swabhasha but he also emphasized the necessity for gradualism. This emphasis split the UNP: S. W. R. D. Bandaranaike, who was identified with a policy of immediate adoption of swabhasha, resigned from the cabinet in 1951 and his party, the Sinhala Maha Sabha (SMS), withdrew from the UNP. The SMS charged the UNP government with procrastination and delay on the language question. Immediately, Bandaranaike disbanded the SMS and founded the Sri Lanka Freedom Party (SLFP). By 1956 it was able to fight the next election almost entirely upon the language issue, which had shifted from swabhasha to Sinhalese-only. Intense and violent communal politics had finally emerged in Ceylon.

The 1956 Election: Sinhalese-Only.[13] In the 1956 election, the issue of Sinhalese-only absolutely overrode all other concerns. Senanayake and the UNP were resoundingly defeated by Bandaranaike, who had built a combined opposition — the Mahajana Eksath Peramuna (MEP: Peoples United Front)—around his Sri Lanka Freedom Party. Both major parties emphasized their adherence to a Sinhalese-only viewpoint. The UNP asked the electorate for a two-thirds majority that would allow it to imple-

---

11. Again figures 3.8 and 3.9 are instructive. The lottery — in this case swabhasha — can be defeated by a more extreme position ("Sinhalese only"). Extremism is efficacious, and all the more obvious, in light of an overwhelming Sinhalese majority.

12. *Op. cit.*, p. 72.

13. See Weerawardana, *op. cit.*, for a detailed Nuffield-type study of the 1956 election.

ment Sinhalese as the sole official language. The MEP also adopted Sinhalese-only as its major campaign theme; they spent much time and effort trying to convince the electorate that the integrity of the UNP on the language issue was suspect, arguing vigorously that UNP promises were not normally kept.[14] The MEP appealed chiefly to up-country Sinhalese who professed anti-Western, anti-English, anti-Christian sentiments, depicting the UNP as the party of the small exclusive English-speaking middle class. During the campaign Bandaranaike promised to make Sinhalese the official language within forty-eight hours if he were elected, while the UNP stated it would require from two to three years—a policy of gradualism.[15] Furthermore, the UNP did not adopt the platform of Sinhalese-only until after the opposition had already invoked it. Timing was crucial. UNP claims for Sinhalese-only suffered a credibility gap, especially since the UNP Prime Minister had hinted in his campaigning that English would still have its place even though Sinhalese would become the official language. Tamils were also informed by the UNP that they would be permitted to use their language in the northern and eastern portions of the island, as they had done previously.[16]

Bandaranaike's claims that the UNP was less than sincere on the language issue appeared consistent with UNP campaign behavior during by-elections held in the 1952-56 period. The UNP generally tended to associate its opponents with international and revolutionary conspiracies, rather than to debate issues of policy,[17] trying consciously to downgrade language. In addition, Bandaranaike's split with the UNP on the grounds that they were laggard and gradualist in the swabhasha movement confirmed for the Sinhalese electorate that the MEP was the genuine expression of Sinhalese-only sentiments.

The result of the general election even surprised the victors. The MEP garnered an absolute majority of fifty-one seats, the UNP was able to retain only eight, and the remaining thirty-six seats were distributed among independents, leftist parties, and Tamil communal parties. The new MEP government immediately promulgated an Official Language Act that declared Sinhalese the one official language of Ceylon. Tamil representatives naturally opposed the measure. On this point Kearney observes that

> the rapid mobilization of Sinhalese-only sentiment in the South, climaxed by the unqualified declaration of Sinhalese as the sole official language of Ceylon, appeared to be the realization of their [the

---

14. *Ibid.*, p. 232.
15. Woodward, *op. cit.*, p. 122.
16. Weerawardana, *op. cit.*, p. 99.
17. Woodward, *op. cit.*, p. 97.

Tamils] worst fears regarding the intentions of the Sinhalese majority.[18]

The new cabinet did not contain even a single Tamil. The passage of the
Official Language Act was viewed by Tamils as a serious threat to their
identity and cultural integrity. When language emerged in 1956 as the
dominant issue, Tamils and their chief spokesman, the Federal Party, became alienated from the main stream of Ceylonese politics, and have
since been either unwilling or unable to cooperate with any Sinhalese
party. Instead, to insure support from their constituents, they have expressed a desire for the establishment of a federal state that would constitutionally enshrine some measure of Tamil autonomy.

The passage of the Official Language Act heightened communal tensions. The victorious MEP coalition, which had planned to provide for
some "reasonable use of Tamil," came under pressure from Sinhalese
extremists within its own ranks and dropped these provisions from its
program. Communal violence at once erupted. A demonstration organized
by the Federal Party led to interethnic violence and further intensification
of extremist positions on both sides.

The Federal Party then threatened a nonviolent direct action campaign
if its demands on language were not met within a year. To forestall violence,
Bandaranaike agreed to recognize Tamil as the language of a national
minority and permit its use for administrative purposes in the Northern
and Eastern provinces. In return, the Federal Party agreed to call off its
campaign. But uncompromising Sinhalese immediately denounced the
pact, and communal tensions swiftly materialized into outright violence.
Tamils in the south were beaten and their homes and shops burned. Reprisals were carried out against Sinhalese in the north. Altogether hundreds
died and thousands were evacuated. A state of emergency was declared
and the army and police were ordered into action.

Shortly after the riot subsided, a Tamil Language Act was enacted,
which defined the "reasonable use of Tamil" to mean use in education,
public service entrance examinations, and "prescribed administrative purposes" in the Northern and Eastern provinces. (Extremist pressures held
up the legislation of regulations to implement the act, however, for seven
more years.) The compromising nature of the Tamil Language Act was
probably responsible for Bandaranaike's assassination in September 1959.
A convicted conspirator in the murder turned out to be a prominent Sinhalese. Kearney points to this incident as an example of "extremist
incendiarism and the opportunistic manipulation of communal passions."[19]

18. *Op. cit.*, pp. 82-83.
19. *Ibid.*, p. 88.

The Tamil response to Sinhalese-only politics has been even greater internal cohesion. The Federalist Tamil leader, Chelvanayakam, became a determined advocate of Tamil political autonomy as the only way of preserving the identity of the Tamil community.

> The Federalists became convinced that the Tamils would never be safe from the threat of domination and assimilation by the Sinhalese majority while the two communities existed together in a unitary state subject to control by the majority.[20]

Since 1956, no Tamil constituency has returned the candidate of any party other than the exclusive Tamil parties.

Elections Since 1956: The Politics of Demand Generation. The next election was held in March 1960. A revivified UNP, led by Dudley Senanayake, carried 50 seats. The Sri Lanka Freedom Party, suffering the loss of its leader, emerged with only 46 seats. As a consequence, neither party commanded a majority in the newly expanded 151-seat Parliament. This deadlock appeared made to order for Sinhalese-Tamil cooperation. The union of the Tamil Federal Party with either of the Sinhalese parties would set up a majority, coalition government, but none materialized. Neither of the Sinhalese parties could find any common ground of cooperation with the Tamils. The Federal Party demanded a federal constitution providing regional autonomy, parity for the Tamil language, and the use of Tamil as the administrative language in the north and east. Neither the UNP nor the SLFP could accept these demands and retain the support of their less compromising members.

Elections were again scheduled for July. The UNP claimed that only it could form a stable government, and accused the SLFP of Marxist tendencies. Mrs. Bandaranaike, who had been persuaded to take over the party of her late husband, actively appealed for support on the basis of his name and policies. The SLFP pledged in the campaign to complete the transition to Sinhalese as the only language of government. They won seventy-five seats, the UNP won only thirty, and the Federal Party emerged as an even more unified group with fifteen seats.

Although the new government straight away embarked on a rigorous implementation of the Sinhalese-only policy, its majority position gradually diminished as its members became dissatisfied on one or more other policies not related to language. The SLFP coalition government was finally defeated on a confidence motion in 1964. Kearney notes that from June 1964 until the March 1965 general election *"communal questions*

---

20. *Ibid.*, p. 96.

were submerged by controversy concerning the coalition's socialist aims, alleged dictatorial actions and designs, and attitude toward Buddhism."[21] Ethnicity did not therefore dominate the 1965 election.

In the 1965 election the three party coalition consisting of the SLFP, the Lanka Sama Samaja Party and the Communist Party captured 55 of 151 elective seats in the House of Representatives. The UNP won 66 seats and was able to form a government with the help of some Federalists, the Tamil Congress, and other Sinhalese. This government marked the first time that a Tamil served as a minister in the cabinet since 1956. In January 1966 the first provisions were announced for the actual use of Tamil since the enactment of the original Tamil Language Act of 1958. The UNP came to power on a campaign which charged Bandaranaike's government with dictatorial practices and economic mismanagement.

The new SLFP opposition harped on communal themes in the hope of splitting the Sinhalese and Tamil supporters of the government or creating a strong Sinhalese reaction against the UNP. Communalism again became the dominant issue of Ceylonese politics.

> The attack on the Government by utilizing language and communal issues appeared to be automatic. . . . The possibility of exploiting Sinhalese reaction to the presence of the Federal Party in the Government and the anticipated announcement of a language settlement must have readily suggested itself to the opposition.[22]

Ceylonese politics demonstrates a periodic regularity. Mrs. Bandaranaike succeeded in 1960 by relying on the ethnic issue, but lost in 1965 when language could not be invoked as a genuine issue. The UNP had succeeded in campaigning on economic and personality issues, *viz.,* Mrs. Bandaranaike's personal dictatorial powers and the general disrepair of Ceylon's economy. By 1970, ethnicity again became salient. Of the 1970 election, *Newsweek* (June 8, 1970) reports that "Mrs. Bandaranaike also had played upon the ethnic chauvinism of the Sinhala-speaking Buddhist majority, whom Senanayake had kept from the throats of the mainly Hindu Tamils."[23] Senanayake and the UNP won only 17 of 151 elective seats whereas the SLFP of Mrs. Bandaranaike won 90 seats. Mrs. B's government represents the first two-thirds victory since independence in 1948 and permits her ruling party to amend the constitution without opposition support. The UNP had campaigned on the theme of maintaining steady economic progress; they lost to the politics of ethnic extremism.[24]

---

21. *Ibid.*, p. 128 (emphasis added).
22. *Ibid.*, p. 133.
23. P. 41.
24. For details of the 1970 election, see *The New York Times*, May 29, 1970, pp. 1 and 3.

Politics in Ceylon: Lessons from the Dominant Majority Configuration.
The conclusions that emerge from a substantive review of Ceylonese electoral politics are consistent with our theoretical expectations.

1. *Little or no interethnic cooperation takes place during the nationalist struggle for independence.* In the dominant majority configuration, a nationalist party of the ethnic majority can secure a majority vote from the entire electorate without support from minorities. British requirements for independence, *viz.*, a responsible party that commands broad support, existed in the United National Party of D. S. Senanayake, which commanded the allegiance of a majority of the Ceylonese population; Tamil participation therefore was not essential in the nationalist struggle. The Tamil-Sinhalese split of 1921 took place only two years after the founding of the multiethnic Ceylon National Congress; nationalism grew primarily as a Sinhalese activity (although the swabhasha campaign had momentarily held Sinhalese together with some non-English-educated Tamils after independence).

2. *Ethnic communities provide the major sources of political support.*
Immediately after the Tamils withdrew from the Ceylon National Congress, they formed their own, ethnically distinct, organizations. The constitutional debates over representation between the two world wars reflected intracommunal consensus (A.1) and intercommunal conflict (A.2): Sinhalese preferred a majoritarian scheme in contrast to the Tamil preference for a "fifty-fifty" balanced arrangement. The debates further reflected the joint belief that communal issues would dominate politics in an independent Ceylon. There existed, then, a perceptual consensus (A.3)—the lines of conflict were drawn, hardened, and in full view of everyone.

3. *The politics of moderation gives way to the politics of outbidding.*
When ethnicity is salient, as we have seen in several other cases, intense communal electorates invariably favor the extremist position in contrast to a more moderate or ambiguous one. The UNP lost the 1956 election on opposition charges of gradualism and recalcitrance in implementing Sinhalese as the sole official language. Again in July 1960, appeals to uncompromising Sinhalese and the memory of the late Prime Minister Bandaranaike forged victory for Mrs. Bandaranaike and the SLFP.

The ethnic issue played a lesser role in the 1965 election. For the first time since 1956, moderate politicians could raise national issues (e.g., economic growth), and make them credible, because the policies of Mrs. Bandaranaike's government had resulted in economic stagnation, widespread corruption and increasingly dictatorial rule. The salience of linguistic issues correspondingly declined. A coalition of dissatisfied minorities gradually increased until Mrs. Bandaranaike's government was defeated on a confidence motion in 1964. She had come to power on the ethnic issue and had now lost her governing majority in spite of it. She was subsequently unable to generate demand for ethnicity in 1965. By 1970, however, she could, as a member of the opposition, charge the UNP government with pro-Tamil policies. Her appeals to the ethnic chauvinism of the Sinhalese majority won for the SLFP the most impressive victory in the history of Ceylonese electoral politics.[25]

4. *Dominant majorities often manipulate the rules of the electoral game to obtain or maintain partisan advantage.* Table 5.1 shows how the disenfranchisement of Indian Tamils has benefitted the Sinhalese, regardless of party. That is, following the 1948 and 1949 Citizenship Acts, which reduced the Tamil electorate by half, the Sinhalese have gained fifteen of the eighteen seats that Indian Tamils might otherwise have won. A gain of five seats immediately accrued to Sinhalese candidates in the 1952 election, the first after the Indian disenfranchisement.

5. *The minority communities, which possess little or no possibility of exercising political power, often resort to extra-legal methods.* The Federal

Table 5.1

Distribution of Parliamentary Seats Among Communal Groups, 1947-65

	Sinha-lese	Ceylon Tamils	Ceylon Moors	Indians	Other	Total
Seats due on population basis	66	12	6	10	1	95
Seats won:						
1947	69	13	5	7	1	95
1952	74	13	7	0	1	95
1956	75	12	7	0	1	95
Seats due on population basis	106	17	10	18	0	151
Seats won:						
1960 (March)	123	18	9	0	1	151
1960 (July)	122	18	10	0	1	151
1965	121	18	11	0	1	151

Source: Calvin A. Woodward, *The Growth of a Party System in Ceylon* (Providence: Brown University Press, 1969), p. 258.

25. Despite the fact that Senanayake and the UNP have no real direction to go but up in the 1975 election (unless it is held sooner), we must note that Mrs. Bandaranaike probably will not be able to invoke the linguistic issue, as defecting members of her government will have left on some other basis even though they agree with her pro-Sinhalese outlook, e.g., the 1971 leftist insurrection. The salient issue of the 1975 election should shift to a nonethnic dimension and the moderate stance of Senanayake should be more attractive to voters. Mrs. B's appeal to the World Bank for development funds and her decision not to nationalize foreign banks in Ceylon in December 1970 to stave off economic regression indicate her awareness of Senanayake's likely future campaign theme.

Party threatened a nonviolent direct action campaign in 1957 to obtain
minimum demands for the Tamil language. During the next year massive
violence rocked Ceylon: Sinhalese officials living in Tamil-majority regions
were set upon and beaten and reprisals were carried out in Sinhalese areas.
Another massive Tamil campaign was conducted in 1961 and additional
rioting took place in Colombo in 1966, also over the language issue. We
should also note that a disenchanted Sinhalese extremist assassinated Mr.
Bandaranaike over his tolerance towards Tamils.

Majority Dominance: Five Additional Cases

As shown above, Ceylon displays a pattern of ethnic politics that differs,
because of its configuration, from the basic model of competitive ethnic
politics. Minority Tamils do not and have generally never shared significantly in governmental decison making. Since the separation of the Tamils
from the Ceylon National Congress in 1921, just two years after the incep-
tion of the modern nationalist movement, there has been little interethnic
cooperation. Instead, abrogation or curtailment of democratic practices
and institutions, albeit by a different route, are the outcomes, legitimate
or not, with which minorities must learn to live.

The cases of Northern Ireland, Cyprus, Mauritius, Rwanda, and Zanzibar also reflect many of the regularities of the dominant majority configuration. They display several variations, however, which pose a minor
classification problem. In Northern Ireland, for example, internal politics
became singularly important after 1920, when the Government of Ireland
Act separated Ulster from the Republic of Ireland and established two
separate parliaments. Ethnic controversy is, however, deeply rooted in
Irish history and still affects the current Catholic-Protestant dispute. The
majority Protestants, who comprise two-thirds of Ulster's population,
agitate for continued membership in the United Kingdom on the one hand,
while, on the other hand, the minority Catholics, comprising one-third of
the population, agitate for union with Ireland. No basis exists for an independence movement as such, but sharp nationalist sentiments often give
rises to outbursts of violence. The Protestants in particular fear submergence in an all-Ireland Catholic state, whereas the Catholics claim job,
housing and political discrimination under the present regime. Although
politics in Ulster is not characteristic of the typical nationalist movement
of the colonial plural society, the regularities of machinations, ethnic parties, violence, and the politics of outbidding still obtain.

Cyprus fits more readily into the model of the recently independent
plural society. Cypriots received their independence from Britain on
August 16, 1960, after several decades of Greek Cypriot agitation. Mauritius, too, is a classic object lesson of the colonial plural society. Inde-

pendence day was celebrated on March 12, 1968, only to be followed by racial violence four days later.

Rwanda and Zanzibar are more difficult to analyze. Rwanda obtained independence on July 1, 1962, after more than fifty years of foreign rule first by the Germans and then, after World War I, by the Belgians. Both colonial powers ruled indirectly through the traditional hierarchical system in which the Tutsi, a small ethnic minority representing one-seventh of the population, had for over four hundred years maintained social, political and economic dominance over the Hutu, who make up about eighty-five percent of the population. Democratization and the franchise, however, radically changed Rwandan politics. As a result of extensive rioting in 1959 and 1960, and an election in 1961, the Hutu majority wrested power from the Tutsi and abolished the traditional monarchy. Independence followed shortly.[26]

Only since 1959 does Rwanda qualify as an element in the dominant majority configuration. Since the 1961 election, the Hutu majority controls the government and thousands of Tutsi have recently fled to neighboring countries. From our perspective of the early 1970s we designate Rwanda as a dominant majority case, even though a minority ruled throughout most of her history.

Zanzibar also escapes easy classification. Between 1800 and 1963 a small Arab oligarchy exercised authority, first under the Omani Sultanate, and then under the status of a British Protectorate. Universal suffrage and parliamentary rule, introduced with postwar constitutional advancement, inaugurated a period of competition between Arabs, indigenous Africans (shirazi), and immigrant mainland Africans. Between 1957 and 1963, these communities contested four general elections with steady African gains. Since the January 1964 revolution and the attendant merger with Tanganyika, Zanzibar is now an example of a dominant majority configuration, although the Arab minority played the major role in government before the revolution.

Since the mid-1960s Rwanda and Zanzibar each exhibit the general features of majority dominance. We therefore choose to subsume these countries under the majority rubric in our analysis of their politics, even though their past histories qualify them for the dominant minority category prior to 1960. Important aspects of the premajority period are noted, though, and can be compared with the observations we record about the minority configuration that appear in the next chapter.

---

26. See Philip Mason, *Patterns of Dominance* (London: Oxford University Press for the Institute of Race Relations, 1970), pp. 13-20; Richard F. Nyrop, et al., *Area Handbook for Rwanda* (Washington: U.S. Government Printing Office, 1969), especially chapters 1, 2, 4, and 6; and René Lemarchand, *Rwanda and Burundi* (New York: Frederick A. Praeger, 1970).

Nationalist Politics: The Absence of Interethnic Cooperation

Ethnic groups in dominant majority societies generally tend not to cooperate with each other. This is probably due to the fact that the majority community commands by itself adequate resources to demand and successfully obtain independence. The five illustrations we present below highlight this characteristic of majority configurations.[27]

Northern Ireland. Northern Ireland is an established European plural society.[28] That part of its history which is relevant for an understanding of contemporary politics begins in 1603 when English rule became strongly entrenched in the north of Ireland following the defeat of the Irish Earls by Crown forces. Native Irish were ordered off the better lands to make room for Protestant settlers from Scotland and England; some remained on the less desirable lands as laborers and rent-payers. The desire of James II to raise and finance a large army in Ireland, where his Catholic sympathizers still had considerable power, further crystallized the Protestant-Catholic division in the late seventeenth century. He called a Parliament in Dublin that confiscated over two thousand Protestant estates. Many Protestants in the north took refuge in Enniskillen and Londonderry and held out until they were finally liberated by William of Orange when he defeated James at the Battle of the Boyne on July 12, 1690. Protestants still regard this victory as a symbol of their deliverance from the forces of Rome, and celebrate it today as a national holiday. The defeat further subordinated Catholics under Protestant rule.

Modern political developments date from 1920 when the promulgation of the Government of Ireland Act partitioned Ireland into Ulster (six counties in the north) and the Republic of Ireland. Since 1920, political power has remained in the hands of the Unionist Party, which is backed by the militant Protestant Orange order. Voting trends have, since the Act of Partition, strictly reflected the main religious divisions. The two communities in Northern Ireland, divided at the start, have retained their

---

27. We remind the reader of our intent to use analytical, not geographical, categories. This may cause some unevenness in presentation at times, but our concern is with cross-national theoretical comparisons. For detailed historical accounts, the reader may refer to the footnote citations.

28. For an excellent summary treatment of the Catholic-Protestant conflict in Northern Ireland see *Orange and Green: A Quaker Study of Community Relations in Northern Ireland* (Yorkshire, England: Northern Friends Peace Board, 1969). An earlier but more detailed treatment is found in Denis P. Barritt and Charles F. Carter, *The Northern Ireland Problem: A Study in Group Relations* (London: Oxford University Press, 1962). More recently Richard Rose has published the results of a study of religious attitudes completed in Ulster in the late 1960s. See *Governing Without Consent: An Irish Perspective* (Boston: Beacon, 1971). Unless otherwise quoted, most of our information is derived from the *Orange and Green* pamphlet.

separateness ever since, and the divisions can be seen in all aspects of religious, political, educational, social, and cultural life.

Cyprus. The nationalist struggle in Cyprus closely approximates the Ceylonese pattern.[29] With the arrival of the first British High Commissioner in Cyprus on July 12, 1878, Ottoman rule was terminated. The immigration of Turks during the previous period of Ottoman rule effectively increased the number of Turkish Cypriot Muslims to 190,000, about one-fourth of the population; Greek Cypriot Orthodox Christians form the remaining three-quarters. Nationalism in Cyprus displayed a near exclusive Greek character, taking the form of a movement of *Enosis,* which symbolized union with Greece. Turkish Cypriot Muslims, behaving much like the Tamil minority in Ceylon, displayed their opposition to Enosis (and independence for that matter) from the very outset. Legislative Council politics reveals the contradictory preference of the two communities. On the council, nine elected votes belonged to Greeks and three to Turks. British administrators, who controlled six votes, depended regularly on the three Turkish votes to offset a unified Greek vote.

> The structure of the Council was such that the government depended on the Turkish minority for the Legislative Council to function. This practice fostered divisiveness between Greeks and Turks. From the very beginning, the Greek members became the permanent opposition to the British-Turkish alliance.[30]

Communalism persisted throughout the independence movement and still pervades politics in independent Cyprus. The Orthodox Church, a strong promoter of Enosis, continually refused to cooperate with British constitutional proposals; the Turks, in defensive reaction, put forth their own demand for partition or double Enosis. Although a compromise constitution was worked out at Zurich and London, the two communities have been generally unable and unwilling to abide by its provisions, as we show in detail below.

Mauritius. Indians, comprising sixty-seven percent of the population, are the overwhelming majority in Mauritius, an island nation in the Indian Ocean. Fifty-one percent of them are Hindus and the remaining sixteen percent Muslims. The balance, consisting basically of Africans,

---

29. Unless otherwise indicated, our data is taken from Stanley Kyriakides, *Cyprus: Constitutionalism and Crisis Government* (Philadelphia: University of Pennsylvania Press, 1968). See also T. W. Adams, "The First Republic of Cyprus: A Review of an Unworkable Constitution," *The Western Political Quarterly* 19, no. 3 (September 1966): 475-90.
30. Kyriakides, *op. cit.,* p. 15.

mixed, and some Europeans, totals about thirty percent. Chinese represent an insignificant minority of about three percent.[31]

No community can lay claim to being the indigenous inhabitants of Mauritius. The French, who claimed the island in 1715, established a plantation system and brought in French colonists from the island of Reunion who, in turn, relied chiefly on slave labor. The island passed into British hands in 1810; the new masters abolished the slave trade in Mauritius in 1813 and freed all resident slaves in 1835. Emancipation, as in Guyana, produced a labor shortage and the planters substituted indentured labor from India between 1835 and 1907 when the system was terminated. Altogether more than 450,000 Indians arrived during this period and only 160,000 returned home after their contract of indenture expired. The Indians, moreover, brought their entire families with them and have, therefore, retained a communally oriented culture. White French creoles, Africans, Indians, and Chinese generally live apart from each other as is the case in Furnivall's description of the plural society.

Ethnic considerations are of paramount political importance in Mauritius. The first constitution, introduced in 1886, contained a restricted franchise that placed political control in the hands of the Europeans. Empire-wide changes after World War II led, however, to a new constitution in 1948 with a vastly expanded franchise. During the first major election contested under this new constitution Indians won twenty-nine of forty elective seats, dropped down to twenty-five in 1963, and the Independence Party (Indian in composition) of S. Ramgoolam, the Prime Minister, won thirty-nine of sixty-two seats in the 1967 preindependence general election. The Parti Maurician, the party of whites and Africans, won only twenty-three seats in 1967, and, not surprisingly, voted unanimously against independence out of fear of Indian domination.[32] The Independence Party, chiefly representative of Indians, commanded sufficient strength by itself to approve the constitutional referendum for independence. Creole and African votes were not crucial and their unanimous opposition did not compel the British to postpone the granting of independence.

Rwanda. Rwanda's history, as previously discussed, shows marked ethnic divisions. The Hutu were subordinated to a Tutsi feudal kingdom for nearly 400 years until the advent of the franchise and representative democracy allowed the numerically dominant Hutu to turn the tables on

---

31. The major work on Mauritius is that of Burton Benedict, *Mauritius: Problems of a Plural Society* (London: Pall Mall Press for the Institute of Race Relations, 1965). The figures reported above are taken from *Mauritius: Fact Sheets on the Commonwealth* (London: British Information Services, 1966), p. 2.
32. See *The New York Times,* August 9, 1967, p. 4.

their former rulers: many Tutsis have since become refugees in neighboring countries.

Zanzibar. Zanzibar's origin as a plural society can be traced to the establishment of the administrative capital of the Sultanate of Oman on the island in the early nineteenth century.[33] The settlement of the Sultanate was followed by the arrival of large numbers of Arab immigrants who brought with them their entire families. The Arab community soon planted cloves as an export crop and, in the process, gradually acquired most of the choice African land. Furthermore, they steadily expanded direct political and judicial powers over Africans with a system of district officers and brought in Indians to work as clerks in the Sultan's administration. Traders from India also arrived. Arabs thus exercised a monopoly of political power and later extended their political control to the island of Pemba (now a constituent part of Zanzibar), whose leaders had requested Arab intervention to relieve the residents of Pemba from their oppressive rulers in Mombasa on the nearby east coast of Africa.

Although the British established a protectorate over Zanzibar in 1890 they did not alter the racial quality of Zanzibar's class structure. Colonial practices were designed to preserve Arab elite status, even in the face of the introduction of the universal franchise after World War II. This decision to preserve the elite status of Arabs is especially intriguing since Africans comprise seventy-six percent of the population, Arabs about seventeen percent, and Asians six percent. And these communities are very tightly knit.

> The strength of communal separatism was exemplified in broad and long-standing acceptance of the practice of racial representation in the Legislative Council, in the presence of innumerable racial and communal bodies, and in the fact that even sports, social life, and the local press were organized on communal lines. The election [1957] demonstrated the persistence of these communal loyalties and revealed that they had entered the modern parliamentary arena as the most powerful basis of political affiliation.[34]

The Zanzibar Nationalist Party, dominated by the Arab elite, was in the forefront of the independence movement. They capitalized on the internal divisions between Pemba Africans and Zanzibari Africans; the former historically had requested, and still viewed themselves as living

---

33. For an excellent treatment of ethnic politics in Zanzibar, and one upon which we rely extensively, see Michael F. Lofchie, *Zanzibar: Background to Revolution* (Princeton: Princeton University Press, 1965.)
34. *Ibid.*, p. 179.

under, benign Arab rule, whereas the latter had been deprived of their land and felt politically oppressed. A coalition party was thus formed consisting of the Arab-based Zanzibar Nationalist Party and the Zanzibar and Pemba People's Party, the latter almost exclusively representing the Pemba shirazis: each of the adherents to this alliance professed common belief in Islam.

African extremists, comprised chiefly of Hadimu (an indigenous tribe) and mainland African immigrants who belong to the Afro-Shirazi Party, had successively increased their share of the vote in the 1957, the two 1961, and the 1963 elections. Due to their disproportionate victories in several heavily African single-member constituencies, they received an absolute majority of the vote in the 1963 election, but only a minority of the seats. Independence was thus granted to a minority Arab government that possessed some Pemba African support. African militant leaders, who believed that peaceful constitutional practices implied permanent Arab rule, revolted in January 1964 — just one month after independence — and immediately placed Afro-Shirazi leaders in control of government. A subsequent merger with Tanganyika rendered the minority Arab position even more tenuous. Thousands of Arabs have perished or become impoverished since the advent of African rule and economic dislocations following the revolution have also significantly diminished Asian fortunes. Since the Africans have come to power, there has been no cooperation with Arabs or Asians.

The Ethnic Basis of Political Cohesion

In those plural societies with dominant majority configurations, ethnicity is customarily the sole grounds for political cohesion, organization and action. For example, the two major parties in Northern Ireland are organized exclusively on religious grounds. Rose finds that very little inclination exists among Ulstermen to cross religious lines in their voting. Ninety-five percent of Unionist supporters are Protestants, and ninety-nine percent of Nationalist supporters are Catholics.[35] The preeminence of the Unionist Party is based upon its identification with the United Kingdom government at Westminster; it is a natural majority party, threatened only by the long-term possibility that higher fertility rates among Catholics might reverse its majority status.

The divisions between Catholics and Protestants, which are hardened and in full view of everyone, eliminate ambiguity in party positions. Rose shows that survey respondents of both religious groups identify the Nation-

---

35. Richard Rose, *op. cit.*, chapter 7, p. 235.

alist Party with unification of Ireland and the Unionist Party with unity with Britain. The Unionists have totally dominated electoral politics since 1920. In many elections Unionist candidates have been returned to the Ulster Parliament unopposed, while defiant, though successful, Nationalist M.P.'s have often refused to take their seats in protest against Protestant rule. With few exceptions in the fifty years of Northern Ireland's separate existence, all elections have been fought between the two major parties over the issue of "for" or "against" continued unity with Britain. Such explicitly nonreligious parties as the Northern Ireland Labor Party and the Liberals have been extremely unsuccessful. As confirmation of the futility of a nonreligious appeal, only six of the fifty-two elective seats for the Stormont assembly were won by candidates from minor parties in 1969. As Rose concludes in chapter 8 of his Irish study

> the observed voting patterns of Protestants and Catholics show that the two major parties are nearly 100 percent sectarian in their support.[36]

In Cyprus, as in Ulster, political organizations mirror ethnic divisions. Turkish and Greek Cypriots each preserve distinct ethnic indentities, express mutual mistrust, and refuse to cooperate with one another. The two ethnic groups are crystallized into opposing political communities, each possessing intense and incompatible preferences. Makarios and the Greek Orthodox Church of Cyprus expressed Greek sentiments in the drive for *Enosis* with Greece while Turkish feelings led to their demands for partition or union with Turkey. Members of each community adhere almost perfectly to the sentiments of their own communal leaders.

Leaders in Mauritius also organized parties along racial dimensions. The most important of these, the Labor Party, is supported primarily by Hindus and some Muslims. It has been the majority party of government since 1959. (It is now a member of the Independence Party.) Whites and Africans, the two other major communities in Mauritius, underpin the Parti Mauricien.[37] This party is led by a mulatto attorney, Gaetan Duval, who has been depicted as the leader of 213,000 ex-slave descendants and 10,000 whites.[38] Voters cross ethnic lines only on rare occasions, so that nearly all political competition is racially oriented. Even the constitution, which incorporated territorial and ethnic criteria as a basis of constituency delimitation, explicitly recognizes the ethnic and religious diversity of the island. And, elections in 1959 and 1963 show a close correlation between

36. *Ibid.*, p. 266.
37. See Figure 3.5 and the discussion pertaining to it for a theoretically suggestive interpretation of cooperation between minority communities.
38. *Time*, August 18, 1967, pp. 30-31.

the seats obtained by members of the principal ethnic communities and their corresponding percentages in the overall population.[39] Hindus, who make up just over half the population, obtained twenty-four of forty seats in 1959, and twenty in 1963. Muslims, at sixteen percent, won five seats each time. Creoles and whites, comprising thirty percent, gained eleven and fourteen seats respectively.

Rwanda also reveals a near unbridgeable gap between its Hutu and Tutsi elements. Hierarchical rule in a Tutsi-dominated feudal kingdom lasted over 400 years, until Belgians were charged by the United Nations Trusteeship Council to prepare Rwanda for independence. Changes were initially made in the system of electing members to advisory councils and, with the introduction of the secret ballot, the Hutu achieved marked gains on the lower councils. Shortly after the Hutu success in these elections, nine important Hutu leaders publicized a document which declared Rwanda's principal problem to be Tutsi domination in political, social and economic activities. The publication of this document was followed by the formation of the Party of the Hutu Emancipation Movement (PARME-HUTU) in 1959. Two years later (1961) PARMEHUTU began its domination of electoral politics. Although Tutsi interests were mobilized and expressed in the Rwanda National Party (UNAR), it could only obtain 16.8 percent of the vote in the balloting for the 1961 Legislative Assembly election. PARMEHUTU, on the other hand, received 77.7 percent of the vote. And on the question of continuing the monarchy, the vote was 80 percent negative. These election results correspond closely with the distribution of Hutu and Tutsi in the Rwanda population and thus the ethnic basis of politics in contemporary Rwanda seems established.[40]

Ethnic cleavages in Zanzibar are somewhat more complex, due chiefly to the internal divisions among the Africans. Four distinct groups of Africans reside in Zanzibar: the Hadimu, who are the subjects of the most extensive Arab repression and loss of land; the Tumbatu, a generally uninvolved fishing community; the Pemba, whose relations with Arabs were on the cordial side; and the mainlanders, chiefly urban proletarians who make up the bulk of the African extremists. A small community of Asians also resides in Zanzibar, but they have normally abstained from political activity.

As Lofchie makes clear, these divisions determine the basis of party organization.

> Since the election of 1957, party and racial conflict had become practically synonymous, for party membership was based essentially on racial divisions. Indeed, members of all communities viewed their

---

39. Benedict, *op. cit.*, pp. 43-67.
40. Nyrop et al., *op. cit.*, chapters 1 and 2.

party affiliation as a projection of the ethnic hostilities between their own community and others in the society.[41]

The political expression of these different communities is found, therefore, in separate political parties. Arabs comprised the Zanzibar Nationalist Party, Pemba Africans the Zanzibar and Pemba People's Party, and Hadimu and mainland Africans the Afro-Shirazi Party.

Ambiguity, Moderation, and the Politics of Outbidding

Only in Zanzibar do we observe a conscious effort at ambiguous politics, and it is confined to the platforms and policies of the minority parties. It is easy to account for this observation. The Arab-based Zanzibar Nationalist Party, as a minority party, required African support to win elections.[42] They tried to obtain this support by stressing the themes of Islamic tradition and national loyalty to the Sultanate in their campaigns.

> Arab nationalism, despite its *liberal multi-racial ethos*, was basically a conservative if not altogether reactionary phenomenon. It was an effort to return Zanzibar to a pre-colonial political condition, namely oligarchic rule, by a small landowning minority. While this would have been *disguised in the form of a multi-racial party* operating through formal parliamentary institutions, the political reality of autocratic rule by a small ethnic elite would, for all practical purposes, have been a return to the condition existing in the nineteenth century before the establishment of the Protectorate.[43]

ZNP leaders accentuated nonracial political doctrines and attempted to discredit the racial political thinking of the African extremists in order to undermine the communal appeal of the African-based Afro-Shirazi Party. Arab speakers thus constantly emphasized the Muslim character of the Zanzibar nationalist movement.

The majority Afro-Shirazi Party harped on communal themes alluding that ZNP rule meant continued Arab colonialism. Since the African community constituted a substantial majority, Afro-Shirazi leaders could concentrate squarely on appeals to their potential supporters.

We observe very briefly that two minority parties in Rwanda also appealed for national unity. Both the Rwanda National Union Party and the Rwanda Democratic Rally, supported mainly by the Tutsi minority,

41. *Op. cit.,* p. 204.
42. The existence of a universal franchise in Zanzibar, which is not the case in South Africa, Rhodesia and Burundi (chapter 6), forced the Arab minority to reconcile its electoral strategy with the requirements of majority rule.
43. Lofchie, *op. cit.,* p. 157 (emphasis added).

advocated harmonious relations between Rwanda's constituent groups; each proposed that the constitutional monarchy be maintained (probably to preserve continued Tutsi rule).

Outbidding: The Politics of Ethnic Extremism. From time to time, moderates appear in the electoral arena of plural societies but usually fail to retain long-run support from their constituents. Extremist entrepreneurs resort to ethnic demand generation and moderates are often compelled to adopt a less compromising stance to avoid defeat.

Extremist Catholics in Ulster look to the Irish Republican Army, a small revolutionary group of militant Irish nationalists, whose aim is to unite the two Irelands. The Army is banned in both Southern and Northern Ireland, but its slogans appear on street walls in Belfast, especially during periods of violence. In Protestant circles, steady progress towards moderation during the middle 1960s divided the ruling Unionists into hard-liners and liberals. The latter have moved, albeit slowly, in trying to redress housing and job inequities between the two communities while the former, exemplified by the Reverend Ian Paisley, have warned that even the slightest concessions toward Catholics mean rule by Rome.

The effect of such extremists as Paisley is clearly evident in Ulster politics. When Captain O'Neill took over the Premiership from Viscount Brookborough in 1963, it was thought by many to be the beginning of a new liberal era. O'Neill invited the Prime Minister of Ireland to Belfast for a visit in 1965, the first time leaders in the two countries had met in forty-one years. This visit, though, was singularly unpopular with Unionist hard-liners.

Paisley was arrested and imprisoned in the same year and a clandestine militant Protestant group, the "Ulster Volunteer Force," made its appearance; the government immediately declared it illegal under the Special Powers Act. Meanwhile, militant Catholics began to protest O'Neill's slow implementation of "liberal" reforms that, in turn, led to even more extremist demands by the Protestant hard-liners. Paisley's recent election to Parliament in 1970 demonstrates the resurging sentiment of Protestant extremism. "His election has upset more moderate Protestants who had hoped to build ties with the estranged Catholic community."[44]

Earlier in 1970 Paisley had won a by-election to fill a vacant seat in Northern Ireland's Parliament. He had fought that election as a Protestant Unionist and one of his slogans was "Stop the Sellout" — meaning the concessions that had been made to Catholics in the past three or four years of civil rights movements.[45] The successes of Paisley signal the demise

---

44. *The New York Times,* June 28, 1970, p. 18.
45. *The New York Times,* April 17, 1970, p. 11.

of moderation. Massive communal rioting erupted in August 1969 and its chronic recurrence throughout 1970 and 1971 suggests that Catholics and Protestants are as sharply separated as ever, and that the majority Protestant community is unwilling to support a policy of moderation and compromise — especially since a greater Catholic birth rate threatens to wipe out their majority status. Protestants must be aware of the fact that one-half of Ulster's primary school children are Catholic.

O'Neill and his associates had tried to incorporate Catholics into the Ulster regime. They stressed economic issues and tried to downgrade the religious question. This strategy seemed viable when, in a snap general election in November 1965, his faction gained two seats. Since that election, however, the rise of Paisley and Protestant extremism spells repudiation of the liberal outlook. Extremism and street violence in 1969, 1970, and 1971 have governed ethnic politics in Northern Ireland.

Moderation, we just saw, quickly disappeared as a viable political strategy in Ulster. In Cyprus moderates were unable to command any degree of Greek or Turkish Cypriot support. Intensely held preferences within the two communities and the value of the stakes for which they were playing mitigated against compromise and moderation.

> Among both Greek and Turkish Cypriots there are moderates who do want to try to make the Zurich settlement work. In both communities there are extremists who want it to fail and who are prepared to resort to open violence. The constitution's creaking performance so far has naturally played into the hands of the extremists on both sides.[46]

The history of ethnic politics in Cyprus reveals a steady crystallization and intensification of ethnic hatred; an outbreak of intercommunal conflict in 1963 almost brought Turkey and Greece to the brink of war. A United Nations peacekeeping force intervened in March 1964 to contain the conflict in Cyprus. Kyriakides records that this United Nations force has been instrumental in easing tension and promoting freer movement of the population; all-out war between Turkey and Greece over Cyprus was thus averted.[47] He cautions in his conclusions, however, that undue optimism for a peaceful future of harmonious Greek-Turk relations may be misleading.

Moderation in Mauritius is also notably absent. Indians and Africans are crystallized into two distinct political parties, represented respectively by the Independence Party of the Prime Minister S. Ramgoolam and the Parti Mauricien of Gaetan Duval. Attempts at moderation or compromise

---

46. *The Economist,* January 4, 1964, p. 10.
47. *Op. cit.,* p. 153.

are likely to cost each leader the support of his constituents. The *New Statesman* plainly points to this constraint.

> Both Mr. Duval and Ramgoolam . . . are imprisoned by their parties and forced to adopt racial attitudes. If they come to some real compromise agreement they would both lose the support of influential extremist elements in their parties.[48]

Our final example, Zanzibar, also evinces the demise of moderation in favor of the politics of outbidding. The Pemba African party consciously avoided racial politics since many Pemba shirazi viewed mainland Africans with distrust, out of possible fear of Christianizing influences in Tanganyika. Many believed that mainland immigrants were not loyal to Zanzibar; furthermore, Pemba shirazi owed an historical debt of gratitude to Arabs who had relieved them of oppressive rule from Mombasa.

At the outset, then, Pemba shirazi leaders refused to join in the Afro-Shirazi Party. Pemba politicians appealed almost exclusively to shirazi voters, emphasizing their special needs, and stating their objectives in such terms as constitutional monarchy, rapid evolution towards independence, and nonracial government policies. Spokesmen charged that militant Afro-Shirazi Party leaders would suppress the Muslim faith, convert Zanzibar to Christianity, and hand it over to Tanganyika (the latter fear, in fact, materialized quickly after independence).

The multiracial and Islamic appeals of the Pemba shirazi, in a coalition with the Arab-based ZNP, produced electoral victories in 1957, 1961, and 1963, although with successively diminishing vote totals. Once the African militants were able to make *race* the sole salient issue, the appeals to national loyalty and Islamic devotion proved inefficacious and ethnic identification became decisively important. Thus, the combined ZNP/ZPPP vote totals steadily diminished and finally fell below fifty percent in the final 1963 election.

Machinations: The Manipulation of Ethnic Politics

Dominant majorities often try to insure permanent advantage by manipulating the rules of the political game. These procedures often take the form of gerrymandering, disenfranchisement of minority voters, harassment of opposition leaders, restrictive job and housing policies, etc. Northern Ireland provides an excellent case study of the manipulative practices of a dominant majority.

---

48. May 21, 1965, p. 794.

The predominant fear of the Protestant community is that some day Catholics may comprise a majority of the population. Catholic fertility rates outdistance those of the Protestants and nearly half of the primary school age population is Catholic. Until now, extensive Catholic migration to Britain and overseas has kept Catholics in a minority status. Nevertheless, Protestants practice systematic discrimination against Catholics.

A major bone of contention has been the one man–one vote controversy. Elections from Ulster constituencies to Parliament at Westminster are based upon United Kingdom laws; election to the Stormont Parliament and local councils with Northern Ireland are based on special Ulster laws. These laws serve to overrepresent Protestant interests. Complaints of gerrymandering and plural voting are easily justifiable in the realm of local government. The authors of *Orange and Green* note that there are some 240,000 fewer electors on the Local Government register than the Stormont List. This discrepancy follows from two provisions:

> 1. An elector must be the owner or tenant of a dwelling house of rateable value of ten pounds or over for three months prior to the election, and
>
> 2. Limited Companies are entitled to appoint one nominee to vote for every ten pounds of valuation up to a maximum of six votes. This provision was repealed in November 1968, and it is now agreed that the first will not apply in the next Local Government elections.[49]

Although the granting of one man–one vote will disproportionately enfranchise more Catholics than Protestants, because of large families and more doubling up, it will not totally offset the effects of gerrymandering.

Gerrymandering is particularly effective in maintaining Protestant control of municipal councils in Catholic majority communities. The Local Government Act of 1922 empowers the Ministry of Local Government to alter Urban and County Council boundaries. In many cases a large proportion of poorer property is included in one ward, so that fewer votes are needed in wealthier wards. Since the richer property is usually Protestant, a permanent majority is easily created. Unionist Councils tend to allocate houses to Catholics only in Catholic wards to maintain the voting patterns. The towns of Londonderry, Armagh, and Omagh contain respectively sixty-nine, fifty-nine, and sixty-one percent Catholic residents, yet Unionists are a majority in each Town Council. "The allocation of houses appears to be badly biased, and the main purpose appears to be to maintain the established voting balance, and thus prevent any challenge

---

49. *Op. cit.*, p. 20.

to the party controlling the Council."[50] Protestants comprise a majority in the overall Ulster population and can reasonably expect to seat a majority in Stormont. On the other hand, Catholics are a majority in some local areas. Manipulative practices have enabled Protestant minorities to govern even some of these Catholic majority towns.

Machinations have figured in the politics of independent Cyprus especially between 1961 and 1963. Greece and Turkey each played a significant part in determining the provisions of Cyprus's constitution. The Turks were overly successful in obtaining concessions for their minority compatriots in Cyprus; guarantees, e.g., that Turks be given thirty percent of all Public Service positions, were obtained that were disproportionate to the numerical strength of the Turkish Cypriot community. The Greek community refused to implement fully the seventy-thirty ratio in the Public Service and in retaliation, Turkish Cypriots refused to vote for tax legislation—a majority vote of each community is required to pass such legislation. In response to persistent Turkish recalcitrance, Greeks refused to extend the Municipalities law, and so forth.

These administrative deadlocks persuaded the Greeks to propose sweeping constitutional amendments, which, if implemented, would have established a unitary state, majority rule, and have eliminated the special safeguards for Turks. Turkey rejected Makarios's proposals as inimical to her interests. Violence erupted between the two communities in 1963 and since then they remain fundamentally separated as ever in outlook.

Leaders in Rwanda have not yet felt the need for manipulative practices. Since independence, the population balance has shifted even more in favor of the majority Hutu community; many Tutsi have left the country seeking refuge elsewhere. Their proportion in the population has declined from fourteen percent to about eleven percent. Possessing adequate police and military safeguards, Hutu leaders can allow Tutsis to participate in the political process. Tutsis are too few in number to constitute a threat to the Hutu leadership.

Again we find evidence of manipulation in Zanzibar. Lofchie reports that between the 1963 election and the January 1964 revolution, the ZNP/ZPPP regime consciously strived to maximize their control. Their measures included restricting the activities of opposition groups and the press, staffing the bureaucracy with loyal Arabs, and dismissing many Zanzibari police who had been recruited in mainland African countries. Members of opposition parties were not permitted to travel abroad and arbitrary search and seizure became commonplace. The Control of Soci-

---

50. *Ibid.*, p. 25.

eties Law had the effect of offsetting the Bill of Rights, which would have
ensured the safety of legitimate opposition parties.[51] These machinations,
while carefully conceived, failed in the long run to achieve the objectives
for which they had been designed.

Violence: Communities in Conflict

Ethnic frustrations often give rise to violent conflict. Chronic rioting in
Ulster in 1969, 1970, and 1971 filled considerable space in the world
press.[52] Similarly, massive intercommunal Turkish-Greek hostilities necessitated the presence of a United Nations peacekeeping force. In Mauritius, clashes over proposed independence between Indians and Africans
resulted in two deaths in May 1965, and a major outbreak of racial
violence in January 1968 left twenty-four dead and over one hundred
wounded. British troops were called in to restore order and a state of
emergency was declared. Racial violence again broke out in the week
following independence day.[53]

Preindependence politics in Rwanda also did not escape interethnic
violence. A series of attacks and counterattacks, directed against Hutu
and Tutsi groups, broke out in November 1959. In particular, the death
of two Tutsi notables touched off a wave of violence in which the Hutu
pillaged and burned thousands of Tutsi huts, and Tutsi commando bands
attacked and killed several Hutu political leaders. The administration was
able to restore order only by declaring a state of emergency and calling in
Belgian paratroopers from the Congo. Additional incidents of burnings
increased the number of Tutsi refugees; many fled to Burundi, Uganda
and the Congo.[54]

Our final case, Zanzibar, also typifies this regularity. The seizure of
government by African extremists was followed by their destruction of
the Arab oligarchy and the expropriation of its lands. There was rioting
during the 1961 election campaign as well, a consequence of a year of
intensive campaigning on the racial issue.

The basic features of dominant majority politics bear repeating. The
numerical status of the dominant community permits it to seek and obtain
independence without the cooperation of the minorities. As a result, ethnic
parties are organized and extremists soon come to dominate the electoral

51. Lofchie, *op. cit.*, pp. 265-68.
52. See, for example, Martin Wallace, *Drums and Guns: Revolution in Ulster*
(London: Geoffrey Chapman, 1970).
53. See *The New York Times,* January 23, 1968, p. 14; January 30, 1968, p. 4;
February 29, 1968, p. 3; and *Newsweek,* February 5, 1968, pp. 37-38.
54. Nyrop, *et al., op. cit.,* p. 20.

arena. Once in power they do not hesitate to adjust the rules of the game to secure their political supremacy. During this process violence frequently erupts. Democracy, in these contexts, has little meaning insofar as the protection of minorities is concerned.

CHAPTER 6

The Dominant Minority

As we have seen, the numerical composition of the ethnic communities profoundly affects politics in plural societies. In the case of the dominant minority situation, one consideration especially stands out: the overriding fear held by the minority, whether rightly or wrongly, that they stand to be overwhelmed by a vastly larger majority. To protect themselves in this situation, the minorities often exclude the majority community from legal participation, deprive them of civil rights and other democratic safeguards, and rely heavily on police rule to maintain order. Equality of opportunity, freedom of expression and other egalitarian values are thus openly discarded in such plural societies as South Africa and Rhodesia. As might be expected, many books and articles about politics in these countries are critical of the minority regimes.[1] South African and Rhodesian politics are not compatible with liberal egalitarian norms. However, a normative evaluation of their standards is not our primary concern in this book. Rather, our chief interest lies in identifying the salient features of ethnic politics in dominant minority configurations and in explaining the how and why of the regularities we discover.

South Africa

Two different conflicts have conditioned South African political history. On the one hand, Afrikaners and English-speaking Whites have continuously competed with each other for political control in South Africa, while on the other hand, both White communities have often banded together against their commonly perceived African and colored opponents.

---

1. See, for example, Pierre L. van den Berghe, *South Africa, A Study in Conflict* (Middletown, Connecticut: Wesleyan University Press, 1965), p. 9.

In both cases, however, ethnicity is the dominant theme of South African politics. As van den Berghe observes:

> The power struggle thus takes place at two levels. On the one hand, the two White groups compete within the constitutional framework for the control of Parliament and of the state apparatus, while, on the other hand, Africans and Europeans oppose one another on the extraparliamentary scene. The "Native policy" of the main European political parties has differed in details and in methods, but *the vast majority of Whites, both Afrikaners and English, has always agreed on the perpetuation of White supremacy. Nearly all Africans, on their side, aim at the overthrow of the present system.*[2]

In the discussion that follows, we show a steady intensification of Black-White conflict which, especially since 1948, has dampened and almost eliminated the political relevance of the intra-White Afrikaner-English conflict. Clearly the most important fact of South African political life is the distinction between Blacks and Whites, symbolized by the term "apartheid."

South African History from 1652-1910: Afrikaner-English Competition.
In 1652 the Dutch East India Company established a small colony on the Cape as a half-way station on the route to India. Following the establishment of this colony, a number of Dutch settlers, now called either Boers or Afrikaners, arrived and quickly imposed White rule and a system of slavery. Most of the early slaves, however, were Asians who were shipped from India and the Indonesian Islands, rather than Africans.[3]

The British arrived more than 150 years later in 1806 and subsequently established a permanent governorship over the Cape Province. Prior to the British, the importation of slaves, chiefly from Madagascar, Mozambique, and the East Indies, had already placed the White settlers in the position of a numerical minority. Relations between the newly settled English and the more established Afrikaners were tense from the outset as many Afrikaners feared that their way of life would be submerged under British culture. As a consequence of the British decision to abolish slavery in the Cape Province in 1834, the second phase of South African history known as the "Great Trek" began:

> Until this year [1836], there had been one Cape Colony, whether or not it was a divided settlement. There was one government and one official ruler: Britain. The Great Trek was aimed at the establishment,

---

2. *Ibid.*, p. 98 (emphasis added).
3. Alex Hepple, *South Africa* (New York: Praeger, 1966), p. 9.

in the interior, of Boer Republics, free of British domination and free to practice religion and education in the Dutch language. Here slavery would not be prohibited.[4]

The Boers moved north in large numbers and established what is now known as Transvaal and the Orange Free State. The British, simultaneously, expanded into the northeast and annexed the province of Natal, where they established sugar plantations. For the required cheap plantation labor the planters obtained indentured Indian immigrants, most of whom, following the expiration of their three year contracts of indenture, chose to stay in South Africa and generally engaged in small scale farming or trading. Whether a legitimate concern or not, the steadily expanding size of the Indian community represented a threat to the "purity" of the Afrikaner republics. This threat led directly to the passage of the first discriminatory legislation in South Africa.

> From 1885, the laws of the Orange Free State Republic [a Boer state] restricted their residence, withheld all political rights and prohibited their free entry into the republic. In 1891 the Free State enacted that no Indian could own or occupy land within the republic. . . .[5]

Subsequent legislation altogether ended Indian immigration in 1911; by this time, however, the Indian community numbered 150,000 persons.

From the days of the Great Trek in 1836 until the establishment of the Union of South Africa as a self-governing state in 1910, the intra-White British-Boer division was of especial political salience — it even led to several instances of overt warfare. The first instance was sparked by the discovery of diamonds around Kimberly in 1867 that prompted Britain to annex the diamond fields to the Cape Colony. The Boer Orange Free State was then unable to contest this annexation by force. Ten years later, in 1877, the British moved into and occupied the Transvaal, but withdrew after a short fight and defeat in 1881. This incident is known as the first Anglo-Boer War.

Though the English acknowledged Afrikaner supremacy by their withdrawal from the Boer Republics in 1881, the discovery of gold around the future city of Johannesburg in 1886 produced a gold rush and flooded the Transvaal (a Boer Republic) with White English miners and other White non-Boers (foreigners). Non-Boer settlement in large numbers in the boom town of Johannesburg began to threaten the political supremacy of the Boers. Their response, denying the franchise to these foreigners, justified new British intervention and the second Anglo-Boer War erupted that ended with a British victory in 1902.

---

4. Harm J. De Blij, *South Africa* (Evanston, Illinois: Northwestern University Press, 1962), p. 39.
5. Hepple, *op. cit.*, p. 14.

Shortly after the hostilities subsided the British promulgated the South Africa Act of 1909 which, to all effects, gave political control to the Afrikaners, while allowing English financial magnates to retain control of the economy. Britain sought to insure in the postwar settlement that South Africa would remain a friendly White-settler dominion with security for the dominant English economic interests. Thus the 1909 agreement, which created an independent South Africa in the British Commonwealth of Nations in 1910, restored prewar Boer political supremacy, especially in the Transvaal and the Orange Free State. Among the important provisions that were incorporated into the constitution, two deserve emphasis.(1) English and Dutch were declared as the two official languages—none of the African languages received any recognition. (2) The franchise was restricted chiefly to Whites. Delegations from the Transvaal and the Orange Free State—the former Boer Republics—were adamantly opposed to any extension of the franchise to non-Whites in their provinces. Any attempt by the British to impose such an extension would have threatened the postwar policy of reconciliation. In the Cape, the voting qualifications were raised to entrench political control even more decisively in White hands; only a small community of 10,000 coloreds, the descendants of intermarriages between natives and the early White settlers, retained the franchise. And finally, in Natal, a British colony with few Afrikaners, the 1909 agreement also denied the franchise to non-Whites.

> The end result was a retention of the existing franchise laws in each of the four provinces. The basic agreement on color issues between most Afrikaners and English has been a constant fact of the South African political scene for over a century. . . . the English, as a group, have only shown liberalism (carefully minimized at that) when it suited their interests as opposed to those of the Afrikaners.[6]

1910-1948: Afrikaner-English Cooperation and the Resurgence of Afrikaner Nationalism.[7] The South Africa Act of 1909 signaled an end to the violence between the Boers and the British government and the beginning of a cooperative spirit between the two major groups of White settlers. Louis Botha (1910-19) and Jan Smuts (1919-24), the first two Prime Ministers, each maintained the spirit of compromise that was reflected in the South Africa Act of 1909. Both men, ex-Boer generals, resisted extremist Afrikaner elements and chose, instead, to cooperate with the English. By 1924, however, the successful rise of Afrikaner nationalism produced a government with a more explicit Afrikaner orienta-

---

6. Van den Berghe, *op. cit.*, p. 35.
7. For this section we draw upon van den Berghe, pp. 101-4, and the other references that are cited below.

tion. This government (1924-33) was headed by J. B. M. Hertzog, who had earlier broken away from Botha and had founded the Afrikaner-based Nationalist Party in 1912. Hertzog had successfully formed a coalition with the English-based Labor Party to oppose the government of Jan Smuts, who had supported English big business interests in 1922 when White mine workers, chiefly Afrikaners, went on strike demanding that restrictions be placed on Black mine workers. Thus a seeming alliance of White working-class elements enabled Hertzog to come to power and carry out several more obvious pro-Afrikaner policies. These included the passage of several pieces of national legislation, e.g., Nationality and Flag Act of 1927, substitution of Afrikaans for Dutch as one of the two official languages of South Africa.

Hertzog's openly anti-English policies came to an end in 1933 when he and Smuts, the former Prime Minister, reached an agreement to establish a new coalition government. Although Hertzog remained in his post as Prime Minister, this rapprochement meant that the new government would likely be more favorable to English capital and less disposed to accept extremist Afrikaner demands. As a result of Hertzog's new moderate stance, the militant wing of the Nationalist Party (now the Purified Nationalist Party) split off and eliminated both Hertzog and the other nonnationalists who had entered into Smut's government. This new nationalist Party, led by Dr. D. F. Malan, officially sought the creation of an Afrikaner Republic and South African withdrawal from the British Commonwealth of Nations.[8]

The union of Hertzog and Smuts was institutionalized in the formation of the United Party,which represented the older line of English-Afrikaner compromise, and of cooperation with Britain and the Commonwealth. This compromise was short-lived, however, and dissolved when the two men split over the issue of South African participation in World War II; Hertzog had favored a neutral position while Smuts advocated active South African participation on the British side. Hertzog was defeated in 1939 by a parliamentary vote of eighty to sixty-seven, which enabled Smuts to form his United Party war cabinet. Hertzog subsequently rejoined the Nationalist party, *but this time Malan, with his extremist Afrikaner policies, was the undisputed leader.*

The 1948 election is the crucial turning point in South Africa's electoral history.[9] On March 29, 1948, Dr. D. F. Malan made a campaign speech

---

8. For a brief, but excellent, discussion of modern party history in South Africa, see Newell M. Stultz and Jeffrey Butler, "The South African General Election of 1961," *Political Science Quarterly* 78, no. 1 (March 1963): 86-110, especially pp. 90-94.

9. For an excellent discussion of the 1948 election and its consequences for South African politics see Edward A. Tiryakian, "Apartheid and Politics in South Africa," *The Journal of Politics* 22, no. 4 (November 1960): 682-97.

in which, for the first time, he proposed apartheid — separate development of the races — as a policy of race relations. The issue was immediately ridiculed by the English press and the United Party. Throughout the campaign the Nationalists accused the United Party of promoting racial integration. Smuts, campaigning actively as the election drew near, ridiculed the notions of apartheid, separate development, and placing the natives back on their own land reserves as "so much nonsense."

The election results clearly show that the United Party badly underestimated the appeal of the issues of racial policy and apartheid to the European voter. The United Party of Smuts was shockingly defeated by Malan's Nationalist Party, even though the former polled over 120,000 more votes than the latter. The Nationalist Party emerged with 70 seats, the United Party 65, the Afrikaner Party, led by N. C. Havenga, 9, the Labor Party 3, and minor parties and independents 6. Malan's Afrikaner-oriented party benefitted from the constituency provisions contained within the 1910 South Africa Act, which gave greater representation to the heavily Afrikaner-populated rural areas. With the emergence of race as the sole salient issue in South African politics, moderation gave way to extremism.[10]

After the election, Malan formed a coalition government with Havenga's Afrikaner Party, which had won nine seats, thereby giving the government a narrow parliamentary majority of seventy-nine to seventy-four; the opposition consisted primarily of the United Party and the Labor Party, both of which were chiefly English in composition. The Afrikaner support, though not extensive, which had allowed the United Party to govern between 1939 and 1948, was not forthcoming in the 1948 election. Afrikaner sentiments were reflected almost exclusively by the Nationalist Party. Malan became Prime Minister and appointed an all-Afrikaner cabinet. Three years later the Afrikaner Party joined his Nationalist Party.

> By rallying the mass of the Afrikaner electorate, the Nationalist Party eliminated the necessity of compromise with the English, gained control of the entire country, and *opened the way for more extremist policies.*[11]

1948-1970: Minority Domination and the Politics of Racial Extremism.

Since their rise to a position of preeminence in 1948, Afrikaners have totally monopolized the decision processes of government. At the same time, Afrikaner-English political competition has markedly declined in view of the growing political salience of extraconstitutional conflict between Whites and non-Whites. The English have, since the defeat of their

---

10. *Ibid.*, p. 691.
11. Van den Berghe, *op. cit.*, p. 103 (emphasis added).

moderate program in 1948, apparently become more or less reconciled to the business of making money, leaving the business of government to the Afrikaner Nationalist Party. Meanwhile, the Afrikaners have moved to consolidate their position through a series of legal enactments. These measures included the following: (1) the elimination of Cape Coloreds from the common electoral roll; (2) the abolition of the "Natives Representatives" system, which eliminated from Parliament the White spokesmen for the African community; (3) a reduction in the voting age from twenty-one to eighteen, which increased the voting strength of the more fertile Afrikaners; and (4) the granting of six seats in Parliament to South-West Africa, whose population overwhelmingly supports the Nationalist Party. As a result, Nationalist majorities increased without interruption in the elections of 1953, 1958, 1961, and 1966; a slight reduction from 126 seats in 1966 to 119 seats in 1970 was suffered, but Nationalists have retained a two-thirds control of Parliament since 1961.

An analysis of these election results is very informative. The first point to note is that Malan's electoral manipulations enabled his party to steadily increase its popular vote. Table 6.1 reveals this gain.

Table 6.1

Election Results in South Africa in 1953 and 1958

	1953	1958
Nationalist Party	598,718	642,069
United Party	576,474	503,828
Other	34,730	6,096

Source: Edwin A. Tiryakian, "Apartheid and Politics in South Africa," *Journal of Politics* 22, no. 4 (November 1960): 692.

By 1961, Afrikaner supremacy was openly conceded. Of the 165 seats in the South African Parliament, 70 were unopposed. Of telling importance is the fact that 50 seats, conceded to the Nationalist Party by the opposition, represented either rural provincial constituencies or those in the Afrikaans-speaking towns and working-class sections in Pretoria. The Nationalist Party, in turn, openly conceded 46 constituencies (20 unopposed) to the opposition parties in districts where the English-speakers were predominant. As expected, the major issue in the 1961 campaign was the race policy of the government. The results for the remaining contested seats illustrated the growing strength of appeals to the racial sentiments of the White electorate: the Nationalist Party was successful in 85 percent of these contests (55 seats in all). No Nationalist Party Member of Parliament was unseated; in fact, all of them increased their 1958 majorities. Furthermore, the Progressive Party, which advocated multiracial cooperation, lost 10 of its 11 contests. Many English electors had by now shifted their support to the Nationalist Party and its appeal for White unity.[12]

As the security of the Afrikaner position steadily increased, the policies of the Nationalist government became more extreme. Malan's successor Styrdom and, in turn, his successor Verwoerd adopted even more extremist measures. The latter, in 1958, *eliminated all remaining moderates from his government.* Afrikaner Nationalists gradually secured for themselves the leading positions in the civil service (e.g., the police, railways, education), the diplomatic corps and the judiciary, increased the importance of the Afrikaans language, attacked the autonomy of English-speaking universities, heavily subsidized White Afrikaner farming, and so forth. Their most significant triumph came in 1961 when they declared South Africa a Republic and withdrew from the Commonwealth, policies that Malan's early Nationalist Party had advocated.

Why did the English, who comprise forty percent of the White South African population, stand idly by and permit the Nationalist Party to proceed with these measures, since their economic strength might have permitted them to exert considerable pressure on the government to moderate its policies? In fact, the United Party, as the main official opposition party, has recently *even supported* the government on several pieces of dictatorial legislation.

> The real crux of the answer . . . lies in the "Native problem." The English share all the privileges of the other Whites, and they do not want to change the existing system of White oppression. The dictatorial measures of the government do not affect the daily life of the English, as they are intended to suppress the non-white opposition. . . . In order to maintain White supremacy and privileges, the mass of the English is willing to pay the price of increasing dictatorship, of gradual Afrikanerization, and of a measure of economic interference.[13]

The English have thus acquiesced in Afrikaner political supremacy and increasing repression of the non-White majority because of their paramount interest in economic prosperity. Since 1948, measures have been taken to minimize the threat from non-Whites. These measures, discussed

---

12. Stultz and Butler, *op. cit.*, passim.
13. Van den Berghe, *op. cit.*, p. 106.

below, reveal just how far minority regimes are prepared to go to preserve their advantaged position.

Upon taking office in 1948, the Nationalists legislated still further separation between the races to enhance White racial supremacy. They passed in 1949 the Prohibition of Mixed Marriages Act that forbids any marriage between a White and a non-White. In the following year and again in 1957, they amended the Immorality Act of 1927 to make "immoral or indecent acts" between Whites and non-Whites of opposite sexes an offense punishable by up to seven years of imprisonment. And, as we noted before, they completely eliminated Cape Coloreds from the common electoral role in 1956, and abolished token representation of Africans by White members of Parliament in 1960.

Among the more important provisions was the Group Areas Act of 1950, amended in 1952, 1955, and 1957, which established segregated residential areas for each race. These Acts removed the deferential treatment, which had been accorded to Coloreds and Indians, by restricting their physical movement and area of residence; it also placed a significant bar on Indian economic opportunities. Additional labor and educational legislation served to place all non-Whites at a serious disadvantage both in employment and in universities by prohibiting African workers from competing with Whites in many occupations and forbidding non-Whites from attending English-speaking universities. A number of other laws gave the government wide powers of perquisition, confiscation of property, banning of organizations, exile, extradition, arrest, and detention without trial. These repressive measures have culminated in such regulations as the "pass laws" that require all adult African males to carry "reference books," thereby enabling the police to restrict African migration and keep control over the mass of Africans. In terms of punishments for violations of the law, non-Whites receive distinctly harsher treatments in the courts than Whites for comparable offenses.[14]

In an attempt to justify this increasingly harsh repression of Africans, Whites point to the disastrous cattle-killing by the Xhosas in the 1850s, the Zulu Poll-Tax Rebellion of 1906, and the 1960 revolt of the Pondo peasantry, all of which are seen by the European population as expressions of anti-European ethnic nationalism. Repression, disenfranchisement, differential economic opportunity, and other devices are thus readily employed by Europeans to insure continued White supremacy in all aspects of political, economic and social life.

As a consequence of the intensification of apartheid, Coloreds have now been deprived of those remaining privileges that had distinguished them

14. *Ibid.*, pp. 128-35.

from Blacks, and they are now treated simply as one of South Africa's three non-White groups without the right to participate in the country's government. Indians have also been victims of apartheid policies and their position has been gradually eroded by the acts of several White governments. These enactments include exorbitant taxation, "repatriation" schemes, and even expropriation under the Group Areas Act, under which Indians are required to live within an officially designated segregated area.[15]

Multiracial parties in South Africa are few and far between and have never been successful in moderating the extremist position of the Nationalist Party. Two examples of nonracial political groups are the Communist Party and the Liberal Party, neither of which is represented in Parliament. Most non-White political movements display a Black counter-racialism directed against White domination, and thus it is difficult for well-motivated leaders to bring about genuine interracial cooperation.

What is the likelihood that the Nationalist Party will split and produce a moderate wing that can influence constitutional change attenuating white racial supremacy?

> But the whole evolution of Afrikaner Nationalism in the last thirty years has shown *a trend towards reactionary extremism.* As the Nationalist government becomes more firmly entrenched, its policies become more repressive, *and today the "extremists" are in a stronger position than ever. The influence of "moderate" Nationalist intellectuals and clergymen has become negligible,* and the *Broederbond* [an ultra-secret nationalist organization consisting of prominent Afrikaner elite members of the Dutch Reformed Churches, the professions, business and universities] gradually purged such organizations as the South African Bureau of Racial Affairs of "liberal" dissidents. Within the cabinet and in other leading political posts, the *Broederbond* replaces more and more moderates with extremists, and pressure has been brought upon liberal clergymen to toe the line. . . .[16]

Stultz and Butler also reach a similar conclusion.[17] Since the disagreements between the English and Afrikaners have diminished in importance, it appears unlikely that moderate elements within the White community will emerge to advocate improving the status of non-Whites. The politics of extremism, as the theme of apartheid depicts, seems to preclude the viability of moderation on the racial issue by White politicians who seek electoral victory.

---

15. *Ibid.*, p. 152.
16. *Ibid.*, pp. 173-74.
17. *Op. cit.*, p. 110.

Politics in South Africa: The Salience of Race. 1. *A dominant minority seeks to exclude the majority from legitimate participation in government.* Beginning with the South Africa Act of 1909, the vast majority of non-Whites, excepting about 10,000 Cape Coloreds, were disenfranchised from the common electoral roll. Since Afrikaners began their domination of government in 1948, even these Cape Coloreds have been removed from the electoral lists. Indians, Africans and Coloreds have no basis for legal participation in the electoral process; they cannot vote, cannot run for office, cannot organize legitimate political parties, and generally cannot speak out on political matters. Politics in South Africa is, strictly speaking, the exclusive control over the public sector by a racially defined White minority.

2. *Extremists dominate the political arena.* Since nearly every political movement, whether overt or covert, is predicated upon advancing the interests of some specific racial community, the only attempts at overtly non-racial parties have met with dismal failure. An overriding fear of what the majority Africans are likely to do to the White community if they obtain power encourages extremist Afrikaner Whites, and compels even moderate English Whites, to support official government policy. Politics since 1948 displays a growth of repressive and other extremist measures against the African population, and most Englishmen, it would seem, prefer wealth to social, political, and economic equality for all residents of South Africa.

3. *Interethnic competition strengthens intraethnic cohesion.* Specifically, the English-Afrikaner dispute, marked by thousands of deaths during the two Boer Wars and rooted in a long history dating from 1806, has steadily diminished in importance, especially as Black-White conflict has grown in salience. It appears unlikely that more than a very small number of Whites will diverge from giving support to parties which promote White supremacy. Furthermore, any party leader who advocates moderation is likely to çome under attack from more extremist elements within his party. Leaders of the Afrikaner Nationalist Party must have been aware of this pattern as they moved still further in their extremist position in the 1970 campaign to ward off a possible electoral threat from an even more intensely White supremacist group.

4. *The minority relies heavily upon police rule.* Van den Berghe records a steady growth in the size and expenditures of the police force and army and notes that the police are often used as a deliberate instrument of intimidation and harassment of Africans. They often raid African homes under the cover of enforcing the pass regulations; estimates of arrest and conviction show that one adult African male in three is prosecuted for some criminal offense each year. Police raids also often result in the destruction of African property, in the mistreatment and beating of Afri-

cans, and the use of firearms in the maintenance of order. Law and order for Whites represents abuse and oppression for non-Whites.[18]

Rhodesia

When compared with the White minority which comprises 20 percent of the overall population in South Africa, the tiny White minority in Rhodesia, making up a scant five and one-half percent of its population, appears even more preoccupied with retaining exclusive White political control.[19] Although Africans constitute an overwhelming majority (94.5 percent) of the Rhodesian population, they are only allocated the use of less than half of the country's lands (much of it undesirable), earn on the average one-tenth as much as Europeans, receive a per pupil government expenditure in education approximately one-tenth that accorded to Europeans, and very rarely complete a full course in the secondary schools. In a nutshell, Whites exercise a monopoly on the decision-making structures of government in Rhodesia's plural society; effective African participation in government is negligible and it is unlikely that Whites will relinquish to any degree their position of absolute supremacy. So long as Whites possess adequate police and military forces, Africans are likely to remain, in practice, a disenfranchised, subservient majority.

Ever since Rhodesia unilaterally declared independence from Britain in November 1965, Ian Smith, Rhodesia's Prime Minister, has gradually consolidated White rule. When the Union Jack was hauled down in March 1970, Rhodesia had already adopted a constitution which ensured that the country's overwhelming African majority could never legitimately achieve control of Parliament. *Newsweek* reports that even moderate White voters feel compelled to support the White regime: a typical voter [in the 1970 election] remarked, "We Europeans don't want a dictatorship, but the threat [African rule] to us is very real."[20]

The theoretical paradigm that informs our analysis of ethnic politics in South Africa's dominant minority configuration provides appropriate

18. *Ibid.*, pp. 136-41.

19. These figures and much of our information about Rhodesia are taken from Theodore Bull, *Rhodesia: Crisis of Color* (Chicago: Quadrangle Books, 1967). See especially Appendix I, pp. 159-60. See also James Barber, *Rhodesia: The Road to Rebellion* (London: Oxford University Press for the Institute of Race Relations, 1967); "Rhodesia: The Constitutional Conflict," *Journal of Modern African Studies* 4, no. 4 (December 1966): 457-69; Frank Clements, *Rhodesia: A Study of the Deterioration of a White Society* (New York: Praeger, 1969); and Larry W. Bowman, "Organization, Power, and Decision-Making Within the Rhodesian Front," *Journal of Commonwealth Political Studies* 7, no. 2 (July 1969): 145-65.

20. April 20, 1970, p. 64.

categories for making comparisons with White Rhodesian politics. Even though Rhodesian Whites are not internally divided into distinct sub-cultures as in South Africa, ethnic politics under the two White minority regimes is remarkably similar.

Exclusion of the African Majority from Participation in Government. Africans in Rhodesia have not been totally disenfranchised; a large number are eligible to vote for candidates who run on a special list called the *B*-roll. Qualifications for *B*-roll voting include citizenship, two years continuous residence in the country, 21 years of age, some knowledge of English, a specified minimum income, and fixed assets of a specified value, or the completion of at least a certain minimum number of years of education. As a consequence of these qualifications, some 11,577 Rhodesians were eligible to vote on the *B*-roll in 1965; the vast majority, 10,689 to be exact, were African. *A*-roll franchise qualifications are more demanding, both in terms of income and education. The 1965 list of qualified *A*-roll voters included 92,405 Europeans out of a total listing of 97,284 persons. Requirements of high income, education and ownership of property, therefore, serve to insure White domination of what may legally appear to be a "color-blind" *A*-roll. Africans correspondingly dominate the *B*-roll. Since the constitution of independent Rhodesia provides for 50 *A*-roll seats and 15 *B*-roll seats, Whites are certain to obtain an overwhelming majority in Parliament. Although Africans may campaign for office and vote (if franchise qualifications are met), representatives elected by *B*-roll voters exert little influence in the allocative decisions of government.

Extremism and the Failure of Moderation. As mentioned above, the White community is not subdivided into ethnically separate groupings; rather, most Whites are of British extraction and are culturally quite homogeneous. Most Whites came to Rhodesia to engage in commercial agriculture, especially when it was discovered that mineral wealth claims had been vastly exaggerated. In 1922 these settlers, on the basis of a "color-blind" franchise, voted on the issue of Rhodesia's future political status: approximately sixty percent of the qualified voters indicated their preference for responsible internal government; the remaining forty percent had voted for union with South Africa. Rhodesia was subsequently annexed to Britain in October 1923 with political control firmly in the hands of the resident European population — Africans were in practice excluded from the franchise because of income, property and educational requirements. Most newly arriving European immigrants were easily absorbed into the white Rhodesian way of life, and the White community, therefore, retained its homogeneous character.

The demise of moderation and the rise of extremist politics is found in the 1958 election. Rhodesia had earlier joined in a federation with Northern Rhodesia (now Zambia) and Nyasaland (now Malawi) by a two-thirds majority vote in 1953, but a crisis with the leader of the governing Federal Party, Garfield Todd, emerged in 1956. Federal Party losses to the newly revitalized Dominion Party in by-elections were blamed on Todd and he was removed from office out of fear that he stood for and might become an activist for widely increased African rights. The Federal Party, under its new leader Sir Edgar Whitehead, was transformed into the United Federal Party, the union of the federal and territorial parties, and won seventeen of thirty elective seats in the 1958 election. Bull reports that this was the most crucial election in Rhodesia's political history. Todd's defeat signified to most African leaders that they no longer possessed any prospects for exercising influence within the framework of the established constitution. "The steady flow of repressive legislation and the repeated banning of African nationalist parties by the Whitehead government only served to emphasize that the races had parted ways."[21]

Whitehead's government was chiefly concerned with obtaining a greater measure of freedom from British control. Following a series of talks and conferences with Britain, a constitution was fashioned in 1961 that provided for fifteen *B*-roll seats, most likely to be controlled by middle-class Africans, and fifty *A*-roll seats, the prerogative of the affluent Whites. In a referendum campaign on the constitution, Whitehead secured a two-thirds approval vote but he misinterpreted the victory as a desire for liberal reform.

At the outset Africans refused to cooperate with White Rhodesians[22] and the British were disappointed because the constitution failed to produce genuine racial cooperation. Extremist tendencies were on the rise as is evident in the 1962 electoral contest between Whitehead's United Federal Party and the Rhodesian Front, the latter having been formed in March 1962 out of the dissident extremist forces that included the old Dominion Party (which was split into Federal and Southern Rhodesian wings), the United Group, and the Southern Rhodesian Association. In

---

21. Bull, *op. cit.*, p. 17.

22. Barber believes that the African nationalists miscalculated when they chose to boycott the 1962 election. Although they feared a possible early independence under a White minority government, by not taking their place inside the Assembly they forfeited their capacity to speak out officially for greater reform and more African representation. Furthermore, as an extra-constitutional political group, they left themselves vulnerable to official proscription by the White government. As expected, the two major African nationalist parties were banned and their leaders restricted from political activity in August 1964. See "Rhodesia: the Constitutional Conflict," pp. 462-64.

the campaign Whitehead and the United Federal Party promised to repeal the Land Apportionment Act, abolish racial discrimination, and appoint some African junior ministers. As a counterstrategy, the opposition Rhodesian Front actively fanned the flames of racial fears, painting a picture of rapid African integration in government, the schools, and housing if the electorate chose the United Federal Party. Overconfident after its success in the 1961 referendum, the United Federal Party misjudged the salience of intensely held fears of the White electorate; the Rhodesian Front, using a strategy of demand generation for the racial issue, won thirty-five of fifty *A*-roll seats and formed the new government.

Winston Field became the new Prime Minister but quickly come under suspicion for several reasons. Many party members were upset because he did not take immediate action on the question of Rhodesian independence to insure freedom from British control for Rhodesian Whites. Moreover, he did not appoint a sufficient number of party members to key diplomatic and industrial posts, he ran the government without paying any attention to the party, and he failed to apply suitably strict measures in dealing with African nationalists. Following a near unanimous decision of the entire party, Field was replaced as Prime Minister in April 1964 by Ian Smith. This change signified another victory for the extremist faction in the Rhodesian Front.

The rest of the Rhodesian story is almost common knowledge. Unilateral Declaration of Independence was proclaimed on November 11, 1965, following a referendum held the preceding November: 58,076 (89.1 percent) voted for independence and only 6,101 (10.9 percent) indicated opposition. In the May 1965 election, the Rhodesian Front completely decimated all European opposition to its list of candidates, sweeping all 50 seats on the *A*-roll. An identical success was scored in April 1970. The Rhodesian Front under the leadership of Ian Smith has thus maintained a complete monopoly on political power ever since its extremist appeal first gained victory in the 1962 election, and occupies an impregnable parliamentary (legal) position.

Since Rhodesia's Unilateral Declaration of Independence in 1965, Smith's government has implemented a number of policies that are designed to entrench more deeply the advantaged position Whites now enjoy. Some of these measures involve detention without trial, rigid enforcement of the Land Apportionment Act, a purge of "liberals" from the University College, and the elevation of tribal chiefs — a conservative group of Africans — to more prominent political roles. Rhodesian politics since 1958 thus evinces a steady growth of extremism. White candiates have won elections by stressing the deleterious consequences of integration with the African majority, whereas those candidates espousing moderate positions have been decisively defeated. The Rhodesian Front does not appear likely to moderate its extremist outlook in the near future.

Repressive Legislation and Police Rule. Successive White Rhodesian governments have enacted a number of repressive security measures that in practice entail serious abrogation of African freedoms. Imprisonment without trial, the right to declare unlawful any organization that threatens public safety, wide police powers of entry and search without warrant, and the banning of several African political parties are just a few of the many devices Whites have employed in order to keep the African population under control. The most far-reaching precaution available to Whites is the Emergency Powers Act passed in 1960 that gives the executive branch of government such all-embracing authority as control of business and employees, the right to take possession of any property, complete censorship of all news media, and so forth. Rigid enforcement of repressive legislation thus, for the present, safeguards White supremacy.

We see, therefore, from this brief review that ethnic politics in Rhodesia and South Africa are remarkably alike. Those features which appear in both contexts include:

1. the effective exclusion of the African majorities from legitimate participation in government;
2. the success of extremist strategies and the failure of moderation on the racial issue;
3. the growing cohesiveness of the White communities in view of a perceived fear of the African population; and
4. the frequent recourse to repressive legislation and police rule.

In the final section of this chapter we conclude our examination of ethnic politics in dominant minority configurations with a brief look at the landlocked African country of Burundi.

Burundi

Burundi is the immediate southern neighbor of Rwanda. Although both countries were administered as one unit during the period of rule by successive German and Belgian colonial regimes, each existed as a historically separate kingdom for the four hundred previous years.

The three communities that comprise Rwanda's population are also present in Burundi: the Hutu, who make up about eighty-three percent of the population; the Tutsi, sixteen percent; and the Twa, less than one percent.[23] As in Furnivall's conception of the plural society, the Hutu and Tutsi are socially and economically differentiated from each other. The Tutsi minority has historically filled most administrative posts and today occupies many major government positions while most Hutu are still farmers and laborers.

Politics in Burundi, however, differs slightly from that in Rwanda insofar as those who held power in Burundi were members of favored Tutsi families, the *ganwa,* rather than simply members of a dominant race. The history of precolonial Burundi is characterized by the struggle for power among various clans, which took the form of succession wars between the descendants of the royal family. Cyclical alliances among different social groupings thus produced some historical measure of social cohesion. Competition between the *ganwa* induced them to seek the support of both Hutu and Tutsi, and the Mwami (ruler of Burundi) did the same to reinforce his position against territorial encroachments from rival feudal *ganwa.* This cyclical competition between the *ganwa* helped to attenuate ethnic tensions.

The initial period of European rule did not seriously alter the social or political structure of Burundi. Belgian administrators favored the ruling *ganwa,* and trained their sons disproportionately to fill administrative and civil service slots. But the advent of independence and the introduction of the franchise to the masses drastically altered the rules of the game leading, in short order, to the politicization of ethnic cleavages. But we are slightly ahead of the story at this point.

The old *ganwa* rivalries, which had remained dormant throughout the period of Belgian rule, emerged in the form of competing political groups in the 1950s. Traditional, monarchic values were expressed in the National Unity and Progress Party (UPRONA), the party of the Bezi family. Modern economic and political values were reflected in the party of the Batare family, the Parti Démocrate Chrétien (PDC). Prince Rwagasore, the son of the Mwami, led UPRONA. Married to a Hutu girl, he was immensely popular with both communities. In the Legislative Assembly election of September 1961, Rwagasore's popularity was translated into fifty-eight of sixty-four seats for his party. He was also very conscious to balance Tutsi and Hutu interests by placing members of both communities in important government positions. Unfortunately for

---

23. Gordon C. McDonald, et al., *Area Handbook for Burundi* (Washington: U.S. Government Printing Office, 1969), p. 39. For an excellent discussion of modern political history in Burundi and one upon which we rely heavily see René Lemarchand, "Social Change and Political Modernization in Burundi," *Journal of Modern African Studies* 4, no. 4 (December 1966): 401-33.

Rwagasore, he was assassinated by political opponents on October 13, 1961, just two weeks after the first meeting of his Legislative Assembly. With Rwagasore's death, his party (UPRONA) divided into competing ethnic factions. Burundi thus achieved full independence on July 1, 1962, in the midst of a widening rift between the Hutu and Tutsi factions of the ruling UPRONA party.

UPRONA's ethnic partition was also influenced by the contagion of republican ideas from Rwanda—Burundi was still a monarchy. Many of the majority Hutu community became sensitive to the implications of majority rule, which had just come about in neighboring Rwanda. These majoritarian sentiments were further intensified by the fact that Tutsis obtained the bulk of new bureaucratic posts and held two-thirds of the senior civil service slots that native Burundians occupied. Meanwhile, fleeing immigrants from Rwanda further strengthened Tutsi convictions.

The intraparty UPRONA struggle spread to the National Assembly and permeated the country's entire administration machinery by August 1962. Chaos was averted in 1963 when the Royal Court intervened and gave several key appointments to former *ganwa*. The stability which resulted, however, was short-lived due, in part, to the resentment of these appointments by the new Burundi elites.

On October 18, 1965, Hutu officers staged an unsuccessful coup, but in the confusion the Mwami fled the country. A second coup, this time led by Tutsi officers, was successful on July 8, 1966. Led by Captain Michael Micombero, these new military leaders have deposed the monarch and now rule by decree through an appointed Council of Ministers. The regime maintains an authoritarian style and, as needed, provides appropriate displays of coercion.

This review of modern political history in Burundi shows that prior to independence, political competition was restricted to the prominent *ganwa* and their supporters as they organized political parties to fight for positions of influence in a soon-to-be-independent Burundi state. *The passage from trusteeship status to self-government changed the focus of competition and converted the traditional Hutu-Tutsi rivalry into the country's most salient political division.*

During its brief four years as an independent monarchy, from 1962 to 1966, the nation had been torn by political strife that developed from an ethnic conflict between the Hutu majority and the powerful Tutsi minority.[24]

The emergence of ethnic identity as the primary focus of political combat led quickly to the dissolution of the Legislative Assembly and the

---

24. McDonald, *op. cit*, p. 77.

establishment of a military government, which has replaced the elected representatives, most of them Hutu, with appointed administrators, mainly of Tutsi origin.[25] We therefore see that in still another case of a dominant minority situation, democracy and political stability do not blend well together. Dominant minorities do not allow their subject majorities the legal right to secure political power by the universal franchise.

---

25. *The New Africans* (London: Paul Hamlyn, 1967), p. 30.

CHAPTER 7

Fragmentation

In this chapter we adopt a change of pace: we compare five countries on a topic-by-topic basis without first presenting a detailed analysis of at least one society. We contend herein that ethnic politics in such diverse fragmented plural societies as Lebanon, a middle-Eastern "confessional" culture, the Congo, Sudan, and Nigeria, all replete with tribal diversity, and Yugoslavia, an Eastern European communist country composed of six ethnically separate Republics, display striking regularities. We turn, first, to a brief recapitulation of the properties that fragmented societies exhibit before beginning our analysis.

Properties of Fragmented Societies

Fragmented societies are characterized by the presence of many culturally distinct communities and the failure of any one of them, at the onset of independent status, to dominate the political process. As in the other ethnic configurations, members of each of the ethnic communities in the fragmented society feel very intensely about the values and practices of their respective cultures. With the departure of the colonial or other ruling power, the rewards of politics become a valuable prize. Political parties, which invariably follow ethnic lines, are then organized and actively compete for these rewards. In the fragmented culture this entails a widespread proliferation of parties, each representing the interests of one specific tribe, religious cult, linguistic group, or other ethnic community. Multiparty coalitions become difficult to form and hold together. The absence of popularly supported, nationwide parties creates a conducive environment in which military or paramilitary organizations, which are the only institutions that possess a nationwide communications network and a capability for effective national rule, can rise to power.

Effective party politics, therefore, does not usually emerge in the fragmented setting; no party is large enough to rule and the multiplicity of culture groups frustrates any attempts to form long-run multiethnic coalitions. In settings such as these, democracy frequently gives way to forms of authoritarian rule.

In summary, the cardinal features of fragmentation are (1) a multiplicity of ethnic groups, (2) the absence of effective brokerage institutions, e.g., national political parties and (3) the tendency for authoritarian rule by military or paramilitary organizations. We examine, now, politics in five fragmented settings, Lebanon, the Congo, Sudan, Nigeria, and Yugoslavia, in order to illustrate these conditions.

Fragmentation: The Proliferation of Ethnic Groups

The first characteristic of the fragmented society is contained in the meaning of the classificatory term itself, *viz.*, the existence of a large number of discrete cultural communities. Furnivall's definition of the plural society is thus slightly modified. Instead of several groups living side by side, but separately, within the same political unit, we find *many* groups living a culturally segregated life.

In Lebanon, for example, most persons are immediately identifiable as Christians or Muslims, but for political purposes membership in a particular sect is much more important. As Edward Shils points out,

> People may know they are Lebanese, but this is not as significant a fact for most of them as being Maronite, Orthodox Christian, Sunni, Shi'ite Muslims, or whatever else.[1]

The full list of confessional communities appears in Table 7.1. Although all of the groups (Jewish excepted) in Table 7.1 are loosely defined as either Christian or Muslim, significant denominational divisions exist within each of the two broader groups.

> The radical and clear-cut cleavage between two different groups which prevails among Frenchmen and Arabs in Algeria, Greeks and Turks in Cyprus, Europeans and Africans in South Africa, does not exist in Lebanon. Only those who like to convey, internally or externally, the impression of a Christian-Muslim either/or, try to distort the varied, rich and complex nature of the Lebanese social picture.[2]

---

1. "The Prospects for Lebanese Civility," in Leonard Binder, ed., *Politics in Lebanon* (New York: John Wiley & Sons, Inc., 1966), pp. 1-11 (quotation at pp. 3-4).
2. Hassan Saab, "The Rationalist School in Lebanese Politics," in Binder, *op. cit.*, pp. 271-82 (quotation at p. 272).

Table 7.1

Lebanese Population by Sect, 1956

Sect	Estimated Population
Maronite	424,000
Sunnite	286,000
Shi'ite	250,000
Greek Orthodox	149,000
Greek Catholic	91,000
Druze	88,000
Armenian Orthodox	64,000
Armenian Catholic	15,000
Protestant	14,000
Jewish	7,000
Syrian Catholic	6,000
Syrian Orthodox	5,000
Latins (Roman Catholic)	4,000
Nestorean Chaldeans	1,000
Others	7,000
Total	1,411,000

Source: Michael C. Hudson, *The Precarious Republic: Political Modernization in Lebanon* (New York: Random House, 1968), p. 22.

J. C. Hurewitz agrees with this description, noting that the two major communities are fractured rather than monolithic.[3] An assessment of ethnic groups in Lebanon shows, therefore, that the sects within the major religions are far more significant for political, economic and social purposes than the broader divisions themselves, and that Lebanon is a fragmented rather than competitive configuration.

It is also the case that each major religious sect is heavily concentrated in a particular region of the country.[4] Sectarian differences are thus reinforced by regional rivalries. Such regional concentration strengthens the alternative claims for statehood that minority communities are prone to assert. The Sunnis in northern coastal towns, for example, have on numerous occasions threatened to withdraw from Lebanon and join Syria.

The classification of the Congo as a fragmented political culture is less problematical. René Lemarchand observes that an amazing variety of cultures and political systems are encountered in the Congo, and the very classification of its people is a difficult task.[5] Six major ethnic groups are

3. "Lebanese Democracy in Its International Setting," in *ibid.*, pp. 213-38 (citation at p. 214).

4. Michael W. Suleiman, *Political Parties in Lebanon: The Challenge of a Fragmented Political Culture* (Ithaca, New York: Cornell University Press, 1967), pp. 26-27.

5. *Political Awakening in the Belgian Congo* (Berkeley and Los Angeles: University of California Press, 1964), p. 7. Our assertions of tribalism in the Congo are based on the discussion which appears in chapter 1 of Lemarchand's study. See also Crawford Young, *Politics in the Congo: Decolonization and Independence* (Princeton: Princeton University Press, 1965), chapter 11, "The Politics of Ethnicity," pp. 232-72.

distinguishable: Bakongo, Baluba, Mongo, Kuba, Mangbetu-Azande, and Waregu. In addition to these major "culture clusters," a host of minor tribal groupings can be identified. Altogether in a total population of over 14 million, some 180 culturally distinct tribes exist. The approxi-

Ethnographic Map of the Republic of Congo

mately 2 million Mongo are the largest community, but even so constitute only a small minority of the overall population. As in Lebanon, the proliferation of tribal groups is further exacerbated by regional concentration (see map).

> To be sure, the difficulties of creating an integrated national community from a multitude of ethnic "selves" are not unique to the Congo, as shown by the continuing efforts of African leaders to overcome the actual or potential threat of ethnic separatism. But in no other African territory have these difficulties assumed such magnitude, for in no other territory has the virulence of ethnic and regional particularism been so pronounced.[6]

---

6. Lemarchand, *op. cit.*, p. 1.

Lemarchand further remarks that "some Congolese politicians . . . conceptualize nationhood in terms of linguistic and cultural affinities, . . ."[7] Tribalism in the Congo thus poses severe problems for national unity.

Nigeria shares tribal diversity with the Congo. Eighteen different tribal groupings exist, each with its own language, organization and body of customs.[8] Three of these make up over half of the population: the Hausa-Fulani in the North, the Yorubas in the West, and the now famous Ibos in the East (see map). The Hausa-Fulani, the largest group, is chiefly Muslim

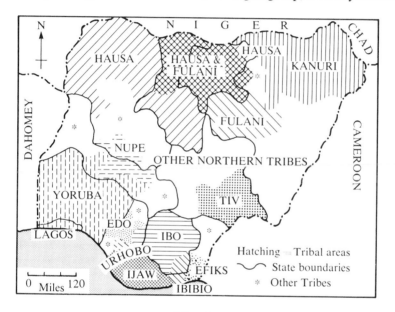

Nigeria

and possesses a traditional Islamic system of authority. Ibos, on the other hand, are noted for their ready acceptance of Christianity and interest in Western education and technology. During the era of British colonial rule that began in the nineteenth century, many Ibos migrated to other parts of Nigeria and filled clerkships in the colonial administration. Yorubas also possess their own distinct cultural traits and tend to be known for their business ability.

The rivalries between these communities are intense and bitter. In addition, rivalries also exist within each region between the dominant group and one or more minority tribes. The interests of the Tiv, the Kanuri and

---

7. *Ibid.*, p. 17.
8. L. Franklin Blitz, *The Politics and Administration of Nigerian Government* (New York: Frederick A. Praeger, 1965), p. 18.

the Nupe are often in opposition to those of the dominant Hausa-Fulani in the North; the Ibibio, Ijaw and Efik occupy a similar minority position in the East, and the same condition applies to non-Yoruba peoples in the West. Altogether, some 400 linguistic groups, large and small, comprise Nigeria's more than 45 million people. Tribalism, thus, aggravates the difficulties most new societies face in their efforts at nation building.

> "Tribalism" continues to bedevil the politics of a nation in which the people still think of themselves as Ibo, Yoruba, Hausa or even Ijebu, Aro or other tribal sub-group, rather than Nigerian.[9]

The Sudan, too, shows a complex ethnic mosaic — the 1956 census recorded some 10,263,000 persons and classified them into 572 tribes and subtribes which range in size from the one million Dinkas down to groups of a few dozen individuals.[10] Even when these tribes and subtribes are aggregated into more inclusive categories, no single community emerges as a majority. Using these broader divisions we find that 39 percent of the population is Arab, 30 percent Southern, 13 percent Western, 12 percent Beja and Nuba, 3 percent Nubian, and 3 percent foreigners

The Sudan

---

9. Walter Schwartz, *Nigeria* (New York: Frederick A. Praeger, 1968), pp. 60-61.
10. Mohamed Omer Beshir, *The Southern Sudan: Background to Conflict* (New York: Frederick A. Praeger, 1965), p. 5.

and miscellaneous. Out of the total population, 52 percent are Arabic-speaking and 48 percent speak a variety of other languages.[11]

Within the Arabic-speaking community, one division has assumed special political importance. We refer to the differences between the Ansar sect, the followers of the late Mahdi who attempted an unsuccessful revolt against Egyptian rule in 1881, and the Khatmiya sect, led by the Mirghani family, which opposed the Mahdi's revolt. Each of these sects have, at various times in modern Sudanese history, dominated one party. Their historical rivalries have often obstructed the formation and/or development of stable, intra-Arabic coalition governments.[12]

The Southern Sudan is considerably more varied than the Arabic North in its ethnic composition. Three main groups of people are ordinarily distinguished: (1) the Nilotics, comprising the Dinka, Nuer, Shilluk and Anuak, who live chiefly in Bahr el Ghazal and Upper Nile Provinces; (2) the Nilo-Hamitics, comprising the Murle, the Didinga, Boya, Toposa and Latuka, who live mostly in Equatoria; and (3) the Sudanese tribes, such as the Azande, which live in the west and southwestern parts of the South (see map).[13] The ethnic differences between tribes are reflected in linguistic, political and religious institutions. Twelve major languages are spoken in the South and none of these has become a *lingua-franca* among all Southerners. In addition, religion does not unify the South since ninety percent of these tribal peoples are pagan.

Yugoslavia is our final example of a fragmented polity. "Yugoslavia, created in 1918 as a new state, was composed of areas which had never enjoyed a common government and which for centuries had been under the domination of different foreign powers."[14] When the Communist Party came to power after World War II, five distinct Slav nationalities were given official recognition: Serbs, Croats, Slovenes, Macedonians, and Montenegrins.[15]

The Serbs, taken together, number approximately seven million and live mainly in the Republic of Serbia. Second in numerical size are the four million Croats who reside chiefly in Croatia but also represent significant minorities in the other Yugoslav republics. The third largest community is the Slovene, a compact national group of one and one-half

---

11. George W. Shepherd, Jr., "National Integration and the Southern Sudan," *Journal of Modern African Studies* 4, no. 2 (July 1966): 193-212 (citation at p. 196).

12. Thomas E. Nyquist, "The Sudan: Prelude to Elections," *Middle East Journal* 19, no. 3 (Summer 1965): 263-72 (see page 265).

13. Beshir, *op. cit.*, pp. 5-6.

14. Jack C. Fisher, *Yugoslavia—A Multinational State* (San Francisco: Chandler Publishing Company, 1966), p. 27.

15. This discussion of ethnic diversity in Yugoslavia follows Paul Shoup, *Communism and the Yugoslav National Question* (New York and London: Columbia University Press, 1968), pp. 3-12.

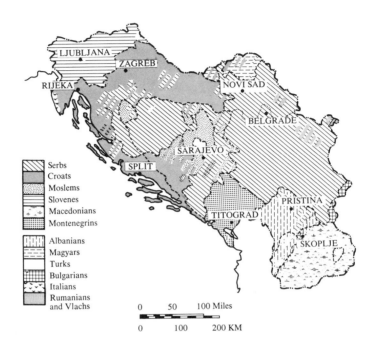

Yugoslavia

million who live in Slovenia. Irredentist movements among Slovenes in
Carinthia still strain current Yugoslav-Austrian relations. Slovenes are
followed in size by Macedonians, numbering on the order of one million,
whose territory (Macedonia) has been claimed at various times by Yugo-
slavs, Bulgarians, and Greeks. Finally, the smallest of the major Slav
communities is the Montenegrin, consisting of 500,000 persons. This
latter people is famous for their proud and warlike ethnic character and
has often disputed its border with neighboring Albania.

Some 700,000 Moslem Slavs, who live mainly in Bosnia and Hercegov-
inia, possess an ambiguous status. Although they have gained recognition
as a nationality in the postwar period, they do not yet enjoy the privileges
(such as a Republic of their own) possessed by the other Slavic communities. Other minorities make up the remaining ten percent of the Yugoslav population. These include Albanians, Hungarians, Turks, Slovaks,
Rumanians, Italians, and Czechs.

These diverse (and regionally concentrated) ethnic communities in
Yugoslavia are separated both by religious and cultural practices. The

Serbs, Montenegrins and Macedonians comprise a large Orthodox bloc, whereas Croats and Slovenes are mainly Catholic. Cultural differences reinforce religious divisions. Different historical experiences have also contributed to national rivalries among the Slavs. During the period of nationalist movements in Central Europe in the nineteenth century, most of the South Slav communities developed their own independent national movements — many of them related to real or imagined glories of past medieval kingdoms.

The achievements of independence and international recognition were not equally shared by all Slavs. On the one hand, for example, Serbia was declared a fully sovereign state by the Great Powers at the Congress of Berlin in 1878, whereas Croatia and Slovenia, on the other hand, failed to win autonomy within the Austro-Hungarian Empire prior to World War I. Although some cooperation developed among the Slavic groups, especially when they were confronted with common enemies, the old issues of national exploitation and intimidation nevertheless hampered the development of harmonious relations among the Slavic groups.

Yugoslavia was finally created as a modern state in 1918, but the union of Slavic peoples did not eliminate the older, more established national loyalties. Genuine Yugoslav patriotism, as might be expected, failed to replace local ethnic feelings: between the two wars, Serbs and Croats moved still further apart as the Croats expressed anxiety over being submerged under a Serbian-dominated government. Other Yugoslav minorities also felt estranged from the government in Belgrade. On top of these fears, atrocities committed during World War II further enlarged the almost irreconcilable gaps among the respective Slav nationality groups: Croatian fascists assaulted Serbs, Serbian Chetniks attacked Moslems, and Bulgarians, Hungarians and Albanians massacred a large number of Serbs.

> When national strife was indeed curbed at the end of the war, it was not as the result of a reconciliation of national differences but because the Communists, by seizing power and carrying out revolutionary changes in Yugoslav society drastically limited the scope given to expressions of national discontent.[16]

Ethnic conflict is thus deeply rooted in Yugoslav history — attempts at reconcilitation must, if they are to be successful, overcome long-established barriers of hate and mistrust, as well as vivid recollections of violence and killing. Yugoslavia's constituent cultural groups are held together now by Tito's Communist Party; even under communist rule, however, traditional ethnic aspirations have remained fundamentally unchanged. Shoup concludes in his study of communism and Yugoslav ethnic groups that,

---

16. *Ibid.*, p. 10.

the Yugoslav Communists, after a decade and a half of experimenta-
tion with a liberal form of Communism, seem to be succumbing to
the sterile pattern of national conflict which so weakened the interwar regime.[17]

The problem that presently confronts the communist rulers is found
in the incompatible, intense ethnic feelings held by the members of the
respective communal groups, and their sensitivity to local interests. These
sentiments are further polarized because of the unevenly developed
character of the economy; the lower developmental level of the South
has strengthened ethnic group ties in that region and its citizens demand
increased public expenditure in their area.[18] Regional grievances are thus
intensified because of real or imagined discrimination by the central government in the allocation of financial assistance and investment funds.
Standards of productivity and efficiency must be relaxed, if necessary, to
prevent an upsurge in regional/ethnic animosities or jealousies. Investment funds are often distributed for political reasons, even though the
maximum marginal productivity gains can only be obtained by concentrated investment in the already industrially advanced North. These investment funds are not viewed by members of each nationality group as public
goods, but rather as private regional goods. Expansion of Yugoslavia's
port capacity, for example, highlights the ethnic competition for public
funds. The Republic of Slovenia is now constructing a major port facility
at Koper, due to Slovenian desire to have a port if its own, regardless of
the actual utility of the port's development.[19] Duplication in other industries is widespread and wasteful of public funds. Thus the rationale for
government, the provision of collective goods, is challenged by communities that suspect they are not receiving their deserved portion of public
funds. Under these conditions, unity is tenuous and perhaps unwarranted.

Summary. We thus see that the fragmented polity is characterized by a
multiplicity of culture groups and the absence of a dominant community
capable of providing stability and orderly government (especially democratic government). This condition holds even though the bases of cultural
pluralism vary from religion in Lebanon, to tribalism in the Congo, Sudan,
and Nigeria,[20] to ethnic regionalism in Yugoslavia. We show in the next

17. *Ibid.*, p. 261.
18. Fisher, *op. cit.*, p. 56.
19. *Ibid.*, pp. 59-60.
20. For further discussion on the problem of tribalism and political integration
in Africa see James S. Coleman, "The Problem of Political Integration in Emergent
Africa," *Western Political Quarterly* 8, no. 1 (March 1955): 44-57; Immanuel Wallerstein, "Ethnicity and National Integration in West Africa," *Cahiers d' Etudes
Africaines* 2, no. 3 (October 1960): 129-39: and Aristide R. Zolberg, "Mass Parties
and National Integration: The Case of the Ivory Coast," *Journal of Politics* 25, no. 1
(February 1963): 36-48.

two sections that such political organizations as parties often follow tribal, religious or lingustic lines, and usually command little support outside their own communities. The absence of such brokerage institutions as national political parties encourages military or paramilitary organizations to seize power — they alone command the resources to provide stable and orderly government.

Political Parties: The Absence of Brokerage Institutions

In competitive, dominant majority, and dominant minority configurations, political parties invariably follow ethnic lines. Racial, religious, linguistic, and tribal communities all represent ready-made sources of political support that political entrepreneurs repeatedly try to tap and mobilize. Leaders in fragmented plural societies are no different. Ethnic communities again constitute the most readily available collection of supporters, especially when these fragmented societies have a history of intercommunal conflict. In the fragmented culture, however, the successful mobilization of even the largest ethnic group, whether it be a tribal, religious or linguistic community, does not provide a basis for majority rule. The formation and maintenance of coalition governments is a formidable task and, as we see shortly, such attempts often meet with failure. Bitter enemies are not easily persuaded to put aside their differences in order to cooperate in government, especially since extremists within each community watch from the sidelines and often seize the first opportunity to discredit men of moderate persuasion with having sold out the interests of their own community. We intend to show in this section that the proliferation of ethnic groups, which defines the fragmented society, encourages a commensurate proliferation of political parties; the plethora of parties, in turn, inhibits cooperative ethnic behavior. The resulting product is instability, or at best a most tenuous stability.

Lebanon. Politics in Lebanon, since its independence from the French Mandate in 1943, is invidious.

> As for national consensus, in one sense it is nonexistent while in another it imposes stiflingly narrow limits: national consensus exists only in the negative form of mutual rivalry and suspicion and an awareness by each group that satisfaction of its own wants must mean the negation of another group's sense of security.[21]

Religious divisions in Lebanese society exert a profound impact upon political behavior and attitudes. These divisions make it difficult for Lebanon to evolve a system of effective party government: no party or

---

21. Malcolm H. Kerr, "Political Decision Making in a Confessional Democracy," in Binder, *op. cit.*, pp. 187-212 (quotation at p. 188).

combination of parties has ever been able to capture a majority in the
Lebanese Parliament. Even in the hard-fought campaigns of 1960 and
1964, some eight to ten parties were able, taken together, to win only
thirty-four and twenty-eight seats (out of ninety-nine), respectively.
Feudal leaders, landlords, and financiers, organized into well-defined
blocs, obtained the majority of seats.[22]

Although party government does not work in Lebanon, it remains true
nevertheless that parties are of a religious character. "Almost in every case
some ethnic or religious group constitutes the predominant element in the
party."[23] In his study of parties in Lebanon, Suleiman identifies some
nineteen distinct parties and classifies them into four categories: (1) transnational parties with non-pan-Arab organizations: the Lebanese Communist Party and the Syrian Social Nationalist Party; (2) transnational
parties that represent the Arab nationalist movement: the Arab Resurrection Socialist Party and the Arab Nationalists' Movement; (3) expressly
religious and ethnic organizations: the Dashnak Party, the Hunchak Party,
and the Ramgavar Azadagan Party; and (4) exclusively Lebanese parties:
An-Najjada Party, the Progressive Socialist Party, the National Appeal
and National Organization Parties (all chiefly Moslem); Phalanges Liban-
aises, the Constitutional Union and National Bloc Parties, and the National Liberals' Party (mainly Christian). What does this proliferation of
parties imply for Lebanese democracy?

> Parties in Lebanon do not meaningfully represent the interests of
> the population, a function which parties in a democratic system are
> supposed to perform. Because they are sectional-confessional in
> their strength and composition, *they are not capable of aggregating
> interests on a national level.* They are generally too doctrinaire and
> *the population is too fragmented to allow for adjustment and balanc-
> ing of divergent views.*[24]

What forces, then, act as a surrogate for parties and provide some
semblance of orderly government? According to Michael Hudson, Lebanon's domestic tranquility is based upon a perpetual stand-off among the
various religious sects.[25] This stand-off is underpinned by an unwritten
agreement called the "National Pact," which was concluded when Muslims

---

22. Suleiman, *op. cit.*, p. xv. For an analysis of the occupational composition of
Lebanese Parliamentary Deputies, and the results of the 1960 election see Jacob M.
Landau, "Elections in Lebanon," *Western Political Quarterly* 14, no. 1 (March
1961): 120-47. Landau concludes from his study of Lebanese politics that as of
1960 parties have been unable to diminish the influence of the feudal lords or cir-
cumscribe their effects.
23. Suleiman, *op. cit.*, p. 267. See also Landau, *op. cit.*, p. 132.
24. Suleiman, *op. cit.*, p. 286 (emphasis added).
25. *The Precarious Republic: Political Modernization in Lebanon* (New York:
Random House, 1968), p. 6.

and Christians united against French rule and restored to high office those officials who had been arrested by French authorities. This "National Pact," an Islamic-Christian accord of which no written text exists, presumably consecrates the voluntary and equal association of Muslims and Christians in the Nation and in the State; Maronites invariably hold the office of President of the Republic, and Sunnis the office of President of the Council.[26] In addition to this sectarian allocation of Lebanon's highest offices, so correspondingly are most other elective posts allocated according to each sect's share of the total population. The 1932 census reported that Christians exceeded non-Christians by a ratio of six to five; seats in the Lebanese Parliament are thereby awarded to the several religious sects on a proportional basis. Cabinet portfolios and other important administrative posts are also reserved on a sect by sect basis.

> In the ninety-nine-member Parliaments of 1960 and 1964 the Maronites were allocated twenty seats, the Greek Orthodox eleven, the Greek Catholics six, the Armenian Orthodox four, the Armenian Catholics, Protestants, and Christian minorities one apiece for a Christian total of fifty-four. The forty-five non-Christian seats were distributed as follows: Sunnites twenty, Shiites nineteen, and Druzes six. These proportions have been maintained in all the Parliaments of the Independent Republic.[27]

A brief review of the Lebanese plural society has shown that a multitude of distinct religious sects has spawned an even larger number of political parties, each with its own sectarian basis. As a consequence, party government is neither responsible nor workable as we know it in other Western democracies. Instead, a small landed gentry has combined with leading businessmen to rule in Lebanon's Chamber of Deputies. Domination of the Lebanese Parliament by these traditional, often nonparty, groups has given Parliament a reputation for being unable to deal with fundamental problems. As a result, Parliament has not been a terribly important institution in Lebanese politics, and sectarian problems have often been contested in the streets. This condition imparts to Lebanon's democracy an extreme sensitivity to destabilizing events and on occasion leads to military rule as a necessary alternative to feudal, factional, regional, and religious party rule in times of crisis.

The Congo. Tribal divisions in the Congo have similarly fostered the origin and growth of an incredibly large number of parties: the 180 or more distinct tribal groups can almost be juxtaposed against the 113 different

---

26. Pierre Rondot, "The Political Institutions of Lebanese Democracy," in Binder, *op. cit.,* pp. 127-41 (citation at pp. 136-37).
27. Hudson, *op. cit.,* p. 23. See also Ralph E. Crow, "Religious Sectarianism in the Lebanese Political System," *Journal of Politics* 24, no. 3 (August 1961): 489-520.

parties that existed just prior to independence; many of these small parties have since dissolved or merged with larger parties.[28] One can, without doing an injustice to an impartial interpretation of Congolese politics, reduce this list to about 19 important parties. In order to stress the point of tribalism and its relationship with multipartyism, we present the full list and indicate in parentheses the provinces in which they are based.[29]

Abako	Alliance des Ba-Kongo (Léopoldville Prov.)
Abazi	Alliance des Ba-Yanzi (Léopoldville Prov.)
A.R.P.	Alliance Rurale Progressiste (Kivu Prov.)
Atcar	Association des Tshokwe du Congo de l'Angola et de la Rhodèsie (Katanga Prov.)
Balubakat	Ba-Luba du Katanga (Katanga Prov.)
Cerea	Centre de Regroupement Africain (Kivu Prov.)
Coaka	Coalition Kasaienne (Kasai Prov.)
Conakat	Confédération des Associations du Katanga (Katanga Prov.)
Luka	No particular meaning (Léopoldville Prov.)
M.N.C.	Mouvement National Congolais: (a) the Lumumba faction (throughout the Congo); (b) the Kalonji faction (Kasai Prov.); (c) M.N.C.-Nendaka
Mederco	Mouvement de l'Évolution et de Developpement Économique Rural du Congo (Equatorial Prov.)
M.U.B.	Mouvement de l'Unité Basonge (Kasai Prov.)
P.N.P.	Parti National du Progrès (throughout the Congo)
P.S.A.	Parti Solidaire Africain (Léopoldville Prov.)
Puna	Parti de l'Unité Nationale (Equatorial Prov.)
R.D.L.K.	Rassemblement Democratique du Lac-Kwango-Kwilu (Léopoldville Prov.)
Reko	Ressortissants de l'"Est de Kongo (Kivu Prov.)
Unimo	Union Mongo (Equatorial Prov.)
U.N.C.	Union Nationale Congolaise (Kasai Prov.)

As is evident from the list, party names often reveal the local basis of organization and tribal support. Even those parties that display a national name are basically tribal in membership.

Most Congolese parties were founded only a few years before independence as a response to the announcement that territorial and communal elections would be held in December 1959; shortly thereafter elections were scheduled for May 1960 for the House of Representatives and the Provincial Assemblies. Tribal support quickly materialized for most of these newly formed Congolese parties.

---

28. Daniel J. Crowley, "Politics and Tribalism in Katanga," *Western Political Quarterly* 16, no. 1 (March 1963): 68-78.
29. Daniel Biebuyck and Mary Douglas, *Congo: Tribes & Parties* (London: Royal Anthropological Institute, 1961), pp. 29-30.

The sudden proliferation of Congolese political groups provides the example of a developmental pattern which finds virtually no counterpart in other African territories. Whereas in November, 1956, the Abako was the only significant party in existence on the Congolese scene, by November, 1959, as many as fifty-three different political groups were officially registered. In the few months preceding independence the number had grown to 120. *This plethoric growth of parties reflects the extent to which they tended to rely on the support of tribal groupings as a means of entry into the political arena.*[30]

Those politicians advocating intertribal cooperation made little headway against tribally based elites. Lemarchand observes, and it is a most crucial observation, that "moderate" groups, either on a uniracial or multiracial basis, were structurally weak and failed to attract widespread national support.[31] For most Congolese, "affiliation to a political party was viewed as secondary to, and derivative from, affiliation with the tribe."[32] The political salience of tribal identification is heavily reinforced since many Congolese can recall a vivid history of intertribal violence.

The first elections, the communal and territorial elections of December 1959, were of little significance because they were boycotted by the three major parties. The Parliamentary and Provincial Assembly elections held the following year, however, are a signpost in recent Congolese history. Throughout the campaign, local interests and tribal rivalries were emphasized.[33] The balloting for seats in the House of Representatives displayed below failed to produce a majority government.[34]

M.N.C. — Lumumba with cartels, Coaka and U.N.C.	41
P.S.A.	13
Abako	12
M.N.C. — Kalonji	8
P.N.P. — A.R.P., Luka, Mederco, Front Commun	15
Reco	4
Puna	7
Cartel Balubakat	7
Conakat	8
Cerea	10
Independents, local interests, Abazi, R.D.L.K., Unimo	12
Total	137

30. Lemarchand, *op. cit.*, p. 191 (emphasis added).

31. *Ibid.*, pp. 210-12.

32. *Ibid.*, p. 187.

33. For details about the 1960 election see Lemarchand, *op. cit.*, pp. 217-32 and Young, *op. cit.*, pp. 302-6.

34. Biebuyck, *op. cit.*, p. 9.

The Congress that was formed almost immediately broke down with the secession of Katanga Province. Although the secession movement ended in 1964, after a period of confusion and conflict that witnessed the intervention of United Nations' forces, popular elections have not yet been restored.

Belgian colonial rule can probably be credited with stimulating rather than reducing tribalism and its political consequences: industrialization produced uneven levels of development that benefitted select tribes and threatened surrounding, less advanced groups; in addition, the tribe became the major focus of personal identification as rural villagers moved into urban areas. Furthermore, Belgian educational policy maintained tribal differences since education was dispensed in the vernacular and few Congolese received higher education. Finally, Belgian administrators tried to adapt district boundaries to tribal divisions, thus "favoring the emergence of separate regional consciousness among Africans."[35]

Even if Belgium had fostered the growth of a national consciousness among Congolese, it is still most unlikely that independence and national elections would have produced a popularly supported majority government. Tribal rioting on behalf of demands placed by various communities for their own autonomous districts, and the subsequent demarcation of twenty-one tribally distinct districts, confirms the salience of tribe in Congolese politics.

Nigeria. Nigerian nationalists never displayed the spirit of cooperative behavior that often appears in competitive, and, on occasion, in dominant majority configurations. As we might expect, political parties in Nigeria originated and grew principally as expressions of tribal/regional interests: Azikiwe, an Ibo, formed the Council of Nigeria and the Cameroons, later renamed the National Council of Nigerian Citizens (NCNC); Yoruba nationalism first appeared in the Egbe Omo Oduduwas, a cultural organization founded in 1948, which subsequently became active in politics as the Action Group (AG); and, finally, Hausa interests were expressed by both the colonial authorities and the traditional rulers until the Northern Peoples' Congress (NPC) was formed to contest the 1951 elections. *Thus by 1950, the alignments that were to characterize Nigerian politics after independence had already solidified: the North against the South, East against West, and the minority groups in each region against their respective dominant communities.*[36] These splits have shaped the history of modern Nigeria.

---

35. Lemarchand, *op. cit.*, p. 66.

36. For an informative account of the position of the minority tribes in the three major Nigerian regions see Richard L. Sklar, "Nigerian Politics in Perspective," *Government and Opposition* 2, no. 4 (July-October 1967): 524-39.

Constitutional development in Nigeria unfolded in the form of a federal government. Major powers of finance, defense and external affairs are allocated to the federal government, and the Eastern, Western and Northern regional governments possess powers in the fields of health, agriculture, and education. Certain powers are shared: trade, labor, industrial development, roads, prisons and public works.[37] During periods of emergency, the federal government also has the right to dissolve the regional legislatures, arrest or detain persons at will, search premises without a warrant, and expropriate any property.

The drawback in the Federal Constitution, at least insofar as Southerners were affected, was the likelihood that Northerners, comprising just over half of all Nigerians, would seek to gain advantages because of their dominant position at the federal level: the Northern region was allocated more seats in the Nigerian House of Representatives than the other two (and later three) regions combined.[38]

Parties and Elections in Nigeria. As mentioned before, parties in Nigeria are tribally based. For example, as of 1958, 59 percent of the major NCNC leaders were of Eastern origin, of whom 49 percent were Ibo. Yorubas in turn comprised 68 percent of the Action Group leadership and 84 percent of the NPC leadership were indigenous Northerners.[39] The regional elections held in 1951 provided the first competitive opportunity for these tribally based parties. As expected, each major party was successful in its own region, and in subsequent regional elections sought to consolidate their power still further. By 1957, the Action Group held 49 of 80 seats in the Western regional assembly, the NCNC controlled 64 of 84 Eastern seats, and in the North the NPC occupied 106 of 131 seats.[40] Minority groups in each region generally allied themselves with major parties outside their own regions in order to strengthen their positions.

The first federal election was scheduled for December 12, 1959. Violence erupted periodically throughout the campaign and "opposition" party members were stoned in all three regions. Each party stressed the unity of its own tribal community and warned its members, who lived as

---

37. Henry L. Bretton, *Power and Stability in Nigeria* (New York: Frederick A. Praeger, 1962), p. 20.

38. The applicability of a federal constitution for Nigeria is explored in S. D. Tansey and D. G. Kermode, "The Westminster Model in Nigeria," *Parliamentary Affairs* 21, no. 1 (Winter 1967/68): 19-37. They conclude that a federal constitution is not likely to work when one member state is more populous than all the rest put together. It was implemented, they suggest, because British sympathies were with the North in any case.

39. Adebayo Adedeji, *Nigerian Administration and Its Political Setting* (London: Hutchinson Education, Ltd., 1968), p. 174.

40. James S. Coleman, *Nigeria: Background to Nationalism* (Berkeley: University of California Press, 1958), pp. 389-95.

minorities in other regions of Nigeria, of likely domination by that region's majority. They, in the language of our theory, adopted an extremist position, resorting to communal demand generation or ethnic chauvinism.

> The Action Group's electoral effort in all three regions during the 1959 pre-independence campaign was based partly on the theme of Yoruba unification and partly on the exploitation of non-Yoruba minority fears in the North and the East. The results indicate that the appeal was successful mainly in the Western Region itself: outside the Region, it succeeded wherever non-Yorubas required outside support against the Hausa-Fulani, the Ibo or other groups of actual or imagined hostile intent. Nearly every argument in favor of these non-Western groups was applied by the NPC and the NCNC against the Yoruba in the Western Region and in support of ethnic argument there.[41]

The final ballot count revealed that each party won a majority of the seats allocated to its region and also received some minority support from areas outside of its region: the NPC controlled 134 seats, the NCNC and its affiliate, the Northern Elements Progressive Union (NEPU) 89 seats, the Action Group 73, and other groups the remaining 16. No one party commanded a majority in the 312-seat House of Representatives.[42]

The 1961 regional elections showed clearly that the different communities were moving further apart from each other instead of becoming reconciled. In the North the NPC overwhelmed its opposition and captured 160 of 170 regional legislative assembly seats. Meanwhile, the Action Group was beset with internal difficulties and several of its dissident members, led by Akintola who was the Premier of the Western Region, split off and formed the United Peoples' Party (UPP). Disturbances erupted in the Western Region's legislative assembly when Akintola was asked to resign his position. The federal government declared a state of emergency and dissolved the Western regional government. Federal intervention infuriated the Yorubas who perceived the emergency as a plot on the part of the NPC and NCNC to intervene in their affairs.[43]

While the Western Region was in a state of chaos, a new region was created in the center of Nigeria: the Mid-Western Region. In keeping with the prevailing pattern of Nigerian politics, a new party was therein formed called the Mid-West Democratic Front, which propagated an anti-Ibo platform and sought to ally itself with the Northern NPC. This alliance

41. Bretton, *op. cit.*, p. 129.

42. K. W. J. Post, *The Nigerian Federal Election of 1959* (London: Oxford University Press, 1963), pp. 356-68.

43. A detailed account of the crisis in the Western Region is given in John P. Mackintosh, "Politics in Nigeria: The Action Group Crisis of 1962," *Political Studies* 10, no. 3 (October 1962): 223-47.

was short-lived as bitter memories of slave raiding led to the flaring of anti-Northern sentiments among the Edo-speaking groups in the Mid-West state.

Relations between the NPC and NCNC, which had earlier set up a coalition government, had badly deteriorated by the time of the 1964 Federal Election. A host of new coalitions were speedily created. The National Progressive Front (NPF), which contained the NCNC and the AG, joined with the NEPU and the United Middle Belt Congress (UMBC) to form the United Progressive Grand Alliance (UPGA). This combination was arrayed against the Nigerian National Alliance (NNA), which consisted of the NPC, the UPP now renamed the Nigerian National Democratic Party (NNDP) and the MDF.[44] Irregularities hampered and prevented the smooth execution of the election: Awolowo, leader of the AG, was imprisoned for his alleged misuse of party funds as revealed in the prior state of crisis in the Western Region; members of the Federal Election Commission became suspect when they decided to accept the list of unopposed nominations provided by the NNA (which seemed to insure the NNA's victory); furthermore, widespread evidence suggests that the NNA used coercion to prevent UPGA candidates from contesting seats in the North. The NNA won a clear victory securing 202 of the 257 elective federal seats.

The results of the 1964 elections are less important than the consequences that followed. The alliance between the NCNC and the AG immediately broke down due to the AG's resentment of its poor showing in the West. In the following year, an election was held for seats in the Western regional assembly. At best it was farcical: AG candidates were not allowed to contest many of the elective seats; government party members received their ballots before polling day; and the counting of votes was haphazard. Calls for a new election went unheeded and violence flared up within the Western Region. Shortly thereafter, in January 1966, the army seized power.

> It appears that a number of army officers, of the rank of major and under, had become inflamed by what they thought to be the incompetence and corruption of the Regional and Federal Ministers, the self-seeking and avarice of the political parties and they thought that the Army would be given the "dirty" work of cleaning up the troubles they strongly believed, and with some truth, had been due to the politicians and to no one else: these factors proved too much for them and they determined to overthrow the civilian administration.[45]

---

44. The reader is asked not to throw his arms into the air in wild confusion. This proliferation of parties and abbreviations terminates shortly in authoritarian military rule; for the moment, please try to struggle with the authors through this welter of parties and coalitions.

45. Rex Niven, *Nigeria* (New York: Frederick A. Praeger, 1967), p. 113.

The Constitution was thrown out and a unitary, military government was established. In the last section of this chapter we discuss the still further deterioration of tribal relations which led to the all too well known civil war.

The Sudan. Electoral politics in the Sudan adheres to the same pattern we have witnessed in the recent histories of Lebanon, the Congo, and Nigeria. A multiplicity of culture groups has spawned a large number of active political groups, each representing the interests of one specific ethnic community. The Umma Party, or Umma for short, was founded by the Mahdi's son and is the spokesman for the Arabic Ansar sect. Its Khatmiya counterpart is the National Union Party, which speaks for the followers of Sayed Ali El Mirghani. (These two Islamic, Arabic communities are distinguished by differences in organization and ritual, and not in matters of faith and doctrine.) These two parties have played an important role in Sudanese electoral history.

Sudan's experience with democracy began in 1943 with the introduction of elections for members on the Provincial Councils. This was followed by elections to the Advisory Council for the Northern Sudan in 1944, for tribal leaders and town councils in 1948, and to a partly elected Legislative Assembly in 1948. These developments prompted the holding of nationwide elections for the Legislative Assembly in 1953.[46]

During these pre-independence days, the ideal of a common struggle against foreign rule helped the rival Islamic factions to forget their narrow affiliations. Sayyid Ismail El Azhari was able to organize the National Unionist Party and, having secured a majority of fifty-one seats in the ninety-seven-member Assembly, was able to lead the country to independence in 1956 as its first Prime Minister. But, as we see below, once the foreign enemy had been removed political life resumed its historical tradition of dissension; all attempts at alignment of the different factions within the democratic framework failed.[47]

The Republic of Sudan began its existence as an independent country on January 1, 1956. Azhari and the Khatmiya, however, were unable to sustain their harmonious relations. On February 26, 1956, Azhari formed a national government without the support of the Khatmiya, who had broken away from the NUP and formed the People's Democratic Party (PDP). As a result of this split Azhari's government was short-lived. It was defeated in a vote of censure, and replaced by a coalition of Umma and the PDP on July 7, 1956. This coalition was sustained by the 1958

---

46. Leo Silberman, "Democracy in the Sudan," *Parliamentary Affairs* 12, nos. 3 and 4 (Summer and Autumn 1959): 349-76 (citation at p. 352).

47. See B. S. Sharma, "Failure of 'Local-Government-Democracy' in the Sudan," *Political Studies* 15, no. 1 (February 1967): 62-71, especially p. 69.

election, but proved unnatural and difficult to maintain. Although Umma, the PDP and some Southern delegates gave the government a comfortable majority of 103 out of 173 seats, the historical conflict between the Mahdists (Umma) and the Mirghanists (PDP) strained the coalition. The resignation of several government ministers in mid-November of 1958 was followed by a military coup on November 17, 1958.[48]

> Since independence on January 1, 1956, the Sudan had struggled under the burden of weak coalition governments. The multiplicity of parties, the constant shifting of party alliances, the lack of discipline over individual members in Parliament all contributed to the inability of parliamentary government to deal decisively with problems facing the new nation.[49]

During the regime of Abdullah Khalil, the Prime Minister between 1956 and 1958, Southern representation in Parliament increased from twenty-two to forty-six members. These Southern delegates presented a demand for a federal solution to the Southern problem, the desire of the South for greater regional autonomy from the Arabic North, but later walked out of Parliament in protest of government's failure to comply. Military rule, which began in 1958, did not improve the Southern situation. The military regime carried out repressive policies in the South: political activity was severely punished, Christian missionaries were expelled from the South, and thousands of Southern Sudanese fled to neighboring countries. By 1963 the Anya-Nya guerrillas began open terrorist activity against the military government stationed in Khartoum. Thus the generally tense relations between Southerners and other Sudanese were even further strained during the first period of military rule.

The military regime was liquidated in October 1964 when it failed to cope with a massive popular uprising led by staff and students of the University of Khartoum.[50] A new caretaker government was formed on February 24, 1965, which included former members of the NUP, Umma, the PDP, the Islamic Charter Front, the Southern delegation, a Communist, and an independent. Although conflicts erupted within the government over the scheduling of elections especially because of turmoil in the South, arrangements were finally made to hold the election on April 21, 1965. They were suspended altogether in the South where twenty-two nominated candidates were unopposed.

---

48. Yusuf Fadl Hasan, "The Sudanese Revolution of October 1964," *Journal of Modern African Studies* 5, no. 4 (December 1967): 491-509, see especially pp. 491-93.

49. Nyquist, *op. cit.*, pp. 263-64.

50. A detailed account of the 1964 popular uprising is found in K. D. D. Henderson, "The Sudan Today," *African Affairs* 64, no. 256 (July 1965): 170-81.

An analysis[51] of the election and its results reveals that tribal, regional and personal loyalties are important determinants of voting behavior. No one party secured enough seats to form the government. An alliance between Umma, which won seventy-five seats, and the NUP, which won fifty-two, was ultimately arranged, though it too had a very limited duration.

The most significant factor in the election, however, was the rise of two racial groupings for the first time: the Beja Congress and the Nuba "Independents." Each party is regionally concentrated. The Beja Congress won ten of fourteen constituencies of the Red Sea Hills in Kassala Province, while the Nubas simultaneously gained eight of thirteen in their region. These candidates appealed to their constituents for support voicing the theme of regional autonomy.

Following the establishment of the new government, a series of negotiations were held between Arabs and Africans that resulted in the Round Table Conference on the Southern Problem at Khartoum in March 1965.[52] Northern extremists were generally opposed to separation for the Southern provinces. In spite of this element of opposition, several reforms in the areas of increased Southern representation in the administration, greater educational opportunities, and more funds for Southern economic development were agreed upon; a twelve-man committee formed after the Conference to implement these reforms, however, soon broke down. Successive prime ministers, Mohammed Mahgoub, Saddik el Mahdi, and Mahgoub again were unable to resolve peacefully the Southern problem.

In May 1969 a new military regime, led by General Gafaar al-Nimeiry, assumed office. Meanwhile, a Nile Provisional Government was formed in the Southern Sudan on March 19, 1969, by representatives of the three Southern provinces.[53] The new nation was christened the "Nile State" and the goal of freedom for the Southern people was announced. Although the General was confronted with overt civil war in the South, he has been unable to maintain unity and cohesion in the North: five attempted coups d'etat had been put down by the new government in just the first year of military rule alone.[54] Moreover, most of these attempts have been led by dissident Moslems, rather than Southern Africans. For example, one assas-

---

51. See B. S. Sharma, "The 1965 Elections in the Sudan," *The Political Quarterly* 37, no. 4 (October-December 1966): 441-52.

52. Shepherd, *op. cit.*, pp. 204-6.

53. The Nile Provisional Government publishes a newsletter called "The Voice of the Nile Republic." In it, they attempt to document claims of Arab repression and genocide. While some of these reported statistics may be exaggerated, these documents do provide an opportunity to study official Southern Sudanese aims and policies.

54. *The New York Times*, January 14, 1970, p. 20.

sination attempt on General al-Nimeiry's life was ultimately traced to an Arab Sudanese of the Ansar sect.[55]

Although the Sudan does not display the impressively large number of parties we find in Nigeria, the Congo, and Lebanon, nevertheless democratic stability does not exist. Repeated terms of military rule highlight the tenuous nature of democratic practices and institutions in the Sudan— the major stumbling block has been and still remains the fundamental differences both within the Islamic Arab North and between it and the African South. The appearance of new political racial groupings in the 1965 election suggests that workable coalitions might be even more difficult to form should elections be reinstated sometime in the future.

Yugoslavia. Electoral history in modern Yugoslavia is divisible into two distinct periods: (1) multiparty competition in 1920 shortly after the establishment of an independent Yugoslavia in 1918, and (2) post-World War II elections which have been dominated almost exclusively by Tito's Communist Party. The first period follows closely the general pattern seen throughout this chapter. An assortment of parties, many of them expressions of particular ethnic communities, contested elections on November 28, 1920, for seats in the Constituent Assembly (Yugoslavia's parliament).[56] A full list of participating parties, which we enumerate below, reveals that political representation of ethnic sentiments in Yugoslavia's fragmented society engendered a panoply of competing groups:

1. the Democratic Party, of which Serbs formed the majority — advocates of a centralized state inspired by Serbia;
2. the Radicals—enthusiasts of Serbia stressing her past glories and the Serbian claim to national leadership;
3. the Communist Party, the only party possessing genuine nationwide backing;
4. the Croatian Republican Peasants Party;
5. the Agrarian Party (a Serbo-Slovene Coalition);
6. the Yugoslav Club;
7. the Yugolsav Moslem Organization;
8. the Social Democrats;
9. the National Club (Croatia);
10. the Džemijet (Turkish Party);
11. the Croat Union;

55. *Ibid.*, March 31, 1970, p. 3.
56. Data about this election are drawn from Frits W. Honduis, *The Yugoslav Community of Nations* (The Hague: Mouton, 1968), pp. 94-95.

12. the Republican Party;
13. the Croatian Law Party;
14. the National Socialists; and
15. the Trumbić-Drinković group.

None of these parties emerged with a majority in the Constituent Assembly. The Democratic Party came out first with 92 seats followed by the Radicals who obtained 91 seats; these two Serbian-based parties, even when taken together, failed to constitute a majority. Other parties polled anywhere from a high of 58 seats (the Communists) to a low of one (the Trumbić-Drinković group) out of a total of 418 seats.

The proliferation of minority parties in the 1920 Yugoslav Constituent Assembly does not appear, in retrospect, to provide a sound basis for stable democratic government. As we might have predicted, disagreements immediately surfaced at the very opening of the Constituent Assembly on December 12, 1920. For example, three delegations (Communists, Yugoslav Club and National Club) refused to take the oath when demands for a two-thirds majority vote acceptance of the constitution were turned down in favor of an absolute majority. Other disagreements centered on such questions as the name of the country, the procedural rules for discussion and adoption of a draft constitution, the number of provinces, and the degree of centralization and decentralization of the new government. The new constitution was finally adopted on June 28, 1921, by a slender majority vote, although the Croatian Peasants, Communists, National Club, and Yugoslav Club members were absent from the vote.

The parliamentary system began to disintegrate in short order. Communist attempts on the life of the Regent and other high officials led the National Assembly to nullify the right of Communist Party delegates to be seated—the party immediately went underground until it reappeared as the leading political force in Yugoslav politics in World War II. The Radical-Democrat coalition broke down in 1922 over an internal Serbian historical problem; meanwhile, the Croatian Peasant Party refused to participate in parliamentary life—the party was outlawed and its leader, Stjepan Radić, was jailed in January 1925. Realignments, new coalitions and other unexpected moves inhibited stable, orderly government; governments succeeded each other in rapid succession.

On 20th June 1928 the parliamentary system broke down. After a sharp discussion in the National Assembly between the Montenegrin Radical delegate Puniša Račic and the opposition, Račic drew his revolver and fired at the Radić group. He instantly killed two

Croatian delegates and wounded three other, including Stjepan
Radic, who died in Zagreb on 8th August.[57]

The King subsequently named an extra-parliamentary government under
General Petar Živkovic: the Constitution was declared no longer in force
and the National Assembly dismissed. Royal rule continued until Germany
defeated the Yugoslav army in 1941. In that interim period, attempts by
the King to reconcile ethnic tensions by including in his governments men
from different parts of the country failed miserably. Most notable was the
refusal of any important Croats to cooperate with the Belgrade government.

The second period of electoral politics dates from the reestablishment
of an independent Yugoslavia immediately following the collapse of Germany in World War II. In the election for a new Constituent Assembly,
the ballot papers were dominated with candidates nominated by the People's Front, and contained only a sprinkling of candidates from other
parties—the People's Front gained over ninety percent of the vote. The
Constituent Assembly met on November 29, 1945, and on December 1
Marshall Tito was appointed head of the Government.

Tito and the Communist Party have ruled Yugoslavia since 1945. Competitive party politics that existed early in the interwar period did not
reappear in the postwar era. Nevertheless ethnic tensions have often materialized within the Communist Party and official government policies
have been designed to grant recognition to the importance of the different
nationality groups.

> The lack of complaints about the system [Yugoslavia's unitary state]
> could not be taken to mean that it met with universal approval,
> *since all opposition to the regime was silenced.*[58]

Shoup goes on to note that a genuine effort was made to establish the
importance of the "nationalities" in Yugoslav life despite the monolithic
character of communist rule set up after the war. The Party generally
staffed government and political posts in the republics with indigenous
personnel representative of the ethnic composition of the region in question.

Although economic and political decentralization was begun in 1949,
following an economic disaster induced by rigid application of Stalinist
measures, the Communist Party, and Tito in particular, continue to hold

---

57. *Ibid.*, p. 104.
58. Shoup, *op. cit.*, p. 119 (emphasis added).

ultimate power. For example, in the Yugoslav election of 1953, an unexpected show of opposition to the regime materialized in Macedonia. The response of the party was stern.

> In the campaign that followed, the contestants began to appeal, among other things, to national feelings, *necessitating the removal of the nonofficial candidates from the ballot.*[59]

Ethnicity is still a political problem for Yugoslav leaders and threatens to become even more severe after Tito steps down from power.

Authoritarian Rule: The Fragility of Democracy

In the final section of this chapter we examine the consequences of a proliferation of parties and other ethnic organizations. The major consequence of this proliferation under the condition of ethnic fragmentation is the tenuous nature of democratic practices and the tendency for military or paramilitary organizations to surface and rule.

Lebanon. Of the five fragmented cultures we have investigated, only Lebanon continues to display democratic features. Even so, civil war, temporary military caretaker governments, and an incredibly rapid turnover of cabinets highlight the fragile character of Lebanese democracy. Edward Shils makes note of these incidents: (1) one of the political parties tried to seize power through a coup d'etat in 1949; (2) a breakdown in the constitutional process of succession occurred in 1952 when the then incumbent President tried to change the constitution to permit an extension of his term of office; and (3) a civil war erupted in 1958 over another crisis of succession.[60] Cabinet instability has remained a recurrent disap-

---

59. *Ibid.*, p. 175 (emphasis added). We might also glance briefly at the condition of ethnic minorities in the Soviet Union. Erich Goldhagen asserts that "the Soviet dictatorship surrounded the nationalities with an iron hedge, ruthlessly suppressing all endeavor for independence, but within these confines the national identity was given considerable freedom of scope." See his "Introduction," in Erich Goldhagen, ed., *Ethnic Minorities in the Soviet Union* (New York: Frederick A. Praeger, 1968), pp. vii-xiv (quotation at p. ix.). Mary Kilbourne Matossian further notes that in the case of the Soviet Union, unity with diversity is not always precarious politically, especially if one ethnic group [the Russians] constitutes a clear majority. See "Communist Rule and the Changing Armenian Cultural Pattern," in Erich Goldhagen, ed., *op. cit.*, pp. 185-95 (citation at p. 195). In other words, *strict totalitarian rule* in the Soviet Union prevents "nationality" sentiments from becoming salient in the political process; otherwise, cultural diversity in such forms as language, dance, etc., are permitted relatively full expression.

60. *Op. cit.*, pp. 1-2.

pointment in Lebanon; Lebanese endured some forty-six Cabinets between 1926 and 1964, or an average of less than eight months per cabinet.[61] Since the Lebanese declaration of independence from the French Mandate in 1943, some thirty-six separate governments have risen and fallen.[62] Stable, orderly government is hard to maintain under conditions of rapid Cabinet turnover.

External events also pose severe strains for the maintenance of democracy. Lebanon has tried to maintain friendly relations with Egypt, on the one hand, and with the United States and France, on the other. The Israeli-Arab disputes perhaps best illustrate the ease with which such national institutions as the army are able to provide an alternative source of rule.

The Arab-Israeli war of 1967 produced an acute domestic crisis in Lebanon. The army's commander General Emile Bustani, a Maronite Christian, refused to obey the orders of Prime Minister Rashid Karami, a Sunnite Moslem, who insisted that the army fight against Israel. As a result of this confrontation, the military temporarily seized power.[63] Twice before, Chehab, a General in the Lebanese army, had been prevailed upon to become President: in 1952 he served as acting head of state after President Khoury felt compelled to resign over fears of impending violence (due to the succession crisis which he himself had created), and again in 1958 he became head of state after the landing of American troops helped end a civil war in which 2,000 to 4,000 casualties were suffered.[64] Palestinian guerrilla raids against Israel from bases in Lebanon continue to pose severe strains on Lebanese democracy.

A brief look at the August 1970 election for President concludes our treatment of Lebanon's plural society. Former Economic Minister Suleiman Franjieh was elected by the slim edge of one vote; the speaker, however, announced that the fifty votes received by Franjieh did not constitute the required simple majority. Tempers soon flared and guns were drawn, but a crisis was averted when the speaker reversed himself and declared Franjieh President.[65] *Newsweek* further reports that Franjieh must cope with two major problems: reform of the archaic political system, specifically the reservation of the Presidency and Prime Ministership for the Maronite Christians and Sunnite Moslems, respectively, and controlling the Palestinian commandos who use Lebanon as a base for operations against Israel. *Newsweek*'s reporter is not sanguine about Franjieh's prospects.

---

61. Kerr, *op. cit.*, p. 192.
62. Hudson, *op. cit.*, p. 5.
63. *Ibid.*, p. 99.
64. *Ibid.*, pp. 105-10.
65. *Newsweek*, August 31, 1970, p. 37.

But given the new President's precarious hold on power, there is no assurance that he will prove able to deal effectively with the guerrillas — or with any of Lebanon's other problems.[66]

The Congo. Military government in the Congo is more the rule than the exception.[67] On September 14, 1960, not long after Congolese independence, Colonel Joseph Mobutu, commander of the Congo army, seized political power in a military coup which was sanctioned by President Kasavubu. The military regime was terminated on February 9, 1961, and Joseph Ileo was appointed as Premier of the provisional government composed of members of the former Parliament. The Katanga secession, which had begun in June 1960, ended on January 15, 1963. Later that year Kasavubu dissolved the central Parliament because of its failure to prepare a draft of a new constitution. New elections were held in May 1965 and Premier Tshombe's Congolese Convention Party obtained an overall majority winning 86 of 125 seats. Parliament met for the first time in two years in September 1965, but two months later General Mobutu again seized control of the government in a new military coup, ousting President Kasavubu. A five year regime of military rule was declared by Mobutu and his new government was almost unanimously approved by Parliament on November 28, 1965. General, now President, Mobutu has ruled continuously since the military coup in 1965.[68]

Nigeria. As we indicated before, a military coup took place in Nigeria in mid-January 1966. At that time, Prime Minister Sir Abubakar Tafawa Balewa and two regional Premiers were killed. A provisional military government headed by an Ibo, Major General Johnson Aguiyi-Ironsi, took over the duties of both the federal and regional governments. Ibos felt they had much to gain from their increased mobility and were consequently in favor of the new regime. Northerners reacted with antipathy and a series of riots developed in the North with attacks aimed principally at resident Ibos. On July 29, 1966, a new military coup led by Northern elements in the Nigerian army overthrew the military regime of Major General Aguiyi-Ironsi and replaced him with Lt. Colonel Yakubu Gowon, who as head of government was later promoted to the rank of Major General. Within a few months the Eastern Region had seceded and declared itself

66. *Ibid.*
67. This discussion is based on data taken from "Deadline Data on World Affairs."
68. We should credit Daniel J. Crowley with having made an astute prediction for the Congo. He speculated, in 1963, that the army or *gendarmerie* would become the elite that the Congo so badly needed. His prediction was borne out by events in 1965 and thereafter (*op. cit.*, p. 77).

the independent state of Biafra. Nearly three years of civil war followed until Biafra surrendered on January 12, 1970. Thus in Nigeria the military has ruled for a considerable portion of the country's postindependence period. Military rule appears to have come about because the animosities shared among Nigeria's tribal communities drained the oil, so to speak, from the country's democratic machinery.[69]

The Sudan. We have already noted that the Sudan has not escaped periods of military rule. General Ibrahim Abboud had seized power earlier on November 17, 1958; he dissolved Parliament, suspended the constitution, and banned all political parties. Six years later the General resigned and a new civilian government was installed. This government, among other things, was unable to resolve peacefully the Southern problem. Consequently, civilian rule was again terminated on May 29, 1969, when Major General Gafaar al-Nimeiry staged a bloodless coup. He immediately nullified the provisional constitution, dissolved all constitutional and legislative bodies, and set up a ten-man Revolutionary Council, consisting of nine officers and one civilian with himself as head of state. Thus, military rule has emerged each time the civilian government has shown itself unable to resolve or cope with major ethnic differences. This result neatly fits the experience of not only the Sudan, but also Nigeria, the Congo, and to a lesser extent, Lebanon.

Yugoslavia. So long as the Communist Party has been willing and able to command nation-wide obedience and compliance with its programs, ethnic demands and grievances have been kept within manageable bounds. Democratic politics in the interwar period soon developed into royal rule because the rival ethnic communities were unable to compromise their differences. A similar pattern now appears to be developing in Yugoslavia: Tito's program of economic and political decentralization, fashioned in response to the economic disasters of the late 1940s, has contributed to a revivification of the old regional rivalries. The Yugoslav constitution grants an exception to Tito for the number of terms the head of state can serve and, as long as he remains competent to rule, the Communist Party appears able to hold together the diverse regions of the country. Still, the Communist Party is more a collection of the Republic Parties of Serbia, Croatia, and Macedonia, and the Regional Parties of Vojovodina and Kossovo-Metohija than it is a genuine, national party. Upon Tito's death

69. For an account of these successive army coups, see Paul Anber, "Modernization and Political Disintegration: Nigeria and the Ibos," *Journal of Modern African Studies* 5, no. 2 (September 1967): 163-79, especially pp. 163-64.

or the passing of his leadership, the future is likely to hold in store a renewed upsurge in the expression of "nationality" sentiments (especially since the previous common enemy, the Soviet Union, no longer provides an external enemy for all the Yugoslav peoples).

Conclusion

This chapter completes our tour of ethnic politics in each of the four different configurations. The prospects for stable democracy appear dim as the historical record has indicated. Does this imply, though, that the problems which plural societies face are insoluble? That democracy and stability in the plural society are incompatible?

We examine these questions in the concluding chapter, paying particular attention to an assessment of the policy implications of our theory as proposed solutions. Let us turn, then, to this task.

CHAPTER 8

Conclusions

The last four chapters vividly display the extent to which ethnic politics governs conflict in plural societies. Eighteen sovereign multiethnic states, scattered throughout the world, show striking regularities in their respective political processes. Multiethnic cooperation, multiethnic conflict, manipulation or opportunistic elimination of democratic procedures, and outright force and discriminatory legislation are just some of these persistent traits. How is it possible, we may ask, that members of separate communal groups can accommodate their differences for one length of time and violently dispute those same differences during some subsequent period?

We are certainly not the first, and probably not the last, to search for a general understanding of political behavior in multiethnic societies. Sociologists and anthropologists still debate the merits of "consensual" versus "conflict" frameworks of analysis, as our review of their treatments in chapter 1 indicates. Political scientists still search for necessary and/or sufficient conditions of democratic political stability in contexts of cultural diversity. Although their work bears considerable fruit, we continue to confront contradictory findings.

History shows that democratic stability and cultural diversity are often incompatible in the postindependence politics of many plural societies. Furthermore, intense ethnic conflict frequently erupts shortly after native peoples obtain their independence. Those scholars who observed a multiethnic nationalist movement reported interethnic cooperation and forecast its continuance. On the other hand, those who studied plural societies in the postindependence period reported interethnic competition and conflict. Thus, the theories resulting from observations in these two different time periods have left us with an inconsistent account of politics in the plural society.

Our task is clear. A valid theory of political behavior in plural societies must account both for patterns of ethnic cooperation and conflict in democratic and nondemocratic situations. Furthermore, this theory should where possible remain free of normative contamination, although the theoretical results can be used by dictators and democrats alike to engineer changes in plural societies. Our main point is that sound policy prescriptions must rest on a firm theoretical foundation.

Part one of this book presents a theoretical account of politics in the plural society, one that illuminates patterns both of cooperation and conflict among communal groups in eighteen plural societies. A completely persuasive treatment, however, must cope with the seeming counterexample that Switzerland represents for our paradigm. We turn in the next section, therefore, to an investigation of linguistic diversity and democratic stability in that landlocked, polyglot society.

Switzerland: The Persistent Counterexample

Proponents of ethnic harmony often cite Switzerland as a model case of cultural coexistence. The Swiss somehow manage to combine ethnic diversity and democratic stability, no mean feat in view of the rarity with which this relationship occurs in other plural societies. Four different language groups that practice two major religions live together in apparent harmony and thus stand as a counterexample to the proposition that plural societies inhere towards instability when their politics are played out in a democratic arena. Yet there is more to ethnic politics in Switzerland than meets the eye.

For a series of unique historical reasons, language is not salient in Swiss national politics.[1] Unlike most European countries Switzerland did not originate as a nation-state. Rather, the Swiss Confederation grew out of a mutual alliance of Swiss Cantons in their common struggle against feudal rulers and the German emperor; this confederation possessed no constitution, no central government, no national army, nor even a capital city. The Swiss Cantons were all sovereign republics bound together by a loose network of treaties entered into for mutual advantage. Nor was this league of cantons a multilingual body. In fact, Switzerland became a multilingual state for the first time in 1798 when

---

1. We draw upon several studies in our reconstruction of the Swiss case. See Kurt B. Mayer, "The Jura Problem: Ethnic Conflict in Switzerland," *Social Research* 35, no. 4 (Winter 1968): 707-41, and James A. Dunn, Jr., *Social Cleavage, Party Systems and Political Integration: A Comparison of the Belgian and Swiss Experiences* (unpublished Ph.D. dissertation, Pennsylvania, 1970).

the confederation collapsed before an invading French army. In the immediately formed Helvetic Republic (decreed from Paris), Switzerland became a centralized state and the right of French, German, and Italian speakers to use their own language on a basis of complete equality was insured by law.

After Napoleon's downfall in 1815 the cantons resumed almost all of their former sovereign independence and German again become the sole official language, as it had been at the Reformation. At the same time, the Swiss Cantons were increased in number to twenty-two as a result of the addition of new territories in 1815 by the Congress of Vienna. These included Italian- and French-speaking areas. Most of these twenty-two cantons are now unilingual: fourteen are German-speaking, three French-speaking, and one Italian-speaking. Three are officially bilingual in French and German (Berne, Fribourg and Valais), and one is trilingual in German, Romansh and Italian (Grisons).[2]

Although the official language of the confederation had reverted to German in 1815, the equality of the sovereign cantons kept the multilingual principle alive. The equality of German, French and Italian was formally established in the constitution of 1848, which transformed the confederation into a modern federal state. But language failed then and still fails to be a salient national issue. The reasons for this are easy to find.

> Based on the heritage of many centuries of sovereign independence, the Swiss Cantons retain today important political powers, and they remain sharply differentiated in customs, dialect and outlook. . . . regional and local variations still persist and the cantons remain viable political units as well as the focus of emotional loyalties. *Specifically, all educational, religious, intellectual, and artistic matters remain subject to cantonal, not federal jurisdiction.*[3]

Put another way, the national government provides few collective goods over which the linguistic communities can fight. Since eighteen of the twenty-two cantons are unilingual, there is no ethnic basis for political competition to control the distribution of public goods that the *canton governments* produce in most of Switzerland. The same is not true, as we see below, for all four of the multilingual cantons. Thus linguistic conflict, if it erupts, is limited to those four only. Furthermore, each canton maintains a policy of nonintervention in the affairs of other cantons. Accordingly, James Dunn observes

---

2. Mayer, *op. cit.*, p. 713.
3. *Ibid.*, p. 716 (emphasis added).

most conflicts could be settled within the cantonal framework. If, however, a conflict proved to be so polarizing, if a cleavage became so salient and severe that the decision of the cantonal majority was totally unacceptable to the minority, then the solution was to split the canton. The two half-cantons thereby created usually would be counted on to be much more stable than the larger one had been.[4]

Thus the Swiss possess a legitimate institutional device for resolving linguistic conflict in multilingual cantons. And since these conflicts are not subject to resolution at the national level, national unity and democratic stability remain unthreatened. Linguistic conflict threatens stability only at the level of canton government. Conflict in one canton does not ordinarily involve the other twenty-one.

It was the peculiar genius of Switzerland to permit political life to remain focused on the canton down to the present, with only a very gradual buildup of the scope and importance of the central government. *Thus most issues in Swiss politics are seen as local issues.*[5]

Let us stop for a moment and emphasize the point we are trying to make. *Switzerland does not constitute a counterexample to or denial of our theoretical propositions.* This is so for the following reasons:

1. Language is not a salient national issue; linguistic conflict is a problem that the individual multilingual cantons must resolve.
2. The national government provides few public goods — these are the responsibility of the canton governments. Leaders perceive few incentives, therefore, to mobilize language groups at the level of national politics. Thus language differences do not threaten national unity or stability.
3. Most salient issues in Swiss politics are local issues.

We need not modify or reject our theory, then, on the basis of the Swiss experience.

We now carry our reasoning one step further. If the cantons possess what we call *independent, decision-making authority,* as they seem to do, then the features of the plural society we delineate in chapter 3 should appear in one or more of the multilingual cantons. This implication is amenable to investigation and, as the title of Mayer's paper suggests, we are indeed correct. The Jura conflict in the Berne canton

---

4. Dunn, *op. cit.*, p. 177. Dunn records that the Swiss had divided cantons in 1597 and 1833.
5. *Ibid.*, p. 178 (emphasis added).

bears out our analysis. By treating the Canton Berne as a "pseudo-sovereign" plural society we find another illustration that fits the general pattern of ethnic conflict in plural societies.

The Jura Conflict: Ethnic Politics in Berne. From the end of the tenth to the eighteenth century, the area that is now known as the Bernese Jura had formed the main part of an ancient clerical principality, governed by the autocratic Prince-Bishop of Basel. Although the northern parts of the Bishopric are still chiefly Catholic, most of the southern Jura residents practice Protestantism as a result of their predecessors' conversion during the Reformation. The northern Catholic area was annexed by France after 1792 (the end of bishopric rule) and the southern Jura, which possessed a protective alliance with Switzerland, held out until French armies overran all of Switzerland. By 1800 France had annexed the entire region.

France was required to relinquish all territories acquired since 1792 by the Congress of Vienna. A provisional governor controlled the former Bishopric of Basel while the Congress of Vienna deliberated the future of the territory. The decision resulted in the union of the Jura with the Canton Berne, although neither party was enthusiastic about this arbitrary territorial marriage. And worse, Berne refused to grant demands by the Jurassian delegates for recognition of French as an official language. Nor did it concede any special minority representation in the legislature or executive of the canton.[6]

By 1831 Jurassians obtained the right to use French as a second official language. Ethnic conflict, however, frequently heated up to the boiling point. A movement to nationalize the Roman Catholic Church and subordinate it to the state created dissatisfaction and a cry for separation in the northern Jura. The Bernese government ordered a military occupation, but backed down in the face of a French threat to intervene, in the process withdrawing its assault upon the Church. The separatist movement thus dissolved.

Another separatist movement, which demanded that the entire French legal code be applied to the whole Jura region, evaporated only after the then liberal government was overturned by a new radical popular movement. A Jurassian leader named Stockmar was permitted to return from exile and participate in the new government. He helped gain for French the status of a fully equal official language.

---

6. We should observe that the opportunity for a multiethnic nationalist movement did not exist for the Bernese and Jurassians. The Congress of Vienna created the new canton against the wishes of the Jurassians and even many Bernese, who preferred the return of two other former subject territories. We focus, therefore, on the Jurassian movement for separation.

Still another separatist movement appeared with the outbreak of World War I. It subsided quickly, however, with the end of the war. Relative calm prevailed between the wars, but separatist passions again flared up in 1947 over the refusal of the Berne legislative assembly to ratify the appointment of a Jurassian to the important post of Director of Public Works and Railways — important because the canton governments bear primary responsibility for the provision of public goods. Evidently the legislators felt that the post should be given to a German speaker. This incident caused a storm of protest and led to the creation of the "Rassemblement jurassien," a separatist movement comprised chiefly of Catholics in the Northern Jura. The Bernese government made several concessions to the Jurassians, but failed to dissipate the movement. This movement has produced a state of continuous instability in Berne for more than twenty years. Its resolution may require the creation of a new Jura canton, a procedure thus far opposed by the Bernese and a majority of Protestant Jurassians who live in the Southern Jura. Protestant Jurassians have formed their own movement — the "union des patriotes jurassiens" — to oppose separatism out of fear of Catholic domination in an independent Jura.[7]

We conclude this discussion of Switzerland with one final observation:

> While it may be true that Switzerland as a Confederation has avoided many of the problems incumbent upon the creation of a modern centralized nation-state, the same cannot be said for the canton of Berne. In many ways Berne has behaved more like a modern state than Switzerland.[8]

---

7. Catholics comprise 55.8 percent of Jurassians and Protestants only 43.1 percent. A referundum for separation in 1959 produced the following results among Jurassian voters:

Jura Region	For Separation	Against Separation
Catholic North	11,108	4,900
Protestant South	3,522	10,004
Laufen (German-speakers)	1,533	1,450
Jura Totals	16,163	16,354
Old Canton of Berne	7,697	63,787

The three Roman Catholic Jura districts returned a two-thirds majority in favor of the measure, while the three Protestant districts voted exactly opposite, with a two-thirds majority opposed. As the table suggests, language is an important issue for Catholic Jurassians and a source of instability in Bernese politics. Separatist French sentiments, for the moment, appear throttled by recalcitrant Protestants. Even though religion plays a role in Jura politics, its presence does not eliminate linguistic pressures. Until Jura is given cantonal status, language will persist as an issue. (However, if it *is* given independent status, one might expect religion to become salient.)

8. Dunn, *op. cit.*, pp. 243-44. Dunn argues convincingly that Berne is the only multilingual canton that should manifest intense separatist sentiments (pp. 33-34).

(R$_X$) Prescriptions for the Plural Society:
Some Applications of the Theory

Our review of ethnic politics in a variety of countries, not to mention the problems that presently confront the urban areas in America or French Canada (Quebec), or a growing ethnocentrism in Wales, Scotland and Cornwall, paints a bleak picture. A future defined by ethnic harmony appears to be most unlikely in the view that parts one and two of this book put forth. In a comparative study of nation building and cultural pluralism, Anderson, von der Mehden, and Young assess and reject the formulae of representation, federalism, cultural neutralism, ideology, assimilation, encapsulation, and expatriation as solutions to the problem of democratic instability in plural contexts. They conclude that "the twin progeny of modernization — cultural pluralism and nationalism — must find reconciliation, because the world offers no other choice."[9] Insofar as protection of minorities and equitable representation of multiple communities in one society has been investigated, two informed scholars concur that no one electoral system is preferable to another and that fair representation in plural societies is a difficult problem from any angle.[10]

We concur with these findings, *viz.*, formulae that serve to guarantee democratic stability in plural societies, are difficult to construct. We intend to present some solutions in the following pages, solutions informed by the preceding theoretical developments. Although these solutions follow from our theoretical concerns, their feasibility and practicability are indeed open to question.

1. Denial of independent, decision-making authority. As we saw time and time again throughout part two, ethnic leaders often cooperate with each other during the period of colonial rule. Colonial or foreign rule represents, therefore, one solution for the problem of ethnic conflict that so often disturbs the peace in plural societies. Since independence provides the prize of decision-making authority over which communal groups inevitably fight, continued colonial rule precludes the crystallization of interethnic hostility.[11]

---

9. *Issues of Political Development* (Englewood Cliffs, N. J.: Prentice-Hall, Inc., 1967), p. 82.

10. See J. A. LaPonce, "The Protection of Minorities by the Electoral System," *Western Political Quarterly* 10, no. 2 (June 1957): 318-39 and W. J. M. Mackenzie, "Representation in Plural Societies," *Political Studies* 2, no. 1 (February 1954): 54-69.

11. It may well be the case, however, that continued or indefinite colonial rule would create more conflict and problems than it would solve. Massive Portuguese expenditures in Africa are testimony to this point.

World opinion and even domestic pressures in Britain discourage perpetual colonial rule. Unusual circumstances in Hong Kong and Gibraltar — the fact that without British protection each are indefensible from China and Spain, respectively — allow the British to disregard the demands that emanate from the United Nation's Trusteeship Council for the worldwide end of colonialism. They appear unlikely, however, to stave off demands for greater, and ultimately total, self-government that black residents in Bermuda and the Bahamas voice today. Prospects of independence in the Bahamas have already led to the formation of a government led by a black Prime Minister, Lynden O. Pindling, which now demands a speed-up in constitutional progress towards independence. Even placid Bermuda has not escaped racial discord: gangs of black youths rampaged in the streets of Hamilton, Bermuda's capital, in October 1970 protesting the visit of Prince Charles.[12] Although the British may succeed in postponing independence for these two colonies in the immediate future, we suspect that they will be unable to speak openly of permanent colonial rule and be forced, after the passage of time, to speed up the granting of independence. Thus this solution, denial of independent authority, is not feasible in light of the anticolonial sentiments shared by most citizens of colonial and imperialist societies alike. How much more difficult it would be, then, to even talk about reestablishing colonial rule in those societies that have already received their independence.[13]

One final version of this prescription deserves examination. Reunion, an island neighbor of Mauritius with similar ethnic composition and size, remains relatively free of ethnic conflict. Why is this so? The answer is found in an examination of the means by which the French govern their overseas territories. Reunion does not possess the status of an independent polity. Rather, Reunion, much like other French overseas possessions, is ruled directly from Paris as an integral part of France. Administrators are appointed in Paris and are often expatriates from France. The threat of French intervention must constrain the

---

12. *The New York Times,* October 9, 1970, p. 14, and October 13, 1970, p. 4.
13. One long-time resident and analyst of Gibraltar suggests that Gibraltarians have much to teach the world about interracial cooperation and goodwill. Talk of genuine independence is equivalent to heresy in Gibraltar. A referendum in 1967 concerning Gibraltar's political future produced a near unanimous judgment that continued colonial rule from Britain is desirable and beneficial. Thus, the writer's description of interracial harmony in Gibraltar is tempered by two factors: (1) Gibraltarians have no independent authority over which they can fight, and (2) regardless of race, the most salient issue in Gibraltar's political life is the joint fear of Spanish domination that implies an end to the political and economic freedoms Gibraltarians now enjoy. See John Stewart, *Gibraltar: the Keystone* (Boston: Houghton Mifflin, 1967). It may well be the case, however, that Gibraltar, and perhaps Hong Kong, are the only two colonies which the British Crown may never have to surrender.

options that are available to indigenous ethnic leaders, who might otherwise choose to generate demand for ethnic chauvinism. Given the extant constitutional structure of French rule in Reunion, there isn't even any basis for a multiethnic nationalist movement to emerge. Perhaps the French can retain perpetual overseas rule in Reunion and, by so doing, prevent the pattern of democratic instability that characterizes Mauritius from ever arising.

2. Restrictions on independent, decision-making authority. The only efficacious technique that seems able to minimize the deleterious effects of ethnic politics is provided in the lesson of Switzerland. Confederation, the relegation of important issues for resolution to local administrative levels, prevents the aggregation of ethnic preferences on a national basis (and its possible harmful consequences). Democratic stability is threatened only at a cantonal level in Switzerland. Twenty years of continuous strife in Berne has not distorted the overall picture of stable democracy in the Swiss polity.

But Switzerland developed as a collective society from a series of alliances among independent cantons that joined together for mutual gains and protection from a common enemy. Loyalties in Switzerland are cantonal, not national. It may be difficult, therefore, to superimpose a decentralized form of government on a plural society that has no tradition of such rule or any institutions to cope with salient issues at a local level of government. We suggest, with hesitation, that Switzerland may stand as the only illustration of this remedy, though Belgium is currently experimenting with it. And even the Swiss are subject to the centralizing pressures of a modern industrial state. Federalism in Nigeria, Malaya, Uganda, Burma, and the West Indies has not met with resounding success.

3. Restrictions on free political competition. In his study of Dutch politics, Lijphart argues that competent leaders can master accommodation and compromise and thereby achieve a measure of democratic stability. They succeed by disregarding the pressures of a mass electorate, or what Lijphart calls practicing the *rule of secrecy.*

> The process of accommodation must, therefore, be shielded from publicity. The leaders' moves in negotiations among the blocs must be carefully insulated from the knowledge of the rank and file. Because an "information gap" is desirable, secrecy is a most important rule. . . . In Holland, covenants are usually, though not always, open, but covenants openly arrived at are rare indeed.[14]

---

14. *The Politics of Accommodation: Pluralism and Democracy in the Netherlands* (Berkeley and Los Angeles: University of California Press, 1968), p. 131.

But Lijphart himself observes that democracy would suffocate under complete secrecy. The question we must ask is whether the Dutch elites in their accommodative maneuvers have significantly infringed on what the common notion of democracy entails? In any event, a successful application of this solution to other societies requires a restriction of the scope of public issues and mass awareness of them.

4. Restrictions on the scope of government. Public goods in the plural society often become the preserve of the advantaged political community and tend to be viewed as public bads by those communities excluded from power. Since the provision of public goods by the state is its primary *raison d'etre*, regime legitimacy often suffers when public funds are used to provide communal goods. If our theory is sound, an agreement to minimize the scope of public goods — and a reliance on the free market — should tone down the invidious quality of ethnic politics in the plural society.

Desirable as this agreement sounds, it is difficult to persuade communities that are at a disadvantage in the competitive marketplace to refrain from using political power to redress a position of economic inferiority. Malay domination of the public sector in Malaya allows them to redistribute, to their communal advantage, some of the wealth that Chinese produce. Their insistence on instituting Malay as the sole official language, on retaining quotas in the Civil Service, in the granting of licenses and university scholarships, is designed to offset the Chinese economic edge. Is it likely that we could persuade Malays to accept a pure *laissez-faire,* competitive market society that in effect reduces their economic opportunities? The answer? Not very likely![15]

5. Creation of homogeneous societies. The division of a plural society into its constituent ethnic components, each as a sovereign society, would certainly (by definition) eliminate cultural diversity and ethnic conflict. Though such a partitioning does not guarantee the disappearance of conflict, it does insure that conflict will no longer follow ethnic lines. Separatists throughout the world speak in these terms: Eritreans in Ethiopia, French-Canadians in Quebec, Muslims in Chad, Africans in the Sudan, to cite a few illustrations. But are their desires feasible and/or practicable? The answer appears to be *no.*

---

15. In Malaya's immediate southern neighbor, Singapore, the Chinese are the dominant economic and political community. They comprise about 75 percent of the population and produce and control most of Singapore's wealth. As a consequence, Singapore's stability is not threatened by the communal pressures which are intrinsic in the Malayan economic and political configuration.

A first objection is that the creation of many new states would pose for most of them questions of economic viability. How is it possible, for example, to demarcate four hundred new nations out of a multitribal African country? Each of these tribal states is not likely to survive as a viable economic or political unit. Thus economic and political pressures do not favor this remedy.

Second, the fact that ethnic groups are not always concentrated in specific regions would make the cost of resettlement almost prohibitively high and the drawing of new political boundaries — in such a way as to satisfy all parties — almost impossible. Most plural societies, therefore, are not amenable to this solution.

Third, and perhaps most important, why should the dominant community, whether it be a majority or minority, give up its position of advantage and privilege — especially when domination is very, very profitable? For these reasons, the creation of new homogeneous societies is likely to take place only after a minority or majority community has carried out a successful revolution. And, as the case of Zanzibar suggests, they are likely to impose rule over the previously dominant community rather than establish a new state.

6. Creation of permanent external enemies. This solution is available for the use of democrats and tyrants alike. The wise leader can often successfully appeal for national unity when his country is threatened by the presence of an external enemy. The failure of the Alliance Party in the 1969 Malayan election suggests, however, that the threat must be credible. Having won a resounding victory in 1964 by labelling opposition candidates as traitors, they flopped in a dismal fashion five years later when confrontation with Indonesia no longer threatened the Malayan polity. Pressures toward ethnic parochialism in Yugoslavia are likely to continue as the threat of Russian intervention steadily declines.

A Final Question

Conclusions are often banal and trite. Important theoretical questions are either begged or isolated as topics for future research. We propose neither to move cautiously towards the formation of a few tentative hypotheses, to allude to problems of measurement, nor to get lost in a maze of methodological discussion (which is very often beside the point). Instead we ask, is the resolution of intense but conflicting preferences in the plural society manageable in a democratic framework? We think not.

Bibliography

I. Theoretical

Alchian, Armen. "The Meaning of Utility Measurement." *American Economic Review* 43, no. 1 (March 1963): 26-50.

Arrow, Kenneth. "Alternative Approaches to the Theory of Choice in Risk-Taking Situations." *Econometrica* 19, no. 4 (October 1951): 404-37.

Axelrod, Robert. *Conflict of Interest.* Chicago: Markham Publishing Company, 1970.

Berry, Brewton. *Race and Ethnic Relations.* 2d ed. Boston: Houghton Mifflin, 1958.

Bottomore, T.B. *Elites and Society.* Harmondsworth, England: Pelican Books, 1966.

Carey, George W. and Willmore Kendall. "The 'Intensity' Problem and Democratic Theory." *American Political Science Review* 62, no. 1 (March 1968): 5-24.

Churchman, C. West. *Prediction and Optimal Decision.* Englewood Cliffs, N.J.: Prentice-Hall, 1961.

Coser, Lewis. *The Functions of Social Conflict.* Glencoe: Free Press, 1956.

Dahl, Robert. *A Preface to Democratic Theory.* Chicago: University of Chicago Press, 1956.

————. *Pluralist Democracy in the United States.* Chicago: Rand McNally, 1967.

Dahrendorf, Ralf. *Class and Class Conflict in Industrial Society.* Stanford: Stanford University Press, 1959.

Deutsch, Karl. *Nationalism and Social Communication.* Cambridge, Massachusetts: Technology Press, 1953.

Downs, Anthony. *An Economic Theory of Democracy.* New York: Harper and Row, 1957.

Etzioni, Amitai. *Political Unification: A Comparative Study of Leaders and Forces.* New York: Holt, Rinehart and Winston, 1965.

Friedman, Milton. *Essays in Positive Economics.* Chicago: University of Chicago Press, 1953.

Frohlich, Norman, Joe A. Oppenheimer and Oran R. Young. *Political Leadership and Collective Goods.* Princeton, N.J.: Princeton University Press, 1971.

Geertz, Clifford. "The Integrative Revolution: Primordial Sentiments and Civil Politics in the New States." In *Old Societies and New States: The Quest for Modernity in Asia and Africa,* edited by Clifford Geertz. New York: Free Press of Glencoe, 1963.

Groennings, Sven, E.W. Kelley, and Michael Leiserson, eds. *The Study of Coalition Behavior.* New York: Holt, Rinehart, and Winston, 1970.

Haefele, Edwin T. "Coalitions, Minority Representation, and Vote-Trading Probabilities." *Public Choice* 8 (Spring 1970): 74-90.

Hildreth, Clifford. "Alternative Conditions for Social Orderings." *Econometrica* 21, no. 1 (January 1953): 81-94.

Jacob, Philip E. "The Influence of Values in Political Integration." In *The Integration of Political Communities,* edited by Philip E. Jacob and James V. Toscano. Philadelphia: Lippincott, 1964.

Kornhauser, William. *The Politics of Mass Society.* New York: The Free Press, 1959.

LaPonce, J.A. "The Protection of Minorities by the Electoral System." *Western Political Quarterly* 10, no. 2 (June 1957): 318-39.

Lijphart, Arend. "Consociational Democracy." *World Politics* 21, no. 2 (January 1969): 207-25.

Lipset, Seymour Martin. *Political Man: The Social Bases of Politics.* Garden City, New York: Anchor Books, 1963.

Luce, R. Duncan and Howard Raiffa. *Games and Decisions.* New York: John Wiley and Sons, Inc., 1957.

MacKenzie, W.J.M. "Representation in Plural Societies." *Political Studies* 2, no. 1 (February 1954): 54-69.

Margolis, Julius. "A Comment on the Pure Theory of Public Expenditure." *Review of Economics and Statistics* 37, no. 4 (November 1955): 347-49.

Marschak, Jacob. "Why Should Statisticians and Businessmen Maximize 'Moral Expectation'?" In *Proceedings of the Second Berkeley Symposium on Mathematical Statistics and Probability,* edited by Jerzy Neyman. Berkeley: University of California Press, 1951.

Mayo, Henry B. *An Introduction to Democratic Theory.* New York: Oxford University Press, 1960.

Mishan, E.J. "The Relationship Between Joint Products, Collective Goods, and External Effects." *Journal of Political Economy* 77, no. 3 (May-June 1969) : 329-48.

Nagel, Ernest, "Assumptions in Economic Theory." *American Economic Review* 53, no. 2 (May 1963) : 211-19.

Olson, Mancur, Jr. *The Logic of Collective Action: Public Goods and the Theory of Groups.* Cambridge: Harvard University Press, 1965.

Pratt, John W., Howard Raiffa, and Robert Schlaifer. "The Foundations of Decision Under Uncertainty: An Elementary Exposition." *Journal of the American Statistics Association* 59, no. 306 (June 1964) : 353-75.

Rabushka, Alvin and Kenneth A. Shepsle. "Political Entrepreneurship and Patterns of Democratic Instability in Plural Societies." *Race* 12, no. 4 (April 1971) : 461-75.

Rae, Douglas W. "Decision – Rules and Individual Values in Constitutional Choice." *American Political Science Review* 63, no. 1 (March 1969) : 40-56.

Riker, William H. "Voting and the Summation of Preferences: An Interpretive Bibliographic Review of Selected Developments During the Last Decade." *American Political Science Review* 55, no. 4 (December 1961) : 900-912.

_____. *The Theory of Political Coalitions.* New Haven: Yale University Press, 1962.

_____. "Arrow's Theorem and Some Examples of the Paradox of Voting." In *Mathematical Applications in Political Science*, Vol.1, edited by John Claunch. Dallas: Southern Methodist University Press, 1965.

Rothenberg, Jerome. *The Measurement of Social Welfare.* Englewood Cliffs, N.J.: Prentice-Hall, Inc., 1961.

Samuelson, Paul A. "The Pure Theory of Public Expenditure." *Review of Economics and Statistics* 36, no. 4 (November 1954) : 387-89.

Sartori, Giovanni. *Democratic Theory.* Detroit: Wayne State University Press, 1962.

_____. "European Political Parties: The Case of Polarized Pluralism." In *Political Parties and Political Development,* edited by Joseph LaPalombara and Myron Weiner. Princeton: Princeton University Press, 1966.

Schattschneider, E.E. "Intensity, Visability, Direction and Scope." *American Political Science Review* 51, no. 3 (September 1957) : 933-42.

_____. *The Semi-Sovereign People.* New York: Holt, Rinehart and Winston, 1960.

Schumpeter, Joseph A. *Capitalism, Socialism, and Democracy.* 3d ed. New York: Harper and Row, 1950.

Sen, Amartya. *Collective Choice and Social Welfare*. San Francisco: Holden-Day, 1970.

Shepsle, Kenneth. "Essays on Risky Choice in Electoral Competition." Unpublished Ph.D. dissertation, University of Rochester, 1970.

_____. "Parties, Voters, and the Risk Environment: A Mathematical Treatment of Electoral Competition Under Uncertainty." In *Probability Models of Collective Decision-Making,* edited by Richard Niemi and Herbert Weisberg. Columbus: Charles Merrill, 1972.

_____. "The Strategy of Ambiguity: Uncertainty and Electoral Competition." *American Political Science Review* 66, no. 3 (September 1972).

Stigler, George. "The Development of Utility Theory." *Journal of Political Economy* 58, nos. 4-5 (August - October 1950): 307-27, 373-96.

Stokes, Donald E. "Spatial Models of Party Competition." *American Political Science Review* 57, no. 2 (June 1963): 368-77.

Thompson, Herbert Fergus, Jr., "Is the Invisible Hand Losing Its Grip?" In *Readings in Economics and Politics,* edited by H.C. Harlan. New York: Oxford University Press, 1961.

Tingsten, Herbert. *The Problems of Democracy*. New York: Bedminster Press, 1965.

Tullock, Gordon. *Toward a Mathematics of Politics*. Ann Arbor: University of Michigan Press, 1967.

von Neumann, John and Oskar Morgenstern. *The Theory of Games and Economic Behavior*. Princeton: Princeton University Press, 1947.

Wagner, Richard E. "Pressure Groups and Political Entrepreneurs: A Review Article." In *Papers on Non-Market Decision-Making,* edited by Gordon Tullock. Charlottesville: Thomas Jefferson Center for Political Economy, 1966.

II. Substantive

Adams, T.W. "The First Republic of Cyprus: A Review of an Unworkable Constitution." *The Western Political Quarterly* 19, no. 3 (September 1966): 475-90.

Adedeji, Adebayo. *Nigerian Administration and Its Political Setting*. London: Hutchinson Education Ltd., 1968.

Anber, Paul. "Modernization and Political Disintegration: Nigeria and the Ibos." *Journal of Modern African Studies* 5, no. 2 (September 1967): 163-79.

Anderson, Charles, Fred R. von der Mehden and Crawford Young. *Issues of Political Development*. Englewood Cliffs, N.J.: Prentice-Hall, Inc., 1967.

Barber, James. "Rhodesia: The Constitutional Conflict." *Journal of Modern African Studies* 4, no. 4 (December 1966): 457-69.

————. *Rhodesia: The Road to Rebellion.* London: Oxford University Press for the Institute of Race Relations, 1967.

Barritt, Denis P. and Charles F. Carter. *The Northern Ireland Problem: A Study in Group Relations.* London: Oxford University Press, 1962.

Benedict, Burton. "Stratification in Plural Societies." *American Anthropologist* 64, no. 6 (December 1962): 1235-46.

————. *Mauritius: Problems of a Plural Society.* London: Pall Mall Press, 1965.

Beshir, Mohamed Omer. *The Southern Sudan: Background to Conflict.* New York: Frederick A. Praeger, 1965.

Biebuyck, Daniel and Mary Douglas. *Congo: Tribes and Parties.* London: Royal Anthropological Institute, 1961.

Binder, Leonard. "National Integration and Political Development." *American Political Science Review* 58, no. 3 (September 1964): 622-31.

Blij, Harm J. De. *South Africa.* Evanston, Illinois: Northwestern University Press, 1962.

Blitz, L. Franklin. *The Politics and Administration of Nigerian Government.* New York: Frederick A. Praeger, 1965.

Bowman, Larry W. "Organization, Power, and Decision-Making within the Rhodesian Front." *Journal of Commonwealth Political Studies* 7, no. 2 (July 1969): 145-65.

Bradley, C. Paul. "Party Politics in British Guiana." *The Western Political Quarterly* 16, no. 2 (June 1963): 353-70.

Bretton, Henry L. *Power and Stability in Nigeria.* New York: Frederick A. Praeger, 1962.

Bull, Theodore. *Rhodesia: The Crisis of Color.* Chicago: Quadrangle Books, 1967.

Butler, Jeffrey and Newell M. Stultz. "The South African General Election of 1961." *Political Science Quarterly* 78, no. 1 (March 1963): 86-110.

Carson, Patricia. *The Fair Face of Flanders.* Ghent: E. Story-Scientia, 1969.

Clements, Frank. *Rhodesia: A Study of the Deterioration of a White Society.* New York: Praeger, 1969.

Coleman, James S. "The Problem of Political Integration in Emergent Africa." *Western Political Quarterly* 8, no. 1 (March 1955): 44-57.

————. *Nigeria: Background to Nationalism.* Berkeley: University of California Press, 1958.

Coleman, James S. and Carl G. Rosberg. *Political Parties and National Integration in Tropical Africa.* Berkeley: University of California Press, 1964.

Collins, B.A.N. "The End of a Colony — II." *The Political Quarterly* 36, no. 4 (October-December 1965): 406-16.

Coombs, David and Richard Norton-Taylor. "Renewal in Belgian Politics: The Elections of March 1968." *Parliamentary Affairs* 22, no. 1 (Winter 1968-69): 62-72.

Crow, Ralph E. "Religious Sectarianism in the Lebanese Political System." *Journal of Politics* 24, no. 3 (August 1961): 489-520.

Crowley, Daniel J. "Plural and Differential Acculturation in Trinidad." *American Anthropologist* 59, no. 5 (October 1957): 817-24.

————. "Politics and Tribalism in Katanga." *Western Political Quarterly* 16, no. 1 (March 1963): 68-78.

Despres, Leo A. *Cultural Pluralism and Nationalist Politics in British Guiana.* Chicago: Rand McNally and Co., 1967.

Deutsch, Karl, et al. *Political Community and the North Atlantic Area: International Organization in the Light of Historical Experience.* Princeton: Princeton University Press, 1957.

Dodge, Peter. "Ethnic Fragmentation and Politics: The Case of Surinam." *Political Science Quarterly* 81, no. 4 (December 1966): 593-601.

Drummond, Stuart and David Hawkins. "The Malaysian Elections of 1969: An Analysis of the Campaign and the Results." *Asian Survey* 10, no. 4 (April 1970): 320-35.

Dunn, James A. *Social Cleavages, Party Systems and Political Integration: A Comparison of the Belgian and Swiss Experiences.* Ph.D. dissertation, Pennsylvania, 1970.

Eckstein, Harry. *Division and Cohesion in Democracy.* Princeton: Princeton University Press, 1966.

Emerson, Rupert. *From Empire to Nation.* Cambridge, Mass.: Harvard University Press, 1960.

Fisher, Jack C. *Yugoslavia — A Multinational State.* San Francisco: Chandler Publishing Co., 1966.

Furnivall, J.S. *Netherlands India.* Cambridge: The University Press, 1939.

————. "Some Problems of Tropical Economy." In *Fabian Colonial Essays,* edited by Rita Hinden. London: George Allen and Unwin, 1945.

————. *Colonial Policy and Practice.* London: Cambridge University Press, 1948.

Haas, Ernst. *The Uniting of Europe: Political, Social and Economic Forces, 1950-1957.* Stanford: Stanford University Press, 1958.

————. "*The Uniting of Europe* and the Uniting of Latin America." *Journal of Common Market Studies* 5, no. 4 (June 1967): 327-28.

Haegendoren, Mieke Claeys-van. "Party and Opposition Formation in Belgium." *Res Publica* 9, no. 3 (1967): 413-35.

Hason, Yusuf Fadl. "The Sudanese Revolution of October 1964." *Journal of Modern African Studies* 5, no. 4 (December 1967): 491-509.

Henderson, K.D.D. "The Sudan Today." *African Affairs* 64, no. 256 (July 1965): 170-81.

Hepple, Alex. *South Africa*. New York: Praeger, 1966.

Honduis, Frits W. *The Yugoslav Community of Nations*. The Hague: Mouton, 1968.

Hudson, Michael C. *The Precarious Republic: Political Modernization in Lebanon*. New York: Random House, 1968.

Hughes, Colin A. "Adult Suffrage and the Party System in Trinidad." *Parliamentary Affairs* 10, no. 1 (Winter 1956-57): 15-26.

Hurewitz, J.C. "Lebanese Democracy in Its International Setting." In *Politics in Lebanon*, edited by Leonard Binder. New York: John Wiley and Sons, Inc., 1966, pp. 213-38.

Kearney, Robert. *Communalism and Language in the Politics of Ceylon*. Durham, N.C.: Duke University Press, 1967.

Kermode, D.G. and S.D. Tansey. "The Westminster Model in Nigeria." *Parliamentary Affairs* 21, no. 1 (Winter 1967-68): 19-37.

Kerr, Malcolm H. "Political Decision Making in a Confessional Democracy." In *Politics in Lebanon,* edited by Leonard Binder. New York: John Wiley and Sons, Inc., 1966, pp. 187-212.

Key, V.O., Jr. *Public Opinion and American Democracy*. New York: Alfred A. Knopf, 1964.

Kyriakides, Stanley. *Cyprus: Constitutionalism and Crisis Government*. Philadelphia: University of Pennsylvania Press, 1968.

Landau, Jacob M. "Elections in Lebanon." *Western Political Quarterly* 16, no. 1 (March 1961): 120-47.

Lane, Robert E. and David O. Sears. *Public Opinion*. Englewood Cliffs, N.J.: Prentice-Hall, 1964.

Lemarchand, René. "Social Change and Political Modernization in Burundi." *Journal of Modern African Studies* 4, no. 4 (December 1955): 401-33.

_____. *Political Awakening in the Belgian Congo*. Berkeley and Los Angeles: University of California Press, 1964.

_____. *Rwanda and Burundi*. New York: Praeger, 1970.

LeVine, Victor T. *The Cameroons: From Mandate to Independence*. Berkeley and Los Angeles: University of California Press, 1964.

Lijphart, Arend. *The Politics of Accommodation: Pluralism and Democracy in the Netherlands*. Berkeley: University of California Press, 1968.

Lofchie, Michael F. *Zanzibar: Background to Revolution.* Princeton: Princeton University Press, 1965.

Lorwin, Val R. "Belgium: Religion, Class, Language in National Politics." In *Political Opposition in Western Democracies,* edited by Robert A. Dahl. New Haven: Yale University Press, 1966.

McDonald, Gordon C., et al. *Area Handbook for Burundi.* Washington: U.S. Government Printing Office, 1969.

Mackintosh, John P. "Politics in Nigeria: The Action Group Crisis of 1962." *Political Studies* 10, no. 3 (October 1962): 223-47.

Mallinson, Vernon. *Belgium.* New York: Praeger, 1970.

Mason, Philip. *Patterns of Dominance.* London: Oxford University Press for the Institute of Race Relations, 1970.

Mauritius: Fact Sheet on the Commonwealth. London: British Information Services, 1966.

Mayer, Kurt B. "The Jura Problem: Ethnic Conflict in Switzerland." *Social Research* 35, no. 4 (Winter 1968): 707-41.

Means, Gordon P. *Malaysian Politics.* New York: New York University Press, 1970.

Melson, Robert and Howard Wolpe. "Modernization and the Politics of Communalism: A Theoretical Perspective." *American Political Science Review* 64, no. 4 (December 1970): 1112-30.

Milne, R.S. *Government and Politics in Malaysia.* Boston: Houghton Mifflin Company, 1967.

Milne, R.S. and K. J. Ratnam. *The Malayan Parliamentary Election of 1964.* Singapore: University of Malaya Press, 1967.

_____. "The 1969 Parliamentary Election in West Malaysia." *Pacific Affairs* 43, no. 2 (Summer 1970): 203-26.

Mitchell, J.D. *Tribalism and the Plural Society.* London: Oxford University Press, 1960.

Molnar, Thomas. *South West Africa: The Last Pioneer Country.* New York: Fleet Publishing Corporation, 1966.

Morris, Stephen. "Indians in East Africa: A Study in a Plural Society." *British Journal of Sociology* 7, no. 3 (October 1956): 194-211.

_____. "The Plural Society." *Man* 57, no. 8 (August 1957): 124-25.

Nicholls, David G. "East Indians and Black Power in Trinidad." *Race* 12, no. 4 (April 1971): 443-59.

Niven, Rex. *Nigeria.* New York: Praeger, 1967.

Nyquist, Thomas E. "The Sudan: Prelude to Elections." *Middle East Journal* 19, no. 3 (Summer 1965): 263-72.

Nyrop, Richard F., et al. *Area Handbook for Rwanda.* Washington: U.S. Government Printing Office, 1969.

Orange and Green: A Quaker Study of Community Relations in Northern Ireland. Northern Friends Peace Board, 1969.

Philippart, André. "Belgium: Language and Class Oppositions." *Government and Opposition* 2, no. 1 (November 1966): 63-82.

Post, K.W.J. *The Nigerian Federal Election of 1959.* London: Oxford University Press, 1963.

Rabushka, Alvin. "The Manipulation of Ethnic Politics in Malaya." *Polity* 2, no. 3 (Spring 1970): 345-56.

Ratnam, K.J. "Constitutional Government and the Plural Society." *Journal of Southeast Asian History* 2, no. 3 (October 1961): 1-10.

_____. *Communalism and the Political Process in Malaya.* Kuala Lumpur: University of Malaya Press, 1965.

Roff, William R. *The Origins of Malay Nationalism.* New Haven: Yale University Press, 1967.

Rondot, Pierre. "The Political Institutions of Lebanese Democracy." In *Politics in Lebanon,* edited by Leonard Binder. New York: John Wiley and Sons, Inc., 1966, pp. 127-41.

Rose, Richard. *Governing Without Consent: An Irish Perspective.* Boston: Beacon, 1971.

Rudner, Martin. "The Malaysian General Election of 1969: A Political Analysis." *Modern Asian Studies* 4, no. 1 (January 1970): 1-21.

Saab, Hassan. "The Rationalist School in Lebanese Politics." In *Politics in Lebanon,* edited by Leonard Binder. New York: John Wiley and Sons, Inc., 1966, pp. 271-82.

Schwartz, Walter. *Nigeria.* New York: Frederick A. Praeger, 1968.

Sharma, B.S. "The 1965 Elections in the Sudan." *The Political Quarterly* 37, no. 4 (October-December 1966): 441-52.

_____. "Failure of Local-Government-Democracy in the Sudan." *Political Studies* 15, no. 1 (February 1967): 62-71.

Shepard, George W. "National Integration and the Southern Sudan." *Journal of Modern African Studies* 4, no. 2 (July 1966): 193-212.

Shils, Edward. "The Prospects for Lebanese Civility." In *Politics in Lebanon,* edited by Leonard Binder. New York: John Wiley and Sons, Inc., 1966, pp. 1-12.

Shoup, Paul. *Communism and the Yugoslav National Question.* New York and London: Columbia University Press, 1968.

Silberman, Leo. "Democracy in the Sudan." *Parliamentary Affairs* 12, nos.3-4 (Summer and Autumn 1959): 349-76.

Sklar, Richard L. "Nigerian Politics in Perspective." *Government and Opposition* 2, no. 4 (July-October 1967): 524-39.

Smith, M.G. *The Plural Society in the British West Indies.* Berkeley and Los Angeles: University of California Press, 1965.

Smith, Raymond T. *British Guiana.* London: Oxford University Press for the Royal Institute of International Affairs, 1962.

Snider, Nancy. "What Happened in Penang." *Asian Survey* 8, no. 12 (December 1968): 960-75.

Stewart, John. *Gibraltar: the Keystone.* Boston: Houghton Mifflin, 1967.

Suleiman, Michael W. *Political Parties in Lebanon: The Challenge of a Fragmented Political Culture.* Ithaca, New York: Cornell University Press, 1967.

Swan, Michael. *British Guiana: The Land of Six Peoples.* London: HMSO, 1957.

Taylor, Sidney, ed. *The New Africans.* London: Paul Hamlyn, 1967.

Tiryakian, Edward A. "Apartheid and Politics in South Africa." *The Journal of Politics* 22, no. 4 (November 1960): 682-97.

Urwin, Derek W. "Social Cleavages and Political Parties in Belgium: Problems of Institutionalization." *Political Studies* 18, no. 3 (September 1970): 320-40.

van den Berghe, Pierre L. *South Africa, A Study in Conflict.* Middletown, Connecticut: Wesleyan University Press, 1965.

―――――. *Race and Racism: A Comparative Perspective.* New York: John Wiley, Inc., 1967.

―――――. "Pluralism and the Polity: A Theoretical Exploration." In *Pluralism in Africa,* edited by Leo Kuper and M.G. Smith. Berkeley and Los Angeles: University of California Press, 1969.

Wallace, Martin. *Drums and Guns: Revolution in Ulster.* London: Geoffrey Chapman, 1970.

Wallerstein, Immanuel. "Ethnicity and National Integration in West Africa." *Cahiers d'Etudes Africaines* 2, no. 3 (October 1960): 129-39.

Weerawardana, I.D.S. *Ceylon General Election 1956.* Colombo: M.D. Gunasena and Co., Ltd., 1960.

Weil, Gordon L. *Benelux Nations: The Politics of Small-Country Democracies.* New York: Holt, Rinehart, and Winston, Inc., 1970.

Weiner, Myron. "Political Integration and Political Development." *The Annals of the American Academy of Political and Social Science* 358 (March 1965): 52-64.

Woodward, Calvin A. *The Growth of a Party System in Ceylon.* Providence: Brown University Press, 1969.

Wriggins, W. Howard. *Ceylon: Dilemmas of a New Nation*. Princeton: Princeton University Press, 1960.

Young, Crawford. *Politics in the Congo: Decolonization and Independence*. Princeton: Princeton University Press, 1965.

Zolberg, Aristide R. "Mass Parties and National Integration: The Case of the Ivory Coast." *Journal of Politics* 25, no. 1 (February 1963): 36-48.

Index